WHITE HOUSE STUDIES

PRESIDENT OR KING? EVALUATING THE EXPANSION OF EXECUTIVE POWER FROM ABRAHAM LINCOLN TO GEORGE W. BUSH

WHITE HOUSE STUDIES

The Great Presidential Triumvirate at Home and Abroad: Washington, Jefferson and Lincoln
William D. Pederson and Frank J. Williams (Editors)
2006. ISBN: 1-60021-318-9 (Hardcover)

The First Woman President
Joseph Caruso (Editor)
2008. ISBN: 1-60021-348-0 (Hardcover)

Filling Advice and Consent Positions in a New Administration
Emmanuel Morel (Editor)
2010. ISBN: 978-1-60741-570-1 (Softcover)

Presidential Advisers and Claims of Executive Privilege
William A. Galvan (Editor)
2010. ISBN: 978-1-60692-552-2 (Softcover)

Advising the President on Science and Technology
Edgar P. Miller (Editor)
2010. ISBN: 978-1-60876-753-3 (Softcover)

Presidents and War
Anthony J. Eksterowicz and Glenn P. Hastedt (Editors)
2010. ISBN: 978-1-61668-917-9 (Hardcover)

Presidential Advisors and Assistants: Background and Issues
Edward R. Murton (Editor)
2010. ISBN: 978-1-61728-884-5 (Hardcover)

President or King? Evaluating the Expansion of Executive Power from Abraham Lincoln to George W. Bush
Meena Bose (Editor)
2011. ISBN: 978-1-61324-655-9 (Hardcover)

This work is published in conjunction with Hofstra University's Peter S. Kalikow Center for the Study of the American Presidency, and is the first in a series of joint publications between the Kalikow Center and Nova

WHITE HOUSE STUDIES

PRESIDENT OR KING? EVALUATING THE EXPANSION OF EXECUTIVE POWER FROM ABRAHAM LINCOLN TO GEORGE W. BUSH

MEENA BOSE
EDITOR

Nova Science Publishers, Inc.
New York

LIBRARY OF CONGRESS CATALOGING-IN-PUBLICATION DATA

President or king? : evaluating the expansion of executive power from Abraham Lincoln to George W. Bush / editor, Meena Bose.
p. cm.
Includes bibliographical references and index.
ISBN 978-1-61324-655-9 (hardcover)
1. Executive power--United States. 2. Presidents--Legal status, laws, etc.--United States. 3. Constitutional law--United States. I. Bose, Meenekshi, 1970-
KF5053.P73 2011
342.73'06--dc22

2011015641

Published by Nova Science Publishers, Inc. ✝ New York

CONTENTS

Introduction **vii**
Meena Bose

PART I: CONSTITUTIONAL LIMITATIONS ON PRESIDENTIAL POWER IN WARTIME **1**

Presidential Ascendancy in Foreign Affairs and the Subversion of the Constitution **3**
David Gray Adler

Presidents Operating Under the Law **27**
Louis Fisher

Institutional Rivalries in Presidential War Powers Cases: A Political Perspective on the Jurisprudence **43**
Rebecca Curry

Reverse Effect: Congressional and Judicial Restraints on Presidential Power **63**
Nancy Kassop

PART II: EXAMINING THE USE OF PRESIDENTIAL POWER IN THE GEORGE W. BUSH ADMINISTRATION **77**

Congressional Abdication and the Cult of the Presidency **79**
Gene Healy

To Be (Unitarian) or Not to Be (Unitarian): Presidential Power in the George W. Bush Administration **99**
Christopher S. Kelley

Bureaucratic Control and the Future of Presidential Power **123**
Andrew Rudalevige

PART III: THE FUTURE OF PRESIDENTIAL POWER **141**

Harm to the Nation from Excessive Executive Branch Secrecy **143**
Frederick A. O. Schwarz, Jr.

Civic Ignorance and the Rise of the President-King **157**
Eric Lane

CONCLUSION **169**

Conclusion: Why the Future of Presidential Power Will Resemble the Past **171**
Julian Ku

About the Contributors **179**

Index **183**

INTRODUCTION

Meena Bose

> "Energy in the Executive is a leading character in the definition of good government. It is essential to the protection of the community against foreign attacks; it is not less essential to the steady administration of the laws; to the protection of property against those irregular and high-handed combinations which sometimes interrupt the ordinary course of justice; to the security of liberty against the enterprises and assaults of ambition, of faction, and of anarchy."
>
> Alexander Hamilton, *Federalist 70* (1788)

While Alexander Hamilton's eighteenth-century argument for "energy in the executive" was fiercely debated between Federalists and Anti-Federalists at the time, its premise seems almost self-evident in modern American politics. With the expansion of the federal government since the 1930s and the rise of the United States as a global power in the twentieth century, the need for a powerful president to direct American priorities and policies is clear. In times of national crisis, domestic and international focus on the president becomes even greater, with the widespread expectation that executive leadership is necessary to combat the challenge. The need for checks on that power by other institutions of American government, namely Congress and the courts, also is evident, though the balancing of presidential power typically has not developed in conjunction with its expansion.

This edited volume analyzes the growth of presidential power from the Civil War era to the present, examining both emergency situations in wartime and developments in non-crisis periods.[1] In so doing, it addresses the following underlying question: Has presidential power expanded beyond constitutional boundaries, and if so, how can it be checked most effectively today? This topic originally was addressed in a 2009 symposium at Hofstra University that recognized the birthday bicentennial of Abraham Lincoln (born 12 February 1809) – a President who exceeded constitutional boundaries in prosecuting the Civil War and is widely considered in scholarly ratings surveys to be one of the top three Presidents of the United States.

In the post-9/11 era, an assessment of the case for and consequences of expanded presidential power is both timely and necessary. Advocates of strong executive leadership argue that the White House must bear primary responsibility for deciding when to use U.S. military force abroad. As legal scholar John Yoo writes:

> With large militaries designed to project overwhelming force throughout the world at his disposal, the president as commander in chief holds the initiative to use force abroad. Congress can always cut off the funding for military adventures, which in the era of modern warfare may mean simply refusing to appropriate new funds or constructing offensive weapons systems. This effective check on the president's power renders unnecessary any formal process requirement for congressional authorization or a declaration of war before hostilities begin.[2]

Other proponents of presidential power employ the concept of a "unitary executive" in making their case. This term refers the president's authority to control the executive branch. Legal scholars Steven G. Calabresi and Christopher S. Yoo define two key features of the unitary executive as "the scope of the president's power to remove subordinates in the executive branch or to direct their actions."[3] They contend that "the Constitution's creation of a unitary executive eliminates conflict in law enforcement and regulatory policy by ensuring that all of the cabinet departments and agencies that make up the federal government will execute the law . . . in accordance with the president's wishes."[4] While Calabresi and Yoo do not apply the concept to emergency situations in wartime, other scholars (such as John Yoo quoted above) do so, as do elected officials, most recently in the George W. Bush administration.[5]

As presidential power has expanded in American politics, a highly controversial aspect of that growth is the ability to maintain the constitutional system of checks and balances. Alexander Hamilton wrote in *Federalist 70* that "energy in the executive" would be checked by "a due dependence on the people, and a due responsibility."[6] Dependence on the people refers to periodic elections, while "due responsibility" essentially means self-restraint; that is, a president's commitment to following the rule of law and fulfilling the duties of the nation's chief executive. Given the limitations of these checks, institutional constraints are needed as well, as the Framers recognized in drafting the Constitution; but the practical application of those constraints has eroded as U.S. responsibilities domestically and globally have expanded.

Unlike proponents of the "unitary executive" concept, scholars who endorse stronger checks on presidential power reject the view that the Framers endorsed executive initiative in going to war. Political scientist Louis Fisher, for example, finds that "the drift of the war power from Congress to the President after World War II is unmistakable,"[7] and he disagrees that the modern era requires broader presidential power. As he explains:

> If the current risk to national security is great, so is the risk of presidential miscalculation and aggrandizement – all the more reason for insisting that military decisions be thoroughly examined and approved by Congress. Contemporary presidential judgments need more, not less, scrutiny.[8]

Fisher advocates congressional assertiveness in war making, calling for legislators "to participate in the daily grind of overseeing administration policies, passing judgment on them, and behaving as a coequal, independent branch."[9]

The relevance of the longstanding scholarly debate about executive power to current American politics became strikingly evident during the George W. Bush administration.

Advocates of administration policies, such as John Yoo, who served in the Justice Department's Office of Legal Counsel in Bush's first term, contend that the president has wide latitude constitutionally to make decisions to protect U.S. national security, while critics declare that many post-9/11 executive decisions by Bush violated constitutional safeguards. An analysis by political scientist James P. Pfiffner focuses on four topics – denial of the writ of habeas corpus to enemy combatants; suspension of the Geneva Conventions in treatment of detainees; surveillance of Americans without legally required warrants; and use of signing statements to assert the president's right not to enforce parts of law based on his interpretation of his power.[10] It finds that the Bush administration created severe constitutional problems through its actions in these areas. Pfiffner contends that "this aggrandizement of executive power threatens fundamental freedoms and dangerously concedes to the president powers that the framers did not intend the executive to have."[11]

This volume examines specific topics about presidential power in wartime, the use of executive power in the George W. Bush administration, and the future of presidential power. In so doing, it evaluates arguments advanced by presidents and their supporters for their actions, particularly in wartime, reactions and rationales from Congress and the courts, and consequences for presidential leadership in the future. The project lays the foundation for further research about the causes and consequences of increased presidential power, which promises to be of particular significance in the twenty-first century for both domestic and international policy making.[12]

Constitutional Limitations on Presidential Power in Wartime?[13]

The first four chapters evaluate the longstanding debate in presidential politics over how executive power is checked in times of external threats to the American republic. This topic is presented as a question because of the practical difficulties that the other institutions of government face in trying to participate in wartime decision making. The size of Congress, with two chambers and 535 voting members, impedes speedy decisions and raises concerns about the feasibility of protecting executive interests while debates are in progress – that is, not revealing information prematurely. Federal courts typically refrain from addressing current policy debates between the President and Congress in foreign affairs, deeming those to be "political questions." Consequently, the parchment barriers to abuse of power may not be sufficient to restrict the chief executive.[14]

In "Presidential Ascendancy in Foreign Affairs and the Subversion of the Constitution," David Gray Adler examines the constitutional foundation of executive power in foreign affairs and finds that the Framers clearly granted primary authority to the first branch of government, the Congress. In reviewing the constitutional debates, Adler argues that the Framers expected Congress to have "senior status in a partnership with the president for the purpose of conducting foreign policy." The Constitution grants Congress the power to declare war, and Adler maintains that the commander-in-chief clause does not grant the president "political authority" in making decisions about going to war. Neither does the "executive power" clause of Article II grant special war-making powers. Consequently,

Adler concludes, "The ascendancy of the president in the area of war and peace finds no foundation in the Constitution."

In "Presidents Operating Under the Law," Louis Fisher examines how presidents use the concept of "inherent" powers to justify actions in wartime that go beyond their constitutional authority. Contrasting the leadership of Abraham Lincoln and George W. Bush, Fisher finds that although Lincoln did exceed his constitutional powers in prosecuting the Civil War in the spring of 1861, he never claimed that Article II of the Constitution gave him the authority to do so. Instead, in the summer of 1861, he asked Congress to approve his actions retroactively, which it did, thereby recognizing Congress's authority in these areas. The Bush administration, however, asserted that executive power over suspected terrorists encompassed indefinite detention, extraordinary rendition, and surveillance without warrants, among other actions, and that information about such actions was privileged. Fisher finds that these actions in the post-9/11 era violated constitutional boundaries, and that Congress and the federal courts largely left executive power unchecked.

In, "Institutional Rivalries in Presidential War Powers Cases: A Political Perspective on the Jurisprudence," Rebecca Curry evaluates Supreme Court rulings on presidential war powers from a political perspective. Focusing on how the three branches of the federal government battle over the separation of powers in such cases, Curry finds that the Supreme Court adopts a "formalist" view of following the constitutional text closely whenever it perceives threats to its own authority. If the executive branch indicates that the judiciary is not equipped to address a particular issue in wartime – such as civilian trials – then the Court is likely to reject such arguments and protect its constitutional powers, thereby restricting executive authority. Curry applies this analysis to several nineteenth- and twentieth-century court cases as well as to more recent rulings on military tribunals and related subjects.

In "Reverse Effect: Congressional and Judicial Restraints on Presidential Power," Nancy Kassop examines both congressional and judicial efforts to restrict presidential power and finds that they often have the opposite effect of legitimizing expanded executive authority. Kassop argues that legislative constraints on executive action in the 1970s focused on procedural issues, which the White House was able to circumvent without difficult. More recent legislation has attempted to establish substantive restrictions, though implementation is still in progress. Supreme Court decisions in the 1970s appeared to deny claims of presidential power, but left openings for future expansion, while cases in the post-9/11 era have imposed some restrictions on independent executive action without addressing underlying claims about "inherent" executive powers.

Evaluating the use of Presidential Power After 9/11[15]

The next three chapters focus on the use of presidential power in the George W. Bush administration. In the aftermath of the September 11, 2001 terrorist attacks, the Bush administration asserted broad claims of executive power, in both foreign and domestic policy. When challenged, the administration typically held that presidential actions were not subject to scrutiny because of the need for secrecy to protect U.S. interests. These chapters evaluate the Bush administration's decisions and discuss their implications for presidential leadership.

In "Congressional Abdication and the Cult of the Presidency," Gene Healy evaluates how legislative deference to the White House has resulted in expanded presidential power in the twenty-first century. In both foreign and domestic affairs, Healy finds that Congress has abdicated its constitutional responsibilities to the president. From waging war against Iraq to managing the bailout of American industries, Congress has repeatedly given the executive branch authority over decision making that should be conducted within its own chambers. Previous efforts by Congress to restrict presidential power, particularly in foreign affairs, have fallen far short of their intended goals; therefore, Healy concludes that only competition from other states in the international arena and growing public skepticism about government action will check presidential power.

In "To Be (Unitarian) or Not To Be (Unitarian): Presidential Power in the George W. Bush Administration," Christopher Kelley evaluates the applicability of the "unitary executive" concept to recent presidential governance, focusing on use of the signing statement. The "unitary executive" concept, developed in the Reagan administration, maintains that Article II of the Constitution gives the chief executive broad powers that he or she must protect scrupulously, though not by intruding upon the powers of the other branches of government. A key component of the unitary executive is the signing statement, which a president may issue verbally or in writing when signing a bill into law. Beginning in the Reagan administration, the signing statement became a tool for asserting how the executive branch would – or would not – implement a law. Kelley finds that the Bush II administration violated the tenets of the unitary executive through its aggressive use of the signing statement to challenge provisions of laws, and its efforts to expand executive power beyond constitutional boundaries. He also concludes that the Obama administration has hued to the tenets of the unitary executive more closely than its predecessor, albeit without referring explicitly to the concept.

In "Bureaucratic Control and the Future of Presidential Power," Andrew Rudalevige examines how modern presidents seek to extend their authority through control of bureaucratic institutions. He argues that George W. Bush continued a practice developed in the Nixon administration of expanding executive authority over the federal bureaucracy to further presidential power. The Bush II White House did so through its close involvement in and direction of executive appointments, evaluation of federal agencies by the Office of Management and Budget, use of signing statements, and other actions. President Barack Obama declared that he would not continue his predecessor's unilateral use of executive power, but Rudalevige points out that Obama himself has acted unilaterally through executive orders and memoranda to reverse some of Bush's policies, and has used signing statements to criticize parts of legislation that might infringe upon executive power. Consequently, Rudalevige concludes, President Obama appears willing to employ the administrative tools of the presidency to protect executive power.

THE FUTURE OF PRESIDENTIAL POWER[16]

The final two chapters in this book examine perennial challenges in modern American democracy with expanding presidential power and offer prospects for reform to check the executive branch in the twenty-first century. They focus on complementary themes: the first evaluates problems with secrecy in the executive branch for American democracy, while the second examines public willingness to accept expanded presidential power, particularly in crisis situations, without sufficient attention to the consequences for American politics. In promoting both greater transparency in government and public education about the constitutional system of shared powers, these papers present feasible measures for consideration that work within the existing political structure.

In "Harm to the Nation from Excessive Executive Branch Secrecy," Frederick A.O. Schwarz, Jr., analyzes the problems created by White House assertions of executive privilege and state secrets, as well as with overclassification of government files. These actions typically result from presidential reliance on a small group of advisers who do not present diverse perspectives and options to the chief executive. Executive secrecy has a long history in modern presidential politics, and Schwarz argues that it has highly detrimental consequences for American democracy as well as limited success for protecting presidential power over the long term. He recommends that presidents promote transparency in government to advance executive accountability.

In "Civic Ignorance and the Rise of the President-King," Eric Lane attributes the expansion of presidential power partly to a complacent public. The structure of American government encourages presidents to seek power for political success, and while presidents are restricted by checks and balances, they sometimes choose to work outside the law rather than within those constraints. Lane contends that the public is particularly willing to defer to executive judgment in wartime, enabling presidents to exceed their constitutional powers by failing to scrutinize their words and actions. Consequently, Lane says, heightened national attention to civic literacy is needed to check presidential power.

CONCLUSION

In his concluding analysis, Julian Ku makes a case for the merits of expanded presidential power that counters some of the above arguments. National crises, particularly threats from abroad, typically prompt strong public and institutional support for heightened executive power, at least until the threat has passed. But even during non-crisis periods, modern presidents often are not restrained by the other branches of government when they assert broad latitude in policy making because of limited active public support for such restraint. The merits of expanded presidential power depend largely on how that power is used; while the "imperial presidency" that Arthur M. Schlesinger, Jr., described in the 1970s was to the detriment of the American republic, other presidents have employed their power judiciously and in the public interest.[17] Furthermore, Ku says, presidents routinely employ secrecy, administrative control, and the other tools discussed in these articles, raising questions about the feasibility of an alternative model of presidential leadership.

The scholarship presented here raises two underlying concluding questions: How do we determine when presidential power expands too much, and how can such power be contained? To address these questions, we must bridge constitutional analyses with political realities, a challenge that these articles address from diverse perspectives. In engaging these debates, we confront a central issue in American politics today, namely, the need to define what "energy in the executive" means in the twenty-first century. These essays guide us in making our own informed assessment.

References

[1] The articles in this volume originally were presented at a November 4-5, 2009 symposium at Hofstra University sponsored by Hofstra University School of Law, the Hofstra Cultural Center, and Hofstra's Peter S. Kalikow Center for the Study of the American Presidency, and were first published in two special issues of *White House Studies* (Vol. 10, Issues 1 and 2). Special thanks to symposium co-directors and Professors Eric Lane and Julian Ku of Hofstra University School of Law; symposium participants; and Hofstra University for supporting and engaging in these important debates about presidential power.

[2] John Yoo, *The Ways of War and Peace: The Constitution and Foreign Affairs After 9/11* (Chicago: University of Chicago Press, 2005), 294.

[3] Steven G. Calabresi and Christopher S. Yoo, *The Unitary Executive: Presidential Power from Washington to Bush* (New Haven, Ct.: Yale University Press, 2008), 3.

[4] .Ibid.

[5] See Elizabeth Drew, "Power Grab," *The New York Review of Books* 53, no. 11 (22 June 2006), which criticizes the George W. Bush administration's use of executive power. In discussing the Detainee Treatment Act of 2005, it quotes from Bush's signing statement, which explicitly mentions the unitary executive: "The executive branch shall construe [the torture provision] in a manner consistent with the constitutional authority of the President to supervise the unitary executive branch." Also see John Yoo, *Crisis of Command: A History of Executive Power from George Washington to George W. Bush* (Kaplan Publishing, 2010).

[6] Alexander Hamilton, *Federalist 70* (1788). Available through the Avalon Project: Documents in Law, History and Diplomacy, Yale Law School, at http://avalon.law. yale. edu/ subject_menus/fed.asp .

[7] Louis Fisher, *Presidential War Power*, 2d ed. (Lawrence, Ks.: University Press of Kansas, 2004), 261.

[8] Idem., 261-62.

[9] Idem., 280.

[10] James P. Pfiffner, *Power Play: The Bush Presidency and the Constitution* (Washington, D.C.: Brookings Institution Press, 2008).

[11] Idem., 4.

[12] Special thanks to Kalikow Center Senior Presidential Fellows Howard Dean and Ed Rollins, and *New York Times* columnist David Brooks for their informative commentary about presidential power in American politics during the November 4-5 symposium at Hofstra University. Their remarks contributed greatly to these assessments.

[13] Special thanks to Michael Genovese of Loyola Marymount University and Carolyn Eisenberg of Hofstra University for their thoughtful and perceptive review of an early

version of these chapters during the November 4-5, 2009 symposium at Hofstra University.

[14] James Madison famously describes the separation of powers as "a mere demarcation on parchment of the constitutional limits of the several departments" in *Federalist 48*, 1 February 1788. The *Federalist Papers* are available on line through The Avalon Project of Yale Law School at http://avalon.law.yale.edu/subject_menus/fed.asp .

[15] Special thanks to Eric Freedman of Hofstra University School of Law and Carolyn Eisenberg of Hofstra University for their thoughtful and perceptive review of an early version of these chapters during the November 4-5, 2009 symposium at Hofstra University.

[16] Special thanks to Michael Genovese of Loyola Marymount University, Julian Ku of Hofstra University School of Law, and Frank Scaturro of Hofstra University School of Law for their thoughtful and perceptive review of an early version of these chapters during the November 4-5, 2009 symposium at Hofstra University.

[17] Arthur M. Schlesinger, Jr., *The Imperial Presidency* (Houghton Mifflin, 1973).

PART I:

CONSTITUTIONAL LIMITATIONS ON PRESIDENTIAL POWER IN WARTIME

In: President or King?
Editor: Meena Bose, pp. 3-26
ISBN: 978-1-61324-655-9

PRESIDENTIAL ASCENDANCY IN FOREIGN AFFAIRS AND THE SUBVERSION OF THE CONSTITUTION*

David Gray Adler

ABSTRACT

This article explores the institutional contributions to presidential hegemony over the nation's foreign policy. Executive aggrandizement of foreign affairs powers rests on a faulty assertion of constitutional and legal claims and misplaced policy assumptions. It hinges, moreover, on extravagant assertions of presidential prerogative and emergency powers and false allusions to historical precedents. At all events, presidential domination of American foreign policy finds no support in the constitutional text, the discussions and debates in Philadelphia or in the architecture of the Constitution.

"The accretion of dangerous power does not come in a day. It does come, however slowly, from the generative force of unchecked disregard of the restrictions that fence in even the most disinterested assertion of authority."

-- Justice Felix Frankfurter. [1]

Presidential domination of American foreign affairs, a commonplace after a half-century of unchecked expansion of executive powers, has triggered a seismic change in the nation's constitutional landscape. [2] Sweeping assertions of unilateral executive power to initiate war, authorize torture, seize and detain American citizens indefinitely, set aside laws, establish military tribunals and suspend and terminate treaties, in addition to claims of authority to order covert operations, extraordinary rendition and warrantless wiretapping, have subverted the bedrock principles of our system —enumeration of powers, separation of powers, checks and balances and collective decision making. This extraordinary concentration of power in the presidency, grounded in the theory of executive supremacy, is pregnant with menace. It has reduced the trumpet sound of the rule of law to tinkling crystal, consigned Congress and

---

* This article was presented to the Hofstra University Symposium on the American Presidency: "President or King: Evaluating the Expansion of Executive Power from Abraham Lincoln to George W. Bush," November 4-5, 2009. My thanks to conference organizers and commentators for their thoughtful remarks and suggestions.

the courts to the role of spectators, and launched the executive on a trajectory toward the realm of unfettered power.

It makes little difference whether we refer to the ascendancy of the executive as the Imperial Presidency, as Arthur Schlesinger Jr. characterized it, or the Plebiscitary Presidency, as Theodore Lowi described it, or whether we consider it in light of the popular exaltation of the president as Superman, as Thomas E. Cronin has explained it, for the innovation of Presidential Government is triumphant in America.[3] The triumph of the executive over the legislature, a reflection of what Gene Healy has rightly depicted as "The Cult of the Presidency," reflects a forbidding historical development. [4] James Madison, who knew something about the construction and maintenance of a republic, wrote in Federalist No. 51 that, "in a republican form of government, the legislature necessarily predominates."[5] Gibbon, who chronicled the rise and fall of the Roman Republic, and also knew something about the frailties and vulnerabilities of republican government, famously declared: "The principles of a free constitution are irrevocably lost when the legislative power is dominated by the executive." [6] The Imperial Presidency, to be sure, threatens republican values. It also threatens fundamental constitutional principles. More pointedly, for our purposes, it violates the constitutional design for the formulation, management and conduct of American foreign policy.

The Imperial Presidency emerged full –grown in the presidencies of Lyndon Johnson and Richard Nixon. It was born of a complex of aggressive presidential claims to unilateral powers, congressional abdication of its powers, responsibilities and duties, executive-friendly judicial decisions dating from the New Deal era and scholarly promotions of a powerful executive. Yet, its most essential, most prominent and most notorious characteristic was the presidential capture and control of powers granted to Congress, including the usurpation of the war power. The cluster of foreign relations powers granted by the Constitution to Congress and, it may be usefully added, thus *denied* to the president, was nevertheless aggrandized by the executive. The treaty power and the critical role of the Senate in foreign policy were overwhelmed by presidential resort to executive agreements. Presidents increasingly claimed authority to withhold information from Congress on diplomatic, military and national security grounds. Covert actions became the norm; secrecy was exalted, and publicity and openness—critical values in a constitutional democracy—were in a state of eclipse.

The Imperial Presidency remains in full flight. It never has been grounded, even if, occasionally, it has flown at a somewhat lower altitude. It remained aloft under Gerald Ford and Jimmy Carter, two presidents whose terms often are derided as disappointments or failures and whose actions, even on their best days in office, it seemed, led to their characterization as "caretaker" presidents. Yet both abused the war power—Ford in the *Mayaguez* incident and Carter in the aborted effort to rescue American hostages in Iran. [7] And Carter, it will be recalled, did not shrink from claiming unilateral authority to terminate treaties, a claim hardly consistent with the constitutional blueprint for foreign affairs. [8] In the hands of more aggressive executives—Ronald Reagan, Bill Clinton and George W. Bush—the embrace of presidential unilateralism and the capacious claims of presidential power were undeterred by constitutional restraints. The mushrooming growth of presidential power is grounded in self-serving missives from the White House adducing newly-contrived assertions of executive authority, but it has been aided and abetted by congressional abdication and judicial acquiescence. It has not always been so, of course, and it need not be so. Executive ascendancy, as we have observed, is of relatively recent vintage. This chapter undertakes a review and discussion of the rise of executive ascendancy, with an emphasis on the constitutional arguments advanced in defense of unilateral executive war making. There is, in our time, a desperate need to halt the tides of power which, for generations, hve steadily flowed to the presidency. We begin with a discussion of the constitutional blueprint for foreign affairs. The work of the Constitutional Convention can be gathered not merely from what the Framers said in Philadelphia, but also from what they did.

THE FRAMERS' DESIGN FOR FOREIGN AFFAIRS

The Framers of the Constitution might have adopted the English model for reasons of familiarity, tradition and simplicity as a means of promoting and securing its vaunted values of unity, secrecy and dispatch—but they did not. Like other nations, Britain concentrated virtually unfettered authority over foreign affairs in the hands of the executive. The Framers, of course, were thoroughly familiar with both the vast foreign relations powers that inhered in the English Crown by virtue of the royal prerogative, and the values, sentiments and policy concerns that justified this arrangement. In his *Second Treatise of Government,* John Locke described three powers of government: the legislative, the executive and the federative. Federative power was the power over foreign affairs—"the power of war and peace, leagues and alliances, and all the transactions with all persons and communities without the Commonwealth." The federative power was "almost always united" with the executive. [9] Locke warned that the [10] separation of executive and federative powers would invite "disorder and ruin." Sir William Blackstone, the great eighteenth-century jurist, explained in his magisterial four-volume work, *Commentaries on the Laws of England* (1765-1769) that the King exercised plenary authority over all matters relating to war and peace, diplomacy, treaties, and military command. Blackstone defined the King's prerogative as "those rights and capacities which the King enjoys alone." [11] The monarch's prerogatives, "those which are 'rooted in and spring from the King's political person,'" include the authority to send and receive ambassadors and the power to make war or peace. [12] The Crown, moreover, could negotiate "a treaty with a foreign state, which shall irrevocably bind the nation."[13] The King, according to Blackstone, possessed the power to issue letters of marque and reprisal which, he explained, was "nearly related to, and plainly derived from, that other of making war." [14] The King, moreover, was "the generalissimo, or the first in military command," and he possessed "the sole power of raising and regulating fleets and armies." [15] In the exercise of this lawful prerogative, Blackstone explained, the King "is, and ought to be absolute; that is, so far absolute that there is no legal authority that can either delay or resist him." [16]

In light of Locke's admonitions, the rejection by the Constitutional Convention of the English model and its promotion of unilateral executive power, grounded in inherent, discretionary and unbridled authority, could not have been more emphatic. The Convention's penchant for enumeration of powers, as a method of avoiding doubt on the repository of key powers and providing protection against executive assertion of inherent authority, was ably explained by Madison in *Federalist No. 45*: "The powers *delegated* by the proposed constitution are *few and defined* . . . [they] will be exercised principally on *external* objects, as war, peace, negotiations, and foreign commerce." [17] The Framers' blueprint for foreign affairs reflects their determination to establish a republic premised on collective decision making, a principle that reflects confidence in the crossfire of discussion and debate as a method for producing superior laws, policies and programs. The preference for collective, rather than unilateral, decision making runs throughout the constitutional provisions that govern American foreign policy.

The Constitution assigns to Congress senior status in a partnership with the president for the purpose of conducting foreign policy. Article 1 vests in Congress broad, explicit and exclusive powers to regulate foreign commerce; raise and maintain military forces; grant letters of marque and reprisal; provide for the common defense; and initiate hostilities on behalf of the United States, including full-blown war. As Article II indicates, the president shares with the Senate the treaty-making power and the authority to appoint ambassadors. The Constitution exclusively assigns two foreign affairs powers to the president. He is designated commander in chief of the nation's armed forces, although, as we shall see, he acts in this capacity by and under the authority of Congress. The president also has the duty to receive ambassadors, but the Framers viewed this as a routine administrative function, devoid of discretionary authority. [18] This list exhausts the textual grant of authority to Congress and the president. The president's constitutional powers are few and modest, and they pale in comparison to those vested in Congress. The American arrangement for the conduct of the nation's foreign affairs bears no resemblance to the English model. In fact, the Convention discarded the British model as obsolete and inapplicable to the republican manners of the United States. [19] Alexander Hamilton captured this sentiment in *Federalist No. 75*:

> "The history of human conduct does not warrant that exalted opinion of human virtue which would make it wise in a nation to commit interests of so delicate and momentous a kind, as those which concern its intercourse with the rest of the world, to the sole disposal of a magistrate created and circumstanced as would be a president of the United States."[20]

The Founders' deep-seated fear and distrust of executive power, which resonated from the colonial period and reflected their studied reading of history, made the quest for an effective foreign affairs system an arduous task. The pervasive fear of a powerful executive, particularly a president who might wield unilateral authority in an area as sensitive and critical as that of foreign relations, was reinforced by the republican ideology that permeated the Convention. The Framers' attachment to collective judgment—joint participation, consultation and concurrence— reflected their adherence to the fundamental premise of republicanism: the conjoined wisdom of the many is superior to that of one. The decision to create a structure of shared powers in foreign affairs, James Wilson told fellow delegates in the Pennsylvania Ratifying Convention, provided "a security to the people." [21] The emphasis on collective decision making came at the expense of unilateral presidential authority, of course, but that consequence was of little moment, given the Founders' overriding aversion to discretionary executive power. [22] But that was the point, precisely. As a result of the pervasive distrust of executive power, the Framers placed control of foreign policy beyond the unilateral capacity of the president. Furthermore, as James Madison, justly known as the Father of the Constitution, declared, the Convention "defined and confined" the authority of the president so that a power not granted could not be assumed. [23] The Framers contrived a new constitutional arrangement for foreign affairs—a distinctively American contribution to politics and political science—and it was epitomized in their judgment that, in the newly-minted Republican Era, the executive unilateralism exalted by prevailing models was a shopworn, outdated method that belonged to an age and a means of foreign affairs governance that they rejected and discarded. As such, the Framers perceived a broad equatorial divide between the hemispheres of monarchism and republicanism, between the values of the Old World and those of the New World. The Convention's deliberate fragmentation of powers relating to diplomacy, treaties and war and peace, and the allocation of various foreign affairs powers to different departments and agencies—in defiance of conventional understandings and the explicit warnings from Locke of disorder, chaos and disaster—reflected the Framers' determination to apply the doctrines of separation of powers and checks and balances, the principle of the rule of law, and the elements of constitutionalism to the realm of foreign relations as rigorously as they had been applied to the domestic realm.

THE WAR POWER

The Constitutional Convention's repudiation of the English model was dramatically illustrated in its decision to vest the war power in Congress. [24] The Framers granted to Congress the sole and exclusive authority to initiate military hostilities, including full-blown, total war, as well as lesser acts of armed force, on behalf of the American people. The constitutional assignment of the War Power to Congress, which Justice William Paterson, a delegate to the Convention, described in United States v. Smith (1806) as the "exclusive province of Congress to change a state of peace into a state of war," reflected the Framers' decision to deny to the president what Blackstone had attributed to the English King—"the sole prerogative of making war and peace." [25] The Framers' perception of the propensity of executives to initiate war for less than meritorious reasons shadowed their discussions. In Federalist No. 4, John Jay, whose impressions, knowledge and conclusions about national security and foreign affairs were banked on his experience as Secretary of Foreign Affairs, summed up the sentiments that lay behind the Framers' aversion to an executive war power. Jay wrote that "absolute monarchs will often make war when their nations are to get nothing by it, but for purposes and objects merely personal, such as a thirst for military glory, revenge for personal affronts, ambition, or private compacts to aggrandize or support their particular families or partisans. These and a variety of other motives, which affect only the mind of the sovereign, often lead him to engage in wars not sanctified by justice or the voice and interests of his people."[26] Madison echoed Jay's warnings and conclusions about executive war making. In 1793, he characterized war as "the true nurse of executive aggrandizement. . . . In war, the honors and emoluments of office are to be multiplied; and it is the executive patronage under which they are to be enjoyed. It is in war, finally, that laurels are to be gathered; and it is the executive brow that they are to encircle. The strongest passions and most dangerous weaknesses of the human breast; ambition, avarice, vanity, the honourable or venial love of fame, are all in conspiracy against the desire and duty of peace." [27] In 1798, in a letter to Thomas Jefferson, Madison declared that the Constitution "supposes, what the History of all Govts demonstrates, that the Ex. Is the branch of power most interested in war, and most prone to it. It has accordingly with studied care, vested the question of war in the Legisl." [28]

The Framers' understanding that the power of war and peace was historically associated with the monarchy, and often exercised for arbitrary purposes, afforded a backdrop for their debates. The War Clause of the Constitution provides that "the Congress shall have power . . . to declare War [and] grant Letters of Marque and Reprisal." The debate on the proper repository of the authority to initiate war occurred at the outset of the Convention. On May 29, 1787, Gov. Edmund Randolph of Virginia proposed a constitution that included a provision "that a national Executive be instituted." The seventh paragraph stated that the executive "ought to enjoy the Executive rights vested in Congress of the Confederation." [29] On June 1, the Convention took up Randolph's proposal. Charles Pinckney stated that he favored "a vigorous executive but was afraid the Executive powers of [the existing] Congress might extend to peace and war and which would render the Executive a Monarchy, of the worst kind, towit an elective one."[30] John Rutledge supported the placement of the executive power in a single person "tho' he was not for giving him the power of war and peace." [31] Roger Sherman considered "the executive magistracy as nothing more than an institution for carrying the will of the Legislature into effect." [32] In a remark that laid bare the Framers' opposition to the notion of executive prerogative powers, James Wilson indicated that he also preferred a single executive, but "did not consider the Prerogatives of the British Monarch as a proper guide in defining the Executive powers. Some of these prerogatives," he explained, "were of a Legislative nature. Among others that of war and peace and c." [33] James Madison agreed that the war power was legislative in character. Rufus King noted: "Mad: agree with Wilson in his definition of executive powers –executive powers . . . do not include the rights of war and peace . . . ." Madison explained that executive powers should be "confined and defined—if large we shall have the Evils of elective Monarchies." [34] There was no vote on Randolph's resolution, but the discussion reflects an understanding that the power of "war and peace"—the power to initiate war—did not belong to the executive but to the legislature.

On August 6, the Committee of Detail circulated a draft constitution which provided: "the legislature of the United States shall have the power . . . to make war." [35] This clause bore sharp resemblance to the Articles of Confederation, which vested the "sole and exclusive right and power of determining on peace and war" to the Continental Congress. [36] This design was thoroughly familiar to the Framers, thirty-five of whom had served in the Continental Congress, and it reflected the fact, as the distinguished legal historian, Charles Warren, observed, that this power, as well as others, came "bodily from the old Articles of Confederation." [37] This provision gave rise to debate. When the War Clause was considered in debate on August 17, Charles Pinckney opposed placing the power in Congress. "Its proceedings were too slow"; he favored the Senate, [38] as Alexander Hamilton had in the plan he presented to the Convention. [39] Pierce Butler, however, "was for vesting the power in the President, who will have all the requisite qualities, and will not make war but when the nation will support it." [40] Butler's opinion shocked Elbridge Gerry, who declared that he "never expected to hear in a republic a motion to empower the Executive alone to declare war." [41] Butler stood alone in the Convention; there was no support for his opinion and no second to his motion. Credit Butler for being a quick study; by the end of the day, he was in full retreat from his initial position. [42]

The proposal of the Committee of Detail to vest the legislature with the power to make war proved unsatisfactory to Madison and Gerry. In a joint resolution, they moved to substitute "declare" for "make," leaving to the Executive the power to repel sudden attacks."[43] The meaning of the motion is unmistakable. Congress was granted the power to make, that is, initiate war; the president, for obvious reasons, could act immediately to repel sudden attacks without authorization from Congress. There was no quarrel whatever with respect to the sudden-attack provision, but there was some question as to whether the substitution of "declare" for "make" would effectuate the intention of Madison and Gerry. Roger Sherman of Connecticut thought the motion "stood very well. The Executive shd. be able to repel and not to commence war. 'Make' better than 'declare' the latter narrowing the power [of the legislature] too much." Virginia's George Mason "was agst. giving the power of war to the Executive, because not [safely] to be trusted with it; or to the Senate, because not so constructed as to be entitled to it. He was for clogging rather than facilitating war; but for facilitating peace. He preferred 'declare' to 'make.'" The Madison-Gerry proposal was adopted by a vote of seven to two. When Rufus King explained that the word "make" might be understood to authorize Congress to initiate as well as to conduct war, which was an "executive function," Connecticut changed its vote so that the verb "declare" was approved, eight states to one. [44]

The debates and vote on the War Clause make it pellucidly clear that Congress alone possesses the authority to initiate war. The war making power was specifically withheld from the president; he was given only the authority to repel sudden attacks. Only one delegate—Pierce Butler—had advanced the concept of an executive power to initiate war. However, by the end of the August 17 debate on the War Clause, he clearly understood the Convention's intention to place the war power under legislative control, as evidenced by his motion "to give the Legislature the power of peace, as they were to have that of war." [45] The motion, which represented a volte-face on Butler's part, drew no discussion, and it failed by a vote of 10-0. In all likelihood, it was viewed by the delegates as utterly superfluous given their understanding that the war power encompassed authority to determine both war and peace. [46] In a telling moment, reflective of an air of self-defense and contrived detachment, Butler explained to his colleagues at the South Carolina Ratifying Convention that the grant of power to "make war" to the president "was objected to, as throwing into his hands the influence of a monarch, having an opportunity of involving his country in a war." [47] Butler did not disclose that the idea was his.

The Framers' aversion to the royal prerogative precluded an assignment of the war power to the president. The Madison-Gerry motion, which provided that the president would possess the power to "repel sudden attacks," would not have been necessary if the war power had been granted to the president. It was the grant to Congress of the war power, precisely, that raised the question of an exception, that is, the need to clothe the president with the authority to "repel sudden attacks." The emergency created by a sudden attack implies that there is no time to consult with Congress. Surely, Gerry, who co-authored the resolution with Madison, cannot be viewed as repudiating his stated opposition that very day to Butler's idea that the executive "alone could declare war." Nor could it be said with any credibility that Madison, who had explained that the power to initiate war was legislative in character, had intended in the resolution to attribute the war power to the president.

With the exception of Butler's remark, there is nothing in the Framers' comments, arguments or train of discussion to suggest even a mild flirtation with the concept of executive war making. The Convention's decision to leave the war power in Congress, where it had been under the Articles of Confederation, and the reasoning on which it was grounded, was embraced by delegates to the various state ratifying conventions, early governmental practice and a series of decisions rendered by the Supreme Court at the dawn of the republic. Space does not permit a comprehensive review of the discussions in the state conventions, but James Wilson, only slightly less important than Madison as an architect of the Constitution, and regarded as the "most learned and profound legal scholar of his generation," explained the rationale behind the design of the War Clause to his colleagues in the Pennsylvania Ratifying Convention in terms that echoed the sentiments of the Framers:

> "This system will not hurry us into war; it is calculated to guard against it. It will not be in the power of a single man, or a single body of men, to involve us in such distress; for the important power of declaring war is vested in the legislature at large: this declaration must be made with the concurrence of the House of Representatives: from this circumstance we may draw a certain conclusion that nothing but our national interest can draw us into war." [48]

As a means of preventing the president from "hurrying" the nation into war, the Framers, as Wilson later explained, conferred upon Congress the bulk of the war powers, and relegated the president to a subordinate role:

> "The power of declaring war, and the other powers naturally connected with it, are vested in congress. To provide and maintain a navy—to make rules for its government—to grant letters of marque and reprisal—to make rules concerning captures—to raise and support armies—to establish rules for their regulation—to provide for organizing . . . the militia and calling them forth in the service of the Union—all these are powers naturally connected with the power of declaring war. All these powers, therefore, are vested in Congress." [49]

The Framers' additional grant to Congress of power to "provide for the common defense" and to make all appropriations to effectuate its exercise of all powers "naturally connected" with war, left the president with no authority to initiate hostilities. The president, moreover, would be barred from exercising any powers vested in Congress by both the separation of powers and the Take Care Clause, which requires the president to "take care to faithfully execute the law."[50] The Convention's denial to the president of constitutional authority to commence war was complete.

CHALLENGES TO A CONGRESSIONAL WAR POWER

In spite of the illuminating debate and vote on the War Clause, the shift from "make" to "declare" has induced revisionists to find in the presidency a power to initiate war. The Vietnam War provided a backdrop for their efforts. Senator Barry Goldwater, writing in the latter, hectic days of the Vietnam War, was among the first to assert that the shift reflected the Framers' intention to "leave the 'making of war' with the President." [51] Leonard Ratner explained that that the "declare war clause" recognized "the warmaking authority of the President, implied by his role as executive and commander-in-chief and by congressional power to declare, but not make, war," an explanation embraced thirty years later by John

Yoo. [52] There is little dispute that Professor Yoo has been the most prominent advocate of broad presidential powers in recent years, from his post at the law school at the University of California, Berkeley, as well as his position as an Assistant Attorney General in the Office of Legal Counsel under the administration of George W. Bush. Yoo has asserted that the Constitutional Convention embraced the foreign affairs and war making powers of the English King, and concludes that "the Framers created a framework designed to encourage presidential initiatives in war." According to Yoo, the congressional role in making decisions about war is derived not from the War Clause, but from its power to constrain the executive through the appropriations and impeachment powers. Congress may not initiate war. The purpose of the "Declare War Clause," rather, is to merely announce to the nations of the world that America is at war. As Yoo states: "A declaration did not create or authorize; it recognized." The provision did not "add to Congress' store of war powers at the expense of the President." Rather, it granted to Congress "a judicial role in declaring that a state of war exists between the United States and another nation." [53] Other scholars have advanced the idea that the president may order military hostilities, so long as they fall short of war. [54]

We shall defer for the moment consideration of the Executive Power and Commander in Chief Clauses, but these revisionist efforts ignore the fact that, at the time of the framing, the word "declare" enjoyed a settled understanding and an established usage. Simply stated, as early as 1552, the verb "declare" had become synonymous with the verb "commence"; they both meant the initiation of hostilities. [55] This was the established usage in international law as well as in England, where the terms to declare war and to make war were used interchangeably. [56] The Framers were familiar with this usage. Chancellor James Kent of New York, one of the leading jurists of the founding period, stated: "As war cannot be lawfully commenced on the part of the United States without an act of Congress, such an act is, of course, a formal official notice to the world, and equivalent to the most solemn declaration." Though Kent interpreted "declare" to mean "commence," he did not assert that the Constitution requires a congressional declaration of war before hostilities could be lawfully commenced but merely that war is initiated by Congress. What "is essential," according to Kent, is "that some formal public act, proceeding directly from the competent source, should announce to the people at home their new relations and duties growing out of a state of war, and which should equally apprise neutral nations of the fact." [57]

Given the equivalence of commence and declare, it is clear that a congressional declaration of war would institute military hostilities. According to international law commentators, a declaration of war was desirable because it announced the institution of a state of war and the legal consequences that it entailed, to the adversary, to neutral nations, and to citizens of the sovereign initiating the war. Indeed, this is the essence of a declaration of war: notice by the proper authority of intent to convert a state of peace into a state of war. [58] But under American law only a joint resolution or an explicit congressional authorization of the use of military force against a named adversary is required. This can come in the form of a "declaration pure and simple" or in a "conditional declaration of war."[59] There are also two kinds of war, those which U.S. courts have termed "perfect" or general and those labeled "imperfect" or limited wars. [60]

It was decided in three early and important Supreme Court cases that the power of determining perfect and imperfect war lay with Congress. These decisions put the meaning of the War Clause beyond doubt. No court since has departed from these precedents, which are as old as *Marbury v. Madison*, the greybeard of all precedents. In 1800, in *Bas v. Tingy*, the

Court determined that Congress might declare an imperfect war or limited war, as well as a perfect or general war. [61] In 1801, in *Talbot* v. *Seeman,* Chief Justice John Marshall, who had been a member of the Virginia Ratifying Convention, delivered the opinion: "The whole powers of war being, by the Constitution of the United States, vested in Congress, the acts of that body can alone be resorted to as our guides in this inquiry. It is not denied, nor in the course of the argument has it been denied, that Congress may authorize general hostilities, in which case the general laws of war apply to our situation; or partial war, in which case the laws of war, so far as they actually apply to our situation, must be noticed." [62] The power of Congress to authorize limited war is, of course, a necessary concomitant of its power to declare general war. If, as John Bassett Moore has suggested, the president might authorize relatively minor acts of war or perhaps covert military operations in circumstances not demanding full-blown war, that power could be wielded in a way that would easily eviscerate the Constitution's placement of the war power in Congress. Moore, perhaps the most eminent American scholar of international law, justly rebuked that proposition:

> "There can hardly be room for doubt that the framers of the Constitution, when they vested in Congress the power to declare war, they never imagined they were leaving it to the executive to use the military and naval forces of the United States all over the world for the purpose of actually coercing other nations, occupying their territory, and killing their soldiers and citizens, all according to his notion of the fitness of things, as long as he refrained from calling his action war or persisted in calling it peace." [63]

In *Little v. Barreme* (1804), a case arising from the war with France from 1798-1800, Marshall held that President John Adams's instructions to seize ships were in conflict with an act of Congress, thus affirming executive subordination to Congress during war. [64] In 1806, in *United States v. Smith,* Justice William Paterson, while riding circuit, held that Congress alone possesses the constitutional authority to initiate military hostilities. Paterson stated that "it is the exclusive province of Congress to change a state of peace into a state of war." [65] In *Smith,* Paterson explained that the rationale for vesting the president with authority to repel sudden attacks rested on the fact that an invasion constituted a state of war, thus rendering a declaration of war by Congress superfluous. In such an event, the president was authorized to initiate offensive action against the attacking enemy. But the president's power of self-defense does not extend to foreign lands. The Framers did not give the president the right to intervene in foreign wars, or to choose between war and peace, or to identify and commence hostilities against an enemy of the American people. Nor did they empower him to initiate force abroad on the basis of his own assessments of U.S. security interests. These circumstances involve choices that belong to Congress under its exclusive province to change a state of peace into a state of war. The president's power is purely defensive and strictly limited to attacks against the United States.

These early decisions have not been disturbed. In the *Prize Cases* in 1863, the Supreme Court considered for the first time the power of the president to respond to sudden attacks. Justice Robert Grier delivered the opinion of the Court:

> "By the Constitution, Congress alone has the power to declare a national or foreign war. . . . If a war be made by invasion of a foreign nation, the President is not only authorized but bound to resist force, by force. He does not initiate the war, but is bound to accept the challenge without waiting for any special legislative authority. And whether the hostile party

> be a foreign invader, or States organized in rebellion, it is none the less a war, although the declaration of it be "unilateral."[66]

All of the offensive powers of the nation, then, were located in Congress. Consistent with this constitutional theory, the Convention gave to Congress the power to issue "letters of marquee and reprisal."[67] Dating back to the Middle Ages, when sovereigns employed private forces in retaliation for an injury caused by the sovereign of another state or his subjects, the practice of issuing reprisals gradually evolved into the use of public armies. By the time of the Convention, the Framers considered the power to issue letters of marque and reprisal sufficient to authorize a broad spectrum of armed hostilities short of declared war. In other words, it was regarded as a species of imperfect war. For example, Madison, Hamilton and Jefferson, among others, agreed that the authorization of reprisals was an act of war and belonged to Congress. [68] As a direct riposte to the revisionists' claim of a presidential power to order acts of war, we may consider what Jefferson said in 1793 of the authority necessary to issue a reprisal: "Congress must be called upon to take it; the right of reprisal being expressly lodged with them by the Constitution, and not with the executive." [69]

In sum, when the Framers granted to Congress the power to declare war, they were vesting in that body the sole and exclusive power to initiate military hostilities on behalf of the American people. The record reveals that no member of the Philadelphia Convention and no member of any state ratifying convention held a different understanding of the meaning of the War Clause. The Supreme Court, as we have seen, shared that understanding as well. If revisionists are to find constitutional authority for executive ascendancy on matters of war and peace and national security, it must derive from another source. Let us turn to their purported legal justifications for presidential warmaking.

THE COMMANDER-IN-CHIEF CLAUSE

The Commander in Chief Clause has become the principal pillar for those who would vest in the president the power of war and peace. Article 2, section 2 of the Constitution provides: "The President shall be Commander in Chief of the Army and Navy of the United States, and of the Militia of the several States, when called into the actual Service of the United States." The commander-in-chief provision, in the words of Justice Robert H. Jackson, has been invoked for the "power to do anything, anywhere, that can be done with an army or navy." [70] Though stated in the context of reviewing President Harry Truman's invocation of the clause to support his seizure of steel mills, Jackson's observation certainly anticipated the claims of executives who have seized the provision as justification for their military adventures. Presidents Harry Truman, Lyndon Johnson, Richard Nixon, Gerald Ford, Jimmy Carter, Ronald Reagan, George H.W. Bush, Bill Clinton and George W. Bush fall into this camp. [71] As the chief architect of the Bush Administration's view of executive power in foreign affairs, in his position in the Office of Legal Counsel, Yoo stated in what became known as the "Torture Memos" that the president possesses an inherent, plenary power in foreign affairs, including a unilateral power to initiate war. He stated in an OLC Memo of September 25, 2001, that "the Constitution vests the president with the plenary authority, as Commander in Chief and the sole organ of the Nation's foreign relations, to use military force abroad . . . ." Yoo added that all three branches "agree that the president has broad authority to use military force abroad, including the ability to deter future attacks."[72] These assertions find no foundation in the text, structure or history of the Constitution.

As Francis D. Wormuth observed, the "office of commander-in-chief has never carried the power of war and peace, nor was it invented by the framers of the Constitution." [73] The office was introduced by King Charles 1 in 1639 when he named the Earl of Arundel commander-in-chief of an army to battle Scottish forces in the First Bishops War. In historical usage, the title was conferred upon the highest ranking military official in a theatre of battle. The commander-in –chief was always subordinate to a political superior. As a consequence, the title carried with it little discretion. At all events, it conferred no authority to initiate war. [74] The Continental Congress continued the usage of the title on June 15, 1775 when it appointed George Washington as general. His commission named him "General and Commander in Chief, of the Army of the United Colonies." In the manner of subordinating the commander in chief to a political superior, Washington was ordered "punctually to observe and follow such orders and directions, from time to time, as you shall receive from this, or a future Congress of these United Colonies, or Committee of Congress." Congress did not hesitate to instruct the commander in chief on military and policy matters. [75]

The practice of entitling the office at the apex of the military hierarchy as commander in chief and of subordinating the office to a political superior, whether a king, parliament or congress, was thus firmly established for a century and a half and thoroughly familiar to the Framers when they met in Philadelphia. Perhaps this settled understanding and the consequent lack of concern about the nature of the post account for the absence of any debate on the Commander in Chief Clause at the Convention. When Hamilton submitted a plan to the Convention on June 18, he probably did not propose the title commander-in-chief, but he undoubtedly had it in mind when he said that the president was "to have the direction of war when authorized or begun." [76]

It was Hamilton's speech, then, that summarized the essence of the president's power as commander-in-chief: when war is "authorized or begun," the president is to command the military operations of American forces. War, it is to be recalled, might be initiated by Congress or by sudden attack on the United States. In both cases, as Hamilton explained in Federalist No. 69, the office of commander in chief "would amount to nothing more than the supreme command and direction of the military and naval forces, as first general and admiral of the Confederacy." [77] In Federalist No. 74, Hamilton explained the rationale for making the president commander in chief. The direction of war, he stated, "most peculiarly demands those qualities which distinguish the exercise of power by a single head," a conclusion widely shared by his contemporaries. [78] Then too, the power of directing war and emphasizing the common strength, he observed, "forms a usual and essential part in the definition of the executive authority." [79] As General Washington's chief aide in the Revolutionary War, Hamilton was familiar with the rationales that the Framers would employ in constructing the office of commander in chief. The conduct of war was better left in the hands of a single officer, to be sure, but that officer might be directed or instructed by a political superior. At all events, neither Hamilton nor any of his contemporaries claimed for the president a unilateral war making power in his capacity as commander in chief.

The president as commander in chief was to be "first General and Admiral" in "the direction of war when authorized or begun." But all political authority remained in Congress, as it had under the Articles of Confederation. As Louis Henkin has observed, "Generals and Admirals, even when they are 'first,' do not determine the political purposes for which troops are to be used; they command them in execution of policy made by others."[80] The commander-in-chief in the tradition of a century and a half was made subordinate to a political superior. The office carried with it no power to declare war; as Hamilton and Iredell explained, that power is the exclusive prerogative of Congress. Proponents of executive war making will find nothing in the origins of the Commander in Chief Clause to support their agenda.

EXECUTIVE POWER CLAUSE

Advocates of presidential domination of matters involving war and peace and national security have sought to adduce an executive war power from Article 2, section 1, which reads: "The executive power shall be vested in the President of the United States." In 1966, for example, the State Department cited the president's role as chief executive to adduce constitutional support for President Johnson's entry into the Vietnam War. [81] Richard Nixon's legal advisers similarly invoked the clause to justify his adventures in Southeast Asia. [82] In 1975, Gerald Ford found constitutional warrant in the "President's Constitutional executive power" the military activities he ordered in Cambodia. On April 26, 1980, Jimmy Carter authorized an attempted rescue of American citizens held hostage by Iran. He justified the attempt as being "pursuant to the President's powers under the Constitution as Chief Executive and as Commander in Chief."[83]

The effort to ground presidential war making on the Executive Power Clause is unavailing. Indeed, the very premise was raised –and rejected—in the Constitutional Convention. It will be recalled that Madison and Wilson, among others, pointed out that writers on the law of nations regarded the war power as "legislative," not "executive," in nature. When Randolph proposed that the executive would have the "executive rights vested in Congress" under the Articles of Confederation, various members of the Constitutional Convention raised objections if that would mean that the president would inherit the power of war and peace. The Convention embraced a narrow view of executive power, and the discussions of it never referred to it as a source of authority to formulate foreign policy or make decisions on matters of war and peace.

The concept of an executive power, flush with far-reaching discretionary authority, held no charm for the Framers. For the Framers, the phrase "executive power" was limited, as Wilson put it, to "executing the laws and appointing officers." Roger Sherman "considered the Executive magistracy as nothing more than an institution for carrying the will of the Legislature into effect." Madison agreed with Wilson's definition of executive power. He thought it necessary "to fix the extent of Executive authority . . . as certain powers were in their nature Executive, and must be given to that department" and added that "a definition of their extent would assist the judgment in determining how far they might be safely entrusted to a single officer." The definition of the executive's powers should be precise, thought Madison; the executive power "shd. be confined and defined." [84] There was no challenge to the definition of executive power offered by Madison and Wilson, nor was there even an alternative understanding advanced. And there was no argument about the scope of executive power; indeed, any latent fears were quickly arrested by assurances from Madison and Wilson that the power of war and peace was not an executive but a legislative function. Given the

Framers' conception of the chief executive as little more than an institution to effectuate the "will of the legislature," that is to execute laws and appoint officers, there was little about the office to fear.

Lockean Prerogative

Extollers of a unilateral executive war making authority also have invoked the Lockean prerogative as a source of inherent presidential power. Drawing on John Locke's defense of the right of an executive to act for the common good, even if it requires breaking the law (salus populi suprema lex), defenders have adduced a similar claim for the president. [85] There is not a scintilla of evidence that the Framers intended to incorporate the Lockean Prerogative in the Constitution. And lacking a textual statement or grant of power to that effect, such intent is indispensable to the claim of constitutional power. In fact, the evidence runs in the other direction. Fears of executive power led the Framers to enumerate the president's power to "define and confine" the scope of h is authority. And clearly, an undefined reservoir of discretionary power in the form of Locke's prerogative would have unraveled the carefully crafted design of Article 2 and repudiated the Framers' stated aim of corralling executive power.

The absence of such authority means that by definition any presidential assertion of a prerogative power to violate the law is an assertion of extra-constitutional power; an action based on such an assertion is definitionally unconstitutional. This claim, then, does not afford a president any constitutional or legal authority to initiate war. The issue is merely whether a president might commence war in violation of the supreme law of the land and then attempt to justify it on grounds of necessity. Of course, he cannot be the judge of his own actions. He must seek immunity and exoneration from Congress in the way of retroactive authorization, a practice that is deeply imbedded in the American tradition. [86] Whether or not congressional approval of the claimed prerogative is granted, the review itself is an admission of presidential usurpation of power.

Executive Precedents

Champions of executive power have fashioned the argument that executive war making, if repeated often enough, acquires legal validity. This is the contention, as expounded by Henry P. Monaghan, among others, that "history has legitimated the practice of presidential war-making." [87] The entire argument rests on the premise that the president frequently has exercised the war power without congressional authorization. The actual number of these episodes varies among the several compilations, but defenders usually list between 100 and 200 unilateral acts, each of which constitutes a legitimizing precedent for future executive wars. [88]

In detail and in conception, the argument is flawed. In the first place, the revisionists' lists are inaccurately compiled. Francis D. Wormuth has thoroughly deflated their claims with what Raoul Berger rightly characterized as a "painstaking analysis." [89] Space does not permit a critical analysis of each alleged assertion of executive precedents. Consider, however, an error common to the lists: the claim that unilateral war making was initiated by the "undeclared" war with France in 1798. The claim, as Professor Wormuth justly observed, "is altogether false. The fact is that President John Adams took absolutely no independent action. Congress passed a series of acts that amounted, so the Supreme Court said, to a declaration of imperfect war; and Adams complied with these statutes."[90] In a detailed analysis of the quasi-war, Dean Alfange concurred in Wormuth's assessment. Adams's action, Professor Alfange explained, "certainly provides no precedent for a claim of presidential prerogative to commit the United States to war without congressional authorization. Adams made absolutely no claim of a general presidential power to initiate hostilities." [91]

Moreover, many of the episodes involved initiation of hostilities by a military commander, not by authorization from the president. If practice establishes law, then the inescapable conclusion is that every commander of every military unit has the power to initiate war. What is perhaps most revealing about presidential understanding of the constitutional locus of the war power is that in the one or two dozen instances in which presidents personally have made the decision unconstitutionally to initiate acts of war, they have not purported to rely on their authority as commander in chief or chief executive. In "all of these cases the Presidents have made false claims of authorization, either by statute or by treaty or by international law." [92]

Moreover, it cannot be maintained that constitutional power, in this case the war power, can be acquired through practice. In *Powell v. McCormack*, Chief Justice Earl Warren wrote: "That an unconstitutional action has been taken before surely does not render that action any less unconstitutional at a later date." Earlier, Justice Felix Frankfurter, writing for a unanimous Court, echoed a centuries-old principle of Anglo-American jurisprudence: "Illegality cannot attain legitimacy through practice." [93] The Court has repeatedly denied claims that the president can acquire constitutional power through a series of usurpations. If it were otherwise, the president might aggrandize all governmental power. Neither Congress nor the judiciary could lawfully restrain the exercise of the president's accumulated constitutional powers. Clearly, this practice would scuttle our entire constitutional jurisprudence. Thus, the most recent act of usurpation stands no better than the first.

The efforts of revisionists to adduce an executive war making power on the basis of a list of "presidential wars" in the nineteenth century is unpersuasive. [94] As we have seen, the occasional president who did in engage in unilateral executive war making sought refuge in casuistry and contrivance. The Mexican War, which lasted from 1846 to 1848, deserves attention in this context. Following the annexation of Texas, a dispute arose over the title to territory between the Nueces River and the Rio Grande. President James K. Polk ordered an army into the area, and it defeated the Mexican forces. In a message to Congress, Polk offered the rationale that "Mexico has passed the boundary of the United States, has invaded our territory and shed American blood on American soil." It was on the basis of this report that Congress declared, "by the act of the Republic of Mexico, a state of war exists between the Government and the United States." [95]

If Polk's rationale was correct, then his action could not be challenged on constitutional grounds, for it was well established that the president had the authority to repel sudden attacks. If, however, he had been disingenuous, if he had in fact initiated hostilities, then he had clearly usurped the war making power of Congress. It is worth noting that he made no claim to constitutional power to make war. The Whigs greatly resented Polk's actions, and in

1847 the two houses of Congress commenced an inquiry into the circumstances surrounding the outbreak of the war. On January 3, 1848, the House concluded, by a vote of 85 to 81, that the war had been "unnecessarily and unconstitutionally begun by the President of the United States." [96] Congressman Abraham Lincoln of Illinois voted with the majority. Lincoln's law partner, William Herndon, had written a letter to Lincoln in which he stated that he assumed that Polk had initiated the hostilities, but nevertheless defended the action as a legitimate means of preventing an invasion by Mexico. Lincoln answered his friend in words that have become famous:

> "Let me first state what I understand to be your position. It is that if it shall become necessary to repel invasion, the President may, without violation of the Constitution, cross the line and invade the territory of another country, and that whether such necessity exists in any given case the President is the sole judge. . . .
>
> Allow the President to invade a neighboring nation whenever he shall deem it necessary to repel an invasion, and you allow him to do so whenever he may choose to say he deems it necessary for such a purpose and you allow him to make war at his pleasure. Study to see if you can fix any limit to his power in this respect, after having given him so much power as you propose. . . .
>
> The provision of the Constitution giving the war-making power to Congress was dictated, as I understand it, by the following reasons: Kings have always been involving and impoverishing their people in wars, pretending generally, if not always, that the good of the people was the object. This our convention understood to be the most oppressive of all kingly oppressions, and they resolved to frame the Constitution that no one man should hold the power of bringing oppression upon us. [97] But your view destroys the whole matter, and places our President where kings have always stood."

As president, Lincoln did not alter his view of the war power. This conclusion may be drawn from his first annual message on December 3, 1861, when he referred to prior congressional authorization for American ships to "defend themselves against and to capture pirates." It was his opinion that congressional authorization was necessary "to recapture any prizes which pirates may make of United States vessels and their cargoes," which was exactly the understanding of the war power held by Madison, Hamilton and Jefferson. [98] It bears reminder, moreover, that none of Lincoln's actions in the Civil War constitutes a precedent for presidential initiation of war. The attack on Fort Sumter represented a "sudden attack" that Lincoln had the constitutional power to repel. [99] Lincoln, it is to be emphasized, clearly understood what the Framers had undertaken in their construction of the War Clause. In the Prize Cases of 1863, Richard Henry Dana, Jr., who was representing the president, acknowledged that Lincoln's actions had nothing to do with "the right *to initiate a war, as a voluntary act of sovereignty.* That is vested only in Congress." [100] Lincoln's views on the war power do not aid the efforts of those who would champion executive ascendancy in matters of war and peace. On the contrary, adherence to the Lincoln Doctrine would force them to abandon their cause.

CONCLUSIONS

The ascendancy of the president in the area of war and peace finds no foundation in the Constitution. It reflects, rather, the tendency among presidents --Republicans and Democrats, conservatives and liberals alike --to aggrandize and abuse power. Usurpation of the war power, particularly in an era that exalts the concept of a personal or Imperial Presidency at the expense of a constitutionally confined presidency, lays bare the paramountcy of a president's personal characteristics. Indeed, it is precisely in the realm of a personal presidency that a decidedly executive perspective, subject to the full measure of the president's talents, strengths and temperament, as well as his judgment, knowledge and self-restraint, will be brought to the policy anvil. The historical portrait may not be pretty. Consider, for example, the arrogance and self-righteousness of Woodrow Wilson, the inclination toward dramatic posturing by Theodore Roosevelt, the inattentiveness of Ronald Reagan, as well as the indiscipline of Bill Clinton and the stunning, yet naïve certainties of George W. Bush. Then, too, there is the question of the president's ambition, political agenda, personal distractions and desire for fame and glory.

A considerable literature urges executive supremacy, and extols the supposed virtues of presidential assertion, domination and control; yet this body of work often ignores the dimensions of executive flaws, foibles, and frailties. The electoral process is not infallible; an elected president may lack the wisdom, temperament and judgment, not to mention perception, expertise and emotional intelligence to produce success in matters of war and peace. Those qualities which, to be sure, are attributes of the occupant and not of the office, cannot be conferred by election. [101] Champions of a unilateral executive war power have ignored and, perhaps, forgotten the institutional safeguards of separation of powers, checks and balances and collective decision making urged by the Framers as protection from the flaws of unilateral judgment and the temptations of power. Among those who have lost their memory of the virtues and values of those institutional safeguards, apparently, are those many members of Congress and dozens of judges over the years, who have acquiesced in the face of presidential usurpation in the realm of national security. Perhaps seduced by the allure of swift, bold military action under the banner of nationalism, patriotism and ideological and political certainty, these representatives, some elected and others appointed, have forgotten their institutional duties and responsibilities. It is not probable, but certain, that the Imperial Presidency would be brought to heel if the other branches duly exercised their powers and responsibilities, but they have lost their way. No less a personage than the late Senator Sam Ervin questioned, in the course of hearings in 1973 on the unchecked executive practice of impoundment, whether the Congress of the United States will remain a viable institution or whether the current trend toward the executive use of legislative power is to continue unabated until we have arrived at a presidential form of government." Senator Ervin justly criticized executive aggrandizement of legislative authority, but he also found Congress culpable for the rise of presidential dominance: "The executive branch has been able to seize power so brazenly only because the Congress has lacked the courage and foresight to maintain its constitutional position." [102] What was true of impoundment, is true of the war power. Only "Congress itself," to borrow from Justice Robert H. Jackson, "can prevent power from slipping through its fingers." [103]

The siren song of unilateral presidential war making ignores the tragedies of Korea, Vietnam and Iraq, and the cost to America of its precious blood and treasure and futures denied and stolen. The American constitutional system is grounded in the conviction, as James Iredell explained it, that there is "nothing more fallible than human judgment." [104]

It is sometimes observed that the intentions of the Framers are outdated and irrelevant. But before we too readily acquiesce in that verdict, we might do well to recall the policy considerations that underlay the decision to vest the war power in Congress and not the president. Painfully aware of the horror and destructive consequences of warfare, the Framers wisely determined that before the very fate of the nation were put to risk that there ought to be some discussion, some deliberation by Congress, the people's representatives. The Founders did not, as James Wilson explained it, want "one man to hurry us into war." [105] As things stand in the United States today, however, the president has been exercising that power. The "accretion of dangerous power," Justice Frankfurter has reminded us, occurs when power is freed from institutional restraints, checks and safeguards. The eminently sound rationales that convinced the Framers to vest the war power exclusively in Congress, however, have been ignored and abandoned in recent decades. There is a cost in that, too. It was the artist, Goya, who in one of his etchings, graphically portrayed the consequences of ignoring reason with the inscription: "The sleep of reason brings forth monsters." [106] There is no comfort to be found in a practice which permits unilateral executive war making, particularly in the age of nuclear weapons, when war might lead to the incineration of the planet. When it comes to the constitutional design for war making, it is clear that the Framers' policy concerns are even more compelling today than they were two centuries ago.

References

[1] Justice Felix Frankfurter, concurring, Youngstown Sheet and Tube co. v. Sawyer, 343 U.S. 579, 594 (1952).

[2] The rise of presidential hegemony in foreign affairs, and particularly the practice of executive abuse of power, has provoked considerable commentary and criticism. For recent discussion see, e.g., Frederick A.O. Schwarz Jr. and Aziz Z. Huq, Unchecked and Unbalanced: Presidential Power in a Time of Terror (2007); Louis Fisher, The Constitution and 911: Recurring Threats to America's Freedoms (2008); Louis Fisher, Military Tribunals and Presidential Power (2005); Gene Healy, The Cult of the Presidency (2008); James P. Pfiffner, Power Play: The Bush Presidency and the Constitution (2008); Jack Goldsmith, The Terror Presidency: Law and Judgment Inside the Bush Administration (2007); Takeover: The Return of the Imperial Presidency and the Subversion of American Democracy (2007); Andrew Rudalevige, The New Imperial Presidency: Renewing Presidential Power after Watergate (2006); Russell A. Miller, ed., US National Security, Intelligence and Democracy (2008); Michael A. Genovese and Lori Cox Han, eds., The Presidency and the Challenge to Democracy (2006); John Dean, Worse Than Watergate: The Secret Presidency of George W. Bush (2004). See, also, David Gray Adler, "George Bush and the Abuse of History: The Constitution and Presidential Power in Foreign Affairs," 12 UCLA Journal of Int. Law and Foreign Affairs 75 (2007); Adler, "George Bush as Commander in Chief: Toward the Nether World of American Constitutionalism, 36 Pres. Stud. Q. 525 (2006). Executive domination of foreign affairs has been promoted and defended by, among others, John Yoo, The Powers of War and Peace: The Constitution and Foreign Affairs

After 911 (2005), and Yoo, War by Other Means: An Insider's Account of the War on Terror (2006).

[3] Arthur Schlesinger Jr., The Imperial Presidency (1973);. Theodore J. Lowi, The Personal President: Power Invested, Promise Unfulfilled (1985); Thomas E. Cronin, The State of the Presidency (1980); James McGregor Burns, Presidential Government (1966).

[4] Gene Healy, The Cult of the Presidency: America's Dangerous Devotion to Executive Power (2008). Professor Lowi could justly say, in 1985, that in the United States, "we have a virtual cult of personality revolving around the White House." Lowi, Personal President at xi.

[5] The Federalist No. 51 at 338 (Modern Library ed. 1937). In a dissenting opinion in Myers v. United States, Justice Louis Brandeis invoked the fundamental belief of the Founders that the people "must look to representative assemblies for the protection of their liberties. . . ." 272 U.S. 52, 294-295 (1926).

[6] 1 Edward Gibbon, The History of the Decline and Fall of the Roman Republic 54 (1897).

[7] For discussion, see Fisher, Presidential War Power, 136-140.

[8] President Carter's termination of the 1954 Mutual Defense Treaty triggered a lawsuit, Goldwater v. Carter, 344 U.S. 997 (1979), in which the Supreme Court invoked the political question doctrine and thus declined to reach the merits. There are good reasons to believe that the president lacks unilateral authority to terminate treaties. For the argument that the termination power is shared by the president and the Senate, see David Gray Adler, "The Framers and Treaty Termination: A Matter of Symmetry," Arizona State L.J. (1981): 891-923, and Adler, The Constitution and the Termination of Treaties (1986).

[9] John Locke, Second Treatise on Civil Government, sec. 146-148 (1690).

[10] 2 William Blackstone, Commentaries on the Laws of England 238 (1803).

[11] Id. At 239.

[12] Id. at 251.

[13] Id. at 258.

[14] Id. at 262.

[15] Id. at 250.

[16] Federalist No. 45 at 303 (emphasis added).

[17] In Federalist No. 69, Alexander Hamilton explained that the authority to receive ambassadors is "more a matter of dignity than authority," "without consequence," in order to avoid the "necessity of convening the legislature . . . upon every arrival of a foreign minister. . . ." Federalist No. 69 at 451. The Framers regarded the reception of an ambassador as a routine, clerk-like administrative function, devoid of discretion. See my article, "The President's Recognition Power," in David Gray Adler and Larry N. George, eds., The Constitution and the Conduct of American Foreign Policy (1996), pp. 133-158.

[18] In the Convention, James Wilson echoed his colleagues when he declared that the English model was "inapplicable" to the "republican" system that that Framers had undertaken to create. Max Farrand, ed., The Records of the Federal Convention of 1787, 4 vols. (1937), 1:66.

[19] Federalist No. 75 at 487.

[20] Jonathan Elliot, ed., The Debates in the Several State Conventions on the Adoption of the Federal Constitution, 5 vols. (1836-1845), 2:507. In the First Congress, Roger Sherman, who had been a delegate to the Constitutional Convention, argued in defense of the shared-powers arrangement in foreign affairs: "The more wisdom there is employed, the greater security there is that the public business will be done." 1 Annals of Congress 1085. Sherman's statement echoed the sentiment expressed by Benjamin Franklin at the close of the Convention, when he urged the delegates to set aside their remaining differences in favor of the collective judgment. 2 Farrand 641-43. For an excellent discussion of republicanism see, generally, Gordon S. Wood, The Creation of the American Republic, 1776-1787 (1969) at 1-124.

[21] Dread of executive power surfaced again and again in the various conventions. See Farrand, Records, 1:66, 83, 90, 101, 113, 119, 153, 425; and 2:35-36, 101, 278, 513, 632, 640; Elliot, Debates, 3:58, 60; and 4:311.

[22] Farrand, 1:70.

[23] In Federalist No. 69, Alexander Hamilton was at pains to distinguish the powers of the English King from those vested in the president. While the King possessed the power of "declaring" war, that power, under the proposed Constitution, would be granted to Congress. Id. at 448. In sum, Hamilton explained, "there is no comparison between the intended power of the President and the actual power of the British sovereign." Id. at 451.

[24] United States v. Smith, 27 F. Cas. 1192, 1230 (C.C.D.N.Y.) (1806).

[25] The Federalist No. 4 at 18. See David Gray Adler, "Presidential Greatness as an Attribute of Warmaking," Pres. Stud. Q. (2003), 33: 466-483.

[26] The Writings of James Madison (Gaillard Hunt, ed., 1900-1910), 6:174.

[27] Id. at 312.

[28] 1 Farrand 121.

[29] 1 Farrand 64-65.

[30] Id. at 65.

[31] Id.

[32] Id. at 65-66.

[33] Id. at 70.

[34] 2 Farrand 182.

[35] Henry Steele Commager, Documents of American History, 7th ed. (1963), at 133.

[36] Warren, The Making of the Constitution (1947), at 389. The provision would maintain significant continuity, moreover, since it would retain legislative control of the war power. While neither the Virginia nor the New Jersey plans mentioned the war power, the former did stipulate that Congress would become the repository of all of the "Legislative Rights" of the Continental Congress, a fact that assumes great importance when it is recalled that the Framers, as Madison and Wilson explained, regarded the war power as "legislative" in nature.

[37] 2 Farrand 318. The Senate, Pinckney believed, was "more acquainted with foreign affairs, and most capable of proper resolutions." Id.

[38] 1 Farrand 292. Hamilton, it is to be emphasized, never asserted an executive power to make war.

[39] 2 Farrand 318.

[40] Id.

[41] See discussion in text accompanying notes [00-000], infra.

[42] 2 Farrand 318.

[43] Id. at 318-319.

[44] 2 Farrand 319.

[45] Id.

[46] 4 Elliot 263.

[47] 2 Elliot 528. Similar assurance was provided in other state conventions. In North Carolina, James Iredell, destined to be a member of the U.S. Supreme Court, stated: "The President has not the power of declaring war by his own authority. . . . These powers are vested in other hands. The power of declaring war is expressly given to Congress." 4 Elliot 107-108. See also, 4 Elliot 287; 2 Elliot 278. Wilson's impact on the Convention, and the early development of the Constitution, should not be underestimated. Robert G. McCloskey, ed., James Wilson, Works, 2 vols. (1967), Introduction, 1.

[48] 1 Wilson Works 433. Wilson is referring to powers vest in Congress by Article I, Section 8 of the Constitution.

[49] It is a necessary predicate of separation of powers that no branch may usurp the powers of another. It is equally true that no branch "may abdicate its powers to either of the others." Panama Refining Co. v. Ryan, 293 U.S. 388, 421 (1935). Art. II, Sec. 3 of the Constitution provides that the president "shall take Care that the Laws be faithfully executed. . . ." A president who usurps congressional power is not complying with the Take Care Clause. Chief Justice Roger Taney, Ex parte Merryman, 17 Fed. Case No. 9, 487 (1861), 262.

[50] 119 Cong. Rec. S14141 (daily ed. 19 July 1973).

[51] Ratner, "The Coordinated Warmaking Power—Legislative, Executive and Judicial Roles," 44 S. Cal. L. Rev.19 (1971); Professor Yoo's views on presidential power to initiate war may be seen in John C. Yoo, The Powers of War and Peace: The Constitution and Foreign Affairs after 9/II (2005). His first substantial foray into the debate appeared in a lengthy article in 1996, " The Continuation of Politics By Other Means," 84 Cal. L. Rev. (1996), pp. 167-305. For critiques of Yoo's work, see, e.g., Louis Fisher, "Unchecked Presidential Wars," 148 U. Penn. L. Rev. (2000), pp. 1637-1672; David Cole, "What Bush Wants to Hear," New York Review of Books, November 17, 2005, pp. 8-12; David Gray Adler, "Presidential Power and Foreign Affairs in the Bush Administration: The Use and Abuse of Alexander Hamilton," Presidential Studies Quarterly (forthcoming, June 2010).

[52] Yoo, Continuation, at 170. Yoo has also invoked the Commander in Chief Clause as a source of presidential authority to commence war. See, infra, text accompanying notes 71-78.

[53] See, e.g., H. Jefferson Powell, The President's Authority Over Foreign Affairs: An Essay in Constitutional Interpretation (2002), pp. 119-125. For a critique of Professor Powell's views, see David Gray Adler, "Constitution, Foreign Affairs and Presidential War-Making: A Response to Professor Powell," 19 Geo. State L. Rev. (2003), pp. 947-1019. See also, John Norton Moore, "The National Executive and the Use of Armed Forces Abroad," in Richard Falk, ed. The Vietnam War and International Law, 4 vols. (1969), 2:814. Senator Paul Douglas defended President Harry Truman's unauthorized venture in Korea on this ground (Cong. Rec. 9648 (1950)).

[54] Huloet's dictionary provided this definition: "Declare warres. Arma Canere, Bellum indicere." We have here two meanings: to summon to arms; to announce war. Quoted in Francis D. Wormuth and Edwin B. Firmage, To Chain the Dogs of War (1986), at 20.

[55] In 1744, Comyn's Digest, an authoritative treatise on English law, stated: "To the king alone it belongs to make peace and war," as well as "the king has the sole authority to declare war and peace." Quoted in Wormuth and Firmage, at 20. For discussion of the founders' understanding of international law, see the excellent article by the historian, Charles Lofgren, "War-Making Under the Constitution: The Original Understanding," 81 Yale L.J. (1972) 672, 685-695.

[56] James Kent, Commentaries on American Law, 2d ed., 4 vols. (1896), 1:55.

[57] Lofgren, "War-Making," at 685-695.

[58] According to Emerich de Vattel, the leading international law publicist, a conditional declaration of war, an ultimatum demanding satisfaction of grievances, ought properly to precede a declaration of general war. Vatttel, The Law of Nations, trans. Charles Fenwick (1916), at 254-57.

[59] Miller v. The Ship Resolution, 2 U.S. (2 Dall.)12, 21 (1782).

[60] 4 Dall. 37 (1800).

[61] 5 U.S. (1 Cranch) 1, 28 (1801).

[62] John Bassett Moore, The Collected Papers of John Bassett Moore, 7 vols. (1944), 5:195-196.

[63] 6 U.S. (2 Cranch) 170, 177-78 (1804).

[64] 27 F. Cas. 1192, 1230 (No. 16342) (C.C.D.N.Y. 1806).

[65] 67 U.S. (2 Black) 635, 668 (1863).

[66] For an excellent discussion of the origins and development of the use of letters of marque and reprisal, with an application to contemporary covert operations, see Jules Lobel, "Covert War and Congressional Authority: Hidden War and Forgotten Power," 134.Penn. L. Rev 1035 (1986).

[67] Id. at 1045-47.

[68] Quoted in Moore, Digest of International Law, 7:123.

[69] Youngstown Sheet and Tube Co. v. Sawyer, 343 U.S. 579, 643 (1952)(concurring opinion).

[70] For example, the State Department justified Johnson's involvement in Vietnam on the basis of his authority as commander in chief. Dept of State Bull., 54: 474, 484 (1966). For the same justification by Reagan with respect to his actions in Lebanon and Grenada, respectively, see 18 Weekly Comp. Pres. Docs. 1181, 1183 (1993). For discussion of presidential invocation of the Commander in Chief Clause, see Adler, "George Bush as Commander in Chief: Toward the Nether World of Amerian Constitutionalism," 36 Pres. Stud. Q. 525 (2006); Fisher, Presidential War Power.

[71] John Yoo, "Memo: The President's Constitutional Authority to Conduct Military Operations Against Terrorists and Nations Supporting Them," September 25, 2001, in Karen J. Greenberg and Justin L. Dratel, eds., The Torture Papers: The Road to Abu Graib (2005), at pp. 3-4. Yoo's argument in this memo, and others, substantively track his academic work, before and after, his stint at the OLC. From the mid 90's through 2008, Yoo has consistently asserted the view that the president inherited the English

King's "plenary power," except where specifically altered in the Constitutional Convention.

[72] Wormuth, "The Nixon Theory of the War Power," 60 Cal. L. Rev., 623, 630 (1972).

[73] Id. at 630.

[74] For example, the Continental Congress ordered George Washington to Massachusetts to take command of the United Colonies. See Journals of the Continental Congress, 34 vols. (1904-1937), 2:101. Washington was directed to intercept two British vessels on October 5, 1775. Id. at 3:276.

[75] 1 Farrand 292.

[76] Federalist No. 69 at 448.

[77] Federalist No. 74, at 482. In the North Carolina Ratifying Convention, for example, James Iredell delivered remarks that mirrored Hamilton's observations. 4 Elliot 197-108.

[78] Federalist No. 74, at 482.

[79] Louis Henkin, Foreign Affairs and the Constitution (1972), at 50-51.

[80] Leonard Meeker, "The Legality of the United States Participation in the Defense of Vietnam," 54 Department of State Bulletin 474 (1966).

[81] William P. Rogers, "Congress, the President and the War Powers," 59 Cal. L. Rev. 1194 (1971), at 1207-12.

[82] Carter justified his attempted rescue of the hostages on April 24, 1980, on his powers as chief executive and commander in chief. 126 Cong. Rec. H2991 (daily ed., April 28, 1980).

[83] 1 Farrand 65-70.

[84] For a detailed discussion of this claim see Adler, "The Steel Seizure Case and Inherent Presidential Power," 19 Constitutional Commentary 155 (2002), at 163-95. See also, Symposium, "Invoking Inherent Presidential Powers," Louis Fisher, ed., 37 Pres. Studies Q 1-152 (2007).

[85] For discussion of this point, see Fisher, Constitutional Conflicts, at 287-92; Adler, Steel Seizure Case, at 173-80.

[86] Henry P. Monaghan, "Presidential War-Making," 50 Boston University L. Rev. 19 (1970). The Clinton Administration, in Campbell v. Clinton, adduced the argument about precedent. Its claims were demonstrably false. See Adler, "The Clinton Theory of the War Power," 30 Pres. Studies Q. 155 (2000), at 164-166.

[87] For example, in 1967 the State Department published a study that listed 137 cases of unilateral presidential action. Department of State, Historical Studies Division, Armed Actions Taken by the United States Without a Declaration of War, 1789-1967 (1967). J. Terry Emerson, legal adviser to Sen. Barry Goldwater, published a list in 1973 in which he alleged 199 incidents of presidential acts of war without congressional authorization. 119 Cong. Rec. S14174 (daily ed. July 20, 1973. In a footnote to the Clinton Administration's brief in Campbell v. Clinton, it was asserted that "US Armed Forces have acted without a declaration of war in scores of instances from the presidency of George Washington to the present." See, "Memorandum of Points and Authorities in Support of Defendant's Motion to Dismiss," p. 27, n. 9, in Clinton v. Campbell, 52 F. Supp. 2d 34 (D.D.C. 1999).

[88] Raoul Berger, Executive Privilege (1974), at 76. See Wormuth, "Nixon Theory," at 652-654, and Wormuth and Firmage, Chain the Dogs, at 133-49.

[89] Wormuth, Vietnam, at 718.
[90] Alfange Jr., "The Quasi-War and Presidential War Making," in David Gray Adler and Larry N. George, eds. (1996), at 281.
[91] Wormuth and Firmage, Chain the Dogs, at 149.
[92] Powell v. McCormack, 395 U.S. 486, 546 (1969); Inland Waterways Corp. v. Young, 309 U.S. 518, 524 (1940).
[93] The phrase was introduced in the literature by Francis D. Wormuth, "Presidential Wars: The Convenience of 'Precedent,'" in The Nation, October 9, 1972, at 301.
[94] 9 Stat. 9, 29th Cong., 1st sess., ch. 16 (May 13, 1846). Richardson, Messages and Papers of Presidents, 3:2292.
[95] Cong. Globe, 30th Cong., 1st sess., at 95.
[96] Richardson, Messages and Papers of Presidents.
[97] Id. at 6:47.
[98] Arthur Schlesinger, Jr., has written: "There is no suggestion that Lincoln supposed he would use this power in foreign wars without congressional consent." Schlesinger, "Congress and the Making of American Foreign Policy," 51 Foreign Affairs 78 (1972), at 89.
[99] The Prize Cases, 67 U.S. 635, 660 (emphasis in original).
[100] Professor Richard Pious has exposed the claims of presidential superiority in matters of information, expertise and experience. Those alleged virtues of executive primacy in foreign affairs were unable to secure accurate information or provide accurate projection in a variety of episodes, which proved costly to America: the Bay of Pigs, the Cuban Missile Crisis, and the attempted rescue of the merchant ship, Mayaguez, were riddled by inaccurate information, poor judgment and deceptive statements. Pious, Why Presidents Fail (2008).
[101] Quoted in Louis Fisher, Congressional Abdication on War and Spending (2000), p. 119. Another indefatigable defender of congressional powers and constitutional responsibilities, Sen. Robert Byrd of West Virginia, has recently lamented the decline of Congress. See Byrd, Losing America: Confronting a Reckless and Arrogant Presidency (2004). Insightful remedies and prescriptions for restoring constitutional balance have been advanced in a very fine work written by Eric Lane and Michael Oreskes, The Genius of America: How the Constitution Saved Our Country and Why it Can Again (2007).
[102] Youngstown Sheet and Tube Co. v. Sawyer, 343 U.S. at 655 (concurring opinion). Professor George Edwards has justly stated: "There is little question that the Constitution allocates to Congress a central role in determining the major elements of national security policy if Congress chooses to do so." George S. Edwards III, "Congress and National Strategy: The Appropriate Role?" in U.S. National Security Strategy for the 1990s. ed. Daniel J. Kaufman, David S. Clark, and Kevin P. Sheehan (1991), p. 82.
[103] 4 Elliot 14.
[104] 2 Elliott 528.
[105] Goya, Caprichos.

In: President or King?
Editor: Meena Bose, pp. 27-42
ISBN: 978-1-61324-655-9

PRESIDENTS OPERATING UNDER THE LAW [1]

Louis Fisher

ABSTRACT

Over the past six decades, presidents have decided to violate the law by invoking the concept of "inherent" powers, claiming that these independent and exclusive actions may not be checked by Congress or the courts. To conceal illegal operations, executive officials lie to Congress and withhold information from courts. Buttressing these unilateral actions is the state secrets privilege, which administrations have relied on to keep documents from federal judges and private plaintiffs. When Congress and the courts defer to executive claims, often in the name of "national security," the political and constitutional system pays a great price and individual liberties are put at risk.

INTRODUCTION

In times of emergency, it is always tempting for presidents to press the limits of their power and do what law prohibits. They and their advisers may satisfy themselves that their motivations are benign because they are operating for the national good. They justify their actions as attempts to defend the country from hostile forces, both outside and within. What safeguards the country, however, is the rule of law and the system of checks and balances. Presidential efforts to go outside the law "for the public good" invariably do great harm to the system of self-government and constitutional government. In the greatest crisis ever for the United States, the Civil War, President Abraham Lincoln understood that he acted outside his constitutional powers, publicly admitted his lack of legal authority, and came to Congress to seek retroactive authority, which Congress granted. What has destabilized the U.S. legal and constitutional system is the claim by presidents that they possess "inherent" powers that are exclusive and plenary and may not be checked by other branches.

EMERGENCY POWERS

The Constitution can be protected in times of crisis. If an emergency occurs and there is no opportunity for executive officers to seek legislative authority, the Executive may take action sometimes in the absence of law and sometimes against it — for the public good. This is called the "Lockean prerogative." John Locke advised that in the event of Executive abuse, the primary remedy was an "appeal to Heaven." The framers of the U.S. Constitution relied on a more secular and constitutional safeguard. Unilateral presidential measures, at a time of extraordinary crisis, must be followed promptly by congressional action through the regular statutory process. Legislative approval must come from the entire Congress, not from some subgroup within it. [2]

To preserve the constitutional order, executive emergency power is subject to two conditions. The president must (1) acknowledge that the emergency actions are not legal or constitutional and (2) for that very reason come to the legislative branch, explain the actions taken, the necessity for the actions, and ask lawmakers to pass a bill making the illegal actions legal. Without those steps, a government loses its democratic and constitutional character. Under Article 48 of the Weimar Constitution, as implemented by the Nazi government, emergency powers were invoked without ever coming to the legislative body. [3]

Lincoln's Exercise of Power

After the firing on Fort Sumter in April 1861, President Abraham Lincoln called up troops, placed a blockade on the South, suspended the writ of habeas corpus, and withdrew funds from the Treasury without an appropriation. He made no claim that he acted legally or constitutionally or that Article II permitted him to do what he did. Instead, he admitted to exceeding the constitutional boundaries of his office and publicly announced that he needed the sanction of Congress. He told lawmakers that his actions, "whether strictly legal or not, were ventured upon under what appeared to be a popular demand and a public necessity, trusting then, as now, that Congress would readily ratify them." He forthrightly admitted that he used not only his Article II powers but the Article I powers of Congress, concluding that his actions were not "beyond the constitutional competency of Congress." [4]

In his book on crisis government, Clinton Rossiter included a section called "The Lincoln Dictatorship." [5] He claimed that Lincoln was "the sole possessor of the indefinite grant of executive power in Article II of the Constitution." [6] Lincoln did not make that argument. He understood that his powers were not indefinite and he understood that his initiatives after Fort Sumter went beyond his Article II powers and invaded those of Congress under Article I. Lincoln's request that Congress review what he had done and independently judge his actions was not the conduct of a dictator, even a constitutional dictator.

Congress debated his request from July 4 to early August. Some lawmakers wanted to move the bill through quickly to support the President. The general mood, however, was to act with care and deliberation and to receive and examine the materials that Lincoln would submit. It was generally understood that Lincoln had exceeded his legal and constitutional powers, especially by increasing the regular army and suspending the writ of habeas corpus. It was for that reason that statutory ratification was essential. The bill became law on August 6, 1861, providing that all of Lincoln's acts, proclamations, and orders after his inauguration on March 4 respecting the army and navy and calling out the military and volunteers "are hereby approved and in all respects legalized and made valid, to the same intent and with the same effect as if they had been issued and done under the previous express authority and direction of the Congress of the United States." [7]

The Blockade

When the Supreme Court in *The Prize Cases* (1863) upheld Lincoln's blockade of ports in the South, it did not give judicial blessing to the exercise of indefinite powers by the president when operating under the Commander in Chief Clause. Both the Lincoln administration and the Court read those powers in a limited manner. Lincoln's initiatives applied to a purely internal, domestic matter of civil war and had nothing to do with exercising the war power outside the United States.

Richard Henry Dana, Jr., serving as Lincoln's lawyer in this case, submitted a brief to the Supreme Court that reviewed the powers of Congress and the president over war. Although Dana argued that the president might have to repel an attack by another country "as a matter of self-defense," that discretionary power did not give the president any power "to initiate a war, as a voluntary act of sovereignty. That is vested only in Congress." [8] Dana reviewed existing legislation to determine if Congress limited what Lincoln could do with blockades and captures of vessels. He found no restrictions. That was an important concession. Even in times of emergency and civil wars, the president's discretion was subject to statutory policy.

For some reason the administration decided to submit a second brief, this one by William M. Evarts, who argued that during time of war all laws, "of whatever dignity and permanence, are silent under the overwhelming fact of war." [9] He implied that the "law of war" supersedes existing statutory law, which Dana did not assert and neither did Lincoln. Evarts further argued that in time of emergency the president could wield whatever power was necessary, "without further needed recourse to the Legislature," making the president "exclusive judge of these emergencies." [10] That position went far beyond Dana. Lincoln specifically went to Congress to seek retroactive authority.

The Supreme Court ignored Evarts' theory of presidential power and borrowed some of the themes advanced by Dana. Writing for a 5 to 4 majority, Justice Grier said the president "has no power to initiate or declare a war either against a foreign nation or a domestic State." [11] If war comes by invasion of a foreign power or by states organized in rebellion, the president is authorized to "resist force by force." [12]

Suspending the Writ

Lincoln also recognized limits on his power to suspend the writ of habeas corpus. He thought it was unreasonable to interpret the Constitution to prevent the president from selectively suspending the writ in the midst of an emergency when Congress was not in session. Implicit in that argument is the admission that the suspension must be selective, not sweeping, and the president's power narrows when the emergency lifts and Congress returns. As he told lawmakers after they had reassembled: "Whether there shall be any legislation upon the subject, and, if any, is submitted entirely to the better judgment of Congress." [13]

The legal analysis by Attorney General Edward Bates was similarly cautious in interpreting presidential power. Bates reasoned that in times of "a great and dangerous insurrection," the president has discretion to arrest and hold in custody persons "known to have criminal intercourse with the insurgents, or persons against whom there is probable cause for suspicion of such criminal complicity." [14] Bates concluded that if the constitutional language in Article I meant "a repeal of all power to issue the writ, then I freely admit that none but Congress can do it." In case of "a great and dangerous rebellion, like the present," the president's power to suspend the privilege was "temporary and exceptional." [15]

Chief Justice Roger Taney, sitting as circuit judge, issued a writ of habeas corpus to the commandant at Fort McHenry in Baltimore, ordering him to bring John Merryman to the circuit courtroom on May 27, 1861. Acting under Lincoln's orders, the commandant refused to produce Merryman. Taney stated that Merryman was "entitled to be set at liberty" but recognized he could not prevail in this standoff with Lincoln. [16] Taney was not the federal official with either the authority or the capacity to preserve the Union. That task fell to Lincoln and to Congress. With his decision in *Dred Scott*, Taney had helped propel the nation toward civil war.

After Lincoln invited Congress to pass legislation on the writ, a bill was enacted on March 3, 1863, directing the Secretary of State and the Secretary of War to furnish federal judges with a list of the names of all persons held as prisoners by order of the president or executive officers. Submitting this list was mandatory. Failure to furnish someone's name to the judiciary could result in the discharge of a prisoner. [17]

INHERENT POWERS

The framers created a federal government of enumerated and implied powers. Express powers are clearly stated in the text of the Constitution; implied powers are those that can be reasonably drawn from express powers. Because Congress has the express power to legislate, it has the implied power to investigate, to issue subpoenas, and to hold individuals in contempt when they interfere with the investigative power. Because the president has the express duty to see that the laws are faithfully executed, he has the implied power to remove department heads who prevent laws from being carried out.

"Inherent" is sometimes used as synonymous with "implied." [18] However, they are radically different. Inherent powers are not drawn from express powers. Inherent power has been defined in this manner: "An authority possessed without it being derived from another.. Powers over and beyond those explicitly granted in the Constitution or reasonably to be implied from express powers." [19] The purpose of a constitution is to specify and confine governmental powers in order to protect individual rights and liberties. Express and implied powers serve that principle. The Constitution is undermined by claims of open-ended authorities that cannot be located, defined, or circumscribed. What "inheres" in the president? The standard collegiate dictionary explains that "inherent" describes the "essential character of something: belonging by nature or habit." [20] How does one determine what is essential or part of nature? Those words and concepts are so nebulous that they invite political abuse, offer convenient justifications for illegal and unconstitutional actions, and endanger individual liberties. [21]

Over the past six decades, presidents have decided to violate the law by invoking "inherent" powers. President Harry Truman seized steel mills in an effort to prosecute the war in Korea. He was stopped by the Supreme Court. [22] President Richard Nixon conducted warrantless domestic surveillance and refused to spend appropriated funds. His actions were reversed by court rulings and congressional statutes. Regarding surveillance, see *United States* v. *United States District Court* (1972) and the Foreign Intelligence Surveillance Act of 1978, which provided the "exclusive means" of conducting such surveillance, thus overriding executive claims of inherent power. The claim of inherent power to impound was reversed by the Impoundment Control Act of 1974 and dozens of judicial rulings. [23]

Without articulating the theory of "inherent" powers, many of the top leaders in the Reagan administration decided to violate statutory limits on assistance to the Contra "freedom fighters" in Nicaragua. Congress had authorized the assistance of humanitarian assistance but Reagan officials worked with private citizens and foreign governments to circumvent Congress and provide military aid to the Contras. To conceal the illegal operation, executive officials lied to Congress and withheld information. The impulse of these officials had a familiar ring: if law prevents the doing of good then law can be violated or circumvented. In their efforts to export democracy and the rule of law to Central America, the administration was willing to undermine democracy and the rule of law at home. After the illegal operation unraveled and became public, administration officials admitted that government cannot function in this manner.

THE BUSH ADMINISTRATION

Following the terrorist attacks of 9/11, President George W. Bush acted unilaterally by creating military tribunals, detaining citizens and aliens indefinitely without charging them or bringing them to trial, sending suspects to other countries for interrogation and torture ("extraordinary rendition"), and using the National Security Agency to conduct warrantless surveillance. Many of these actions evaded normal checks and balances for years because they were done in secret. When private citizens sued the Bush administration, especially in the case of extraordinary rendition and NSA surveillance, the administration invoked the "state secrets privilege" to put a halt to the litigation. In most cases federal judges deferred to these executive claims and prevented private litigants from gaining access to documents to make their case or even pursue their claims on the basis of documents already in their possession. Once again the political and constitutional system paid a great price.

MILITARY COMMISSIONS

On November 13, 2001, President Bush authorized the creation of military commissions. He issued a military order for the detention, treatment, and trial of noncitizens who belonged to al Qaeda, engaged in international terrorism, or harbored such individuals. [24] He relied upon "the authority vested in me as President and as Commander in Chief of the Armed

Forces of the United States and the laws of the United States of America, including the Authorization for Use of Military Force [AUMF] Joint Resolution (Public Law 107-40, 11 Stat. 224) and sections 821 and 836 of title 10, United States Code." The joint resolution, authorizing military action against the Taliban and al Qaeda in Afghanistan, said nothing about military commissions.

In litigation challenging the president's authority to establish and operate military commissions, the Justice Department argued that Bush "had ample authority" to convene them, relying on both the AUMF and Sections 821 and 836. [25] If congressional support for the military order "were not so clear, the President has the inherent authority to convene military commissions to try and punish captured enemy combatants in wartime — even in the absence of any statutory authorization." [26]

In *Hamdan* v. *Rumsfeld* (2006), the Supreme Court found those arguments to be without merit. The commissions created by Bush lacked authority because they violated both the Uniform Code of Military Justice (Sections 821 and 836) and the Geneva Conventions. The constitutional authority over military commissions lay not in inherent powers for the president but under the Article I powers of Congress to enact Sections 821 and 836. The claim of inherent presidential power fell to the statutory policy already adopted by Congress.

DETAINING U.S. CITIZENS

The military commissions created by President Bush applied to any individual "not a United States citizen." A number of suspected alien terrorists were prosecuted in civil court or taken before a military tribunal. Others were designated "enemy combatant" and held incommunicado without access to an attorney. Two U.S. citizens, Yaser Esam Hamdi and Jose Padilla, were treated in that fashion by being placed in military confinement without ever being charged or tried.

In the case against Hamdi, the Justice Department insisted that whenever the president designates a U.S. citizen an enemy combatant, federal judges may not interfere with his judgment. According to a government brief, the Constitution vests the president "with exclusive authority to act as Commander in Chief and as the Nation's sole organ in foreign affairs." [27] Therefore, courts "may not second-guess the military's determination that an individual is an enemy combatant and should be detained as such. . . . Going beyond that determination would require the courts to enter an area in which they have no competence, much less institutional expertise, intrude upon the constitutional prerogative of the Commander in Chief (and military authorities acting at his control), and possibly create 'a conflict between judicial and military opinion highly comforting to enemies of the United States'." [28]

In *Hamdi* v. *Rumsfeld* (2004), eight Justices of the Supreme Court rejected the administration's central argument that Hamdi's detention was quintessentially a presidential decision and could not be reviewed and rethought by the judiciary. Writing for the plurality, Justice Sandra Day O'Connor announced: "We necessarily reject the Government's assertion that separation of powers principles mandate a heavily circumscribed role for the courts in such circumstances. . . . We have long since made clear that a state of war is not a blank check for the President when it comes to the rights of the Nation's citizens. . . . Whatever power the United States Constitution envisions for the Executive in its exchanges with other nations or with enemy organizations in times of conflict, it most assuredly envisions a role for all three branches when individual liberties are at stake." [29]

DETAINEES AT GUANTANAMO

Legal analyses within the Bush administration concluded that neither courts nor Congress could interfere with how the president decided to treat noncitizen detainees. On December 28, 2002, two attorneys within the Justice Department reasoned that the "great weight" of legal authority indicated that a federal district court "could not probably exercise habeas jurisdiction" over noncitizens detained at Guantánamo. [30] Under this interpretation, detainees at the naval base were beyond the jurisdiction of federal courts to hear their cases.

Some lower courts accepted that argument, relying heavily on *Johnson* v. *Eisentrager* (1950). [31] A district judge in 2002 found a parallel between the detainees at the naval base and the defendants in *Eisentrager*, noting that the plaintiffs in these cases were aliens held outside the territory over which the United States was sovereign. [32] However, the cases were quite different. Unlike the detainees at the naval base, the individuals in *Eisentrager* had been charged, given counsel, tried, and found guilty. No such elementary procedural safeguards had been extended to the detainees at the naval base. The prisoners in *Eisentrager* were aliens of a country (Germany) at war with the United States. The detainees at the naval base were not nationals of countries at war with the United States and had denied being engaged in or plotting acts of aggression against the United States.

A third fundamental difference between *Eisentrager* and Guantánamo is the status of the naval base, which the United States has occupied under a lease entered into with the Cuban government in 1903, giving the Unticd States "complete jurisdiction and control," although not sovereignty. During oral argument before the Supreme Court, Solicitor General Ted Olson told the Justices that on the issue whether the naval base was outside the jurisdiction of U.S. federal courts, the "question of sovereignty is a political decision" and it would be "remarkable for the judiciary to start deciding where the United States is sovereign and where the United States has control." [33] Olson compared the situation at the naval base to detainees "in a field of combat where there are prisons in Afghanistan where we have complete control with respect to the circumstances." The Justices found this analogy unpersuasive, noting that Afghanistan "is not a place where American law is, and for a century, has customarily been applied to all aspects of life," as is the case with the naval base.[34] In a 6 to 3 decision, the Court in *Rasul* v. *Bush* (2004) held that the detainees at Guantánamo had access to federal courts. [35]

EXTRAORDINARY RENDITION

In 2002, a 50-page memo from the head of the Office of Legal Counsel to White House Counsel Alberto Gonzales interpreted the president's authority as Commander in Chief in broad fashion to decide that any statute or treaty regarding torture would be unconstitutional "if it impermissibly encroached on the President's constitutional power to conduct a military campaign." [36] This line of analysis encouraged a policy of subjecting detainees to abuse and torture if it could be justified under the president's constitutional authority as Commander in Chief, including efforts to gain intelligence needed for the war on terrorism. Part of this Justice Department policy led to "extraordinary rendition": sending detainees to another country for interrogation and torture.

For most of U.S. history, Attorneys General concluded that presidents may not surrender someone to a foreign jurisdiction without statutory or treaty authority, as with extradition. [37] At times U.S. officials would resort to kidnappings, renditions, and forcible abduction to transfer someone from another country to the United States, but the purpose was not for interrogation and torture but to bring the individual to court for trial, with all procedural safeguards available to the accused. [38]

Placing the adjective "extraordinary" in front of the noun rendition suggests that a policy previously governed by law (statutes, treaties, and judicial procedures) had entered the realm of executive-made law. Under this theory, the president could act not only in the absence of statutes and treaties but in direct violation of them. Officials in the Bush administration claimed that the policy of extraordinary rendition had been developed in consultation with the National Security Council and disclosed to the appropriate committees of Congress. [39] Nothing in the process of consultation within the executive branch or with selected committees of Congress has anything to do with providing legal authority or justifying violations of law.

When the policy of extraordinary rendition was challenged in court, the Justice Department argued that individuals subjected to this process were barred from litigating their grievances because a lawsuit would risk the disclosure of "state secrets" damaging to national security and encroach upon independent, plenary presidential authority: "The state secrets privilege is based on the President's Article II power to conduct foreign affairs and to provide for the national defense, and therefore has constitutional underpinnings." [40] The success of that argument depends on how independently federal courts wanted to exercise their Article III power to assure fairness and fact-finding in the courtroom. Unfortunately, federal judges have a pattern of granting "deference" and even "utmost deference" to executive claims of state secrets. [41]

One case involved Khalid El-Masri, born in Kuwait, raised in Lebanon, and then moved to Germany where he became a German citizen in 1995. During a vacation trip to Macedonia at the end of 2003, he was detained by border officials because of confusion about his name. They thought he was Khalid al-Masri, a suspect from the al Qaeda Hamburg cell. Macedonian officials transferred him to the CIA and he was flown to a secret prison in Kabul, Afghanistan, held there for five months in squalid conditions until the U.S. recognized and admitted that it had imprisoned the wrong man. At that point he was able to return to Germany and be reunited with his family.

On December 6, 2005, El-Masri sued CIA Director George Tenet, the airlines used by the CIA, and current and former employees of the agency. The Bush administration invoked the state secrets privilege to block litigation. On May 12, 2006, a federal district court held that the privilege was validly asserted and dismissed the case. Although the judge insisted that courts "must not blindly accept the Executive Branch's assertion" of state secrets and "must instead independently and carefully determine whether, in the circumstances, the claimed secrets deserve the protection of the privilege." He also said that courts "must also bear in mind the Executive Branch's preeminent authority over military and diplomatic matters." [42]

Under that test, judges will dismiss the case early, before plaintiffs have an opportunity to seek documents through the discovery process. That is what happened here.

After the judge's decision was affirmed by the Fourth Circuit, the Supreme Court refused to take the case. [43] The Fourth Circuit claimed that the case "pits the judiciary's search for truth against the Executive's duty to maintain the nation's security." [44] Courts cannot search for truth if they prevent plaintiffs from obtaining documents. The nation's security is not endangered when judges insist that executive officials at least disclose to the court, meeting in camera, evidence central to the case. Courts cannot maintain their independence and their function as neutral magistrate if they are uninformed and routinely defer to executive claims and assertions. Accepting those assertions without searching inquiry and analysis is one form of judicial abdication. [45]

The same pattern was repeated with the extraordinary rendition case of Maher Arar. Born in Syria, he moved to Canada with his parents when he was 17, studied at McGill University and the University of Quebec, and obtained a Master's degree in telecommunications. In September 2002, while vacationing with his wife and two children in Tunis, he was called back to Canada to consult with a prospective client. At JFK airport in New York, he was prepared to make a connecting flight to Montreal but was questioned by immigration officials, New York police, and FBI agents over a period of days, during which time he learned that he was suspected of being a member of a foreign terrorist organization. He advised U.S. officials that if he were sent to Syria, as was planned, he would be tortured. Country reports from the State Department warned every year of Syria's torture methods. [46] Nevertheless, the United States sent him to Syria where he was tortured for almost a year before being released and returned to Canada.

In 2005, Arar filed a civil suit seeking money damages and declaratory relief from a number of U.S. officials in their individual and official capacities. The Justice Department filed a memorandum invoking the state secrets privilege. On February 16, 2006, a federal district court held that Arar lacked standing to bring the suit. Any access to remedies, said the court, was foreclosed by national security and foreign considerations. It underscored the importance of secrecy in foreign affairs: "One need not have much imagination to contemplate the negative effect of our relations with Canada if discovery were to proceed in this case and were it to turn out that certain high Canadian officials had, despite public denials, acquiesced in Arar's removal to Syria." [47]

What the court contemplated occurred seven months later, when Canada released a three-volume, 822-page judicial report that Canadian intelligence officials had passed false warnings and bad information about Arar to the United States. The report found no involvement by Arar in Islamic extremism and no evidence that he did anything wrong or was a security threat. [48] On January 26, 2007, Prime Minister Stephen Harper of Canada publicly apologized to Arar and his family. The government of Canada provided $9.75 million in compensation. [49]

Arar appealed his case to the Second Circuit. On June 30, 2008, the court held that he failed to state a claim for a violation of the Torture Victim Prevention Act. Dismissing the case on that and other grounds, the Second Circuit saw no need to consider the issue of state secrets. [50] The Second Circuit agreed to hear the case *en banc*. A hearing was held on December 9, 2008. Eleven months later, on November 2, 2009, the Second Circuit divided 7 to 4 in rejecting Arar's suit. It held that he could not sue for damages because Congress had not authorized such suits. Given the division among the appellate judges, an appeal to the Supreme Court is likely.

Reconsidering State Secrets

In 2008 and 2009, the House and Senate Judiciary Committees held hearings to consider legislation that would authorize federal courts to exercise greater independence in reviewing executive branch claims of state secrets. Judges would be expected to look at disputed classified documents in their chambers rather than simply accept assertions made in executive branch declarations and affidavits. Judges would be able to convert classified documents into substitute documents that would enable plaintiffs to pursue their case without the risk of damage to national security or foreign policy. [51]

On May 21, 2009, President Barack Obama issued a number of remarks on national security, including the observation that the state secrets privilege is "absolutely necessary in some circumstances to protect national security" but has been "over-used." He said his administration "must not protect information merely because it reveals the violation of a law or embarrassment to the government." He promised to "apply a stricter test to material that can be protected under the state secrets privilege." [52] During this review period, the position of the Obama administration on state secrets did not differ from that of the Bush administration. The privilege was regularly invoked to prevent private litigants from pursuing their case.

The "stricter test" was unveiled in a memorandum released by Attorney General Eric Holder on September 23, 2009. He said the Justice Department had adopted a new policy "to strengthen public confidence that the U.S. Government will invoke the privilege in court only when genuine and significant harm to national defense or foreign relations is at stake and only to the extent necessary to safeguard those interests." [53] Procedures were created to require an Assistant Attorney General for the division with jurisdiction to determine whether invocation of the state secrets privilege is warranted, followed by evaluations by a State Secrets Review Committee and approval either by the Attorney General or the Deputy Attorney General. [54]

Those procedures are wholly unrelated to the need of creating within the federal judiciary an opportunity to examine disputed documents, at least in camera, and to propose substitute documents that can allow the case to move forward without risk of disclosing information damaging to national security. Unless judges look at the underlying evidence, they are necessarily dependent on assertions by the executive branch and have no capacity to render an informed and independent ruling. A Justice Department press release, issued on the same day as Holder's memo, said that the Department "will submit evidence to the court for review."[55] However, Holder's four-page memo made no mention of that crucial step. As Senator Russ Feingold noted, the Holder memo "amounts to an approach of 'just trust us.' Independent court review of the government's use of the state secrets privilege is essential."[56]

NSA SURVEILLANCE

On December 16, 2005, the *New York Times* reported that President Bush, in the months following the 9/11 attacks, secretly authorized the NSA to listen to Americans and others inside the United States without a court-approved warrant. On December 17, in a weekly radio address, President Bush acknowledged that he had authorized the NSA, "consistent with U.S. law and the Constitution, to intercept the international communications of people with known links to Al Qaeda and related terrorist organizations."[57] What he did was not only inconsistent with U.S. law but directly in violation of the Foreign Intelligence Surveillance Act of 1978, as amended, which provided the "exclusive means" for national security surveillance.

In a news conference on December 19, Bush stated: "As President and Commander in Chief, I have the constitutional responsibility and the constitutional authority to protect our country. Article II of the Constitution gives me that responsibility and the authority necessary to fulfill it." He noted that Congress after 9/11 had passed the AUMF granting him "additional authority to use military force against Al Qaeda."[58] The Constitution does grant the president broad responsibility for repelling sudden attacks, but if a President decides it is necessary to act against the law, or without it, as Lincoln did, then the next step is to come to Congress, concede the legal violation, and seek retroactive authority. Bush did not do that.

Also on December 19, at a press briefing on the NSA program, Attorney General Alberto Gonzales claimed that "the President has the inherent authority under the Constitution, as Commander-in-Chief, to engage in this kind of activity."[59] When asked why the administration did not seek a warrant from the FISA Court, as required by law, Gonzales replied that it was not "legally required" to do that, in part because the AUMF statute provided alternative statutory support. Nothing in the AUMF, either expressly or by implication, amended FISA. If the administration wanted to revise FISA it knew how to do it: bring it up on the floor of Congress and subject it to amendments (as it had done over the years and would again after 9/11). Claims of "inherent" authority are legally hollow.

On January 19, 2006, the Justice Department produced a 42-page "white paper" defending the legality of the NSA program. It concluded that the NSA activities "are supported by the President's well-recognized inherent constitutional authority as Commander in Chief and sole organ for the Nation in foreign affairs to conduct warrantless surveillance of enemy forces for intelligence purposes to detect and disrupt armed attacks on the United States. The President has the chief responsibility under the Constitution to protect America from attack, and the Constitution gives the President the authority necessary to fulfill that solemn responsibility." Later in the paper, the Justice Department linked "sole organ" to the 1936 Supreme Court decision of *United States* v. *Curtiss-Wright.* [60] These references to inherent authority and the erroneous dicta in the Court's decision are empty of constitutional reasoning.

The Justice Department also argued in this paper that "Congress by statute has confirmed and supplemented the President's recognized authority under Article II of the Constitution to conduct such warrantless surveillance to prevent catastrophic attacks on the homeland." Here the Department recognizes a statute (the AUMF) not as a freestanding and separate source of authority but one that confirmed what the President already had, according to this analysis, under Article II. The Department warned that any statute interpreted to impede the president's ability to use electronic surveillance to detect and prevent future attacks by an enemy "would be called into very serious doubt" as to constitutionality. If FISA were so interpreted to limit presidential power, it "would be unconstitutional as applied in this narrow context." [61] Essentially, then, the Department was relying on Article II authority.

Was the NSA program legal? When Michael Hayden appeared before the Senate Select Committee on Intelligence on May 18, 2006 to testify on his nomination to be CIA Director, he defended the constitutionality of the NSA program on constitutional, not statutory, grounds. He did not attempt to use the AUMF as legal justification. In recalling his service as NSA Director after 9/11, he told the committee that when he talked with NSA lawyers, "they were very comfortable with the Article II arguments and the President's inherent authorities."[62] Elsewhere in the hearing he referred to the "real comfort level" these lawyers had about the president's Article II authority, but their legal advice was not put in writing. [63]

During this hearing, Hayden repeatedly claimed that the NSA program was legal and that the CIA "will obey the laws of the United States and will respond to our treaty obligations." [64] These references to lawfulness were misleading. Hayden made it clear that he was willing, as NSA Director, to violate law (FISA) when the president's team argued it was necessary. The phrase "laws of the United States" therefore meant whatever the administration wanted to do under claims of Article II and inherent power, even when the actions violated statutes, treaties, and the Constitution. Hayden explained: "I had two lawful programs in front of me, one authorized by the President, the other one would have been conducted under FISA as currently crafted and implemented."[65] He was willing to violate statutory law in order to carry out a presidential policy. CIA Director George Tenet asked Hayden after 9/11 whether he could "do more" to combat terrorism with surveillance. Hayden replied: "Not within current law."[66] He knew that the NSA program was illegal under FISA.

Although the Bush administration decided to work with telecoms in violating the law, and did so in secret, on July 20, 2008 Congress gave retroactive immunity to the telecoms. Civil actions against them in federal or state court could be dismissed if the Attorney General certified to a court that the activity was "authorized by the President" and "determined to be lawful."[67] Through this procedure, what was illegal under FISA becomes "legal" if the president "authorized" it and someone, for whatever reason, determined that the action was "lawful." Some lawsuits against the government, not the telecoms, have continued.

SECRET LAW

With extraordinary rendition, abusive interrogation, NSA surveillance, and other programs, the Bush administration prepared secret legal memos. Many of them became public when leaked or released many years later. Some legal memos remain secret. A society cannot remain faithful to the rule of law when governed by secret law, especially policies that promote broad and unchecked presidential power. Secret memos, circulated among a narrow circle of people for review and comment, are likely to be poorly informed, reasoned, and substantiated. If the memos contain sensitive information, such as names, those items can be redacted and the balance of the analysis made public. No plausible case can be made for withholding legal reasoning. Secret policy means that the rule of law is not pursuant to statute or treaty, enacted in public, but done through confidential executive policies unknown to citizens, federal courts, and lawmakers. The general public and executive agencies cannot comply with secret law. Lawmakers are unable to review and amend legal interpretations never released by the executive branch.

CONCLUSION

What we have learned, time after time, is what the framers understood long ago as elementary: political officials will abuse power if left unsupervised and unchecked. The primary check on government power is structural: the capacity of all three branches to fight off encroachments and expose illegal conduct. Justice Robert Jackson reminded us about the meaning of the rule of law: "With all its defects, delays and inconveniences, men have discovered no technique for long preserving free government except that the Executive be under the law, and that the law be made by parliamentary deliberation."[68]

REFERENCES

[1] The views expressed in this article are personal, not institutional.

[2] After 9/11, the Bush administration met only with the "Gang of Eight" to reveal what became known as the "Terrorist Surveillance Program." The Gang of Eight consists of four party leaders in the House and the Senate and the chair and ranking member of the two Intelligence Committees. The administration did not seek congressional authorization until the program had been disclosed by the *New York Times* in December 2005.

[3] Joseph W. Bendersky, Carl Schmitt: Theorist for the Reich (Princeton University Press, 1983), pp. 195-98; John E. Finn, Constitutions in Crisis: Political Violence and the Rule of Law (Oxford University Press, 1991), pp. 146-78; Ingo Müller, Hitler's Justice: The Courts of the Third Reich (Harvard University Press, 1991), pp. 33-34, 46-47; Ellen Kennedy, Constitutional Failure, Carl Schmitt in Weimar (Duke University Press, 2004), pp. 154-69.

[4] A Compilation of Messages and Papers by the Presidents (Bureau of National Literature, 1897-1925, James D. Richardson ed.) (hereafter "Richardson"), vol. 7, p. 3225.

[5] Clinton Rossiter, Constitutional Dictatorship: Crisis Government in the Modern Democracies (Harcourt, Brace and World, 1963 ed.), p. 224.

[6] Ibid., p. 225.

[7] 12 Stat. 326 (1861). For legislative debate, see Cong. Globe, 37th Cong., 1st Sess. (1861), pp. 2, 16, 21, 40-50, 64-71, 127, 137-44, 208, 220, 234-35, 276, 288-97, 332-35, 391-95, 451-58, and the speech by Senator Bayard, "Executive Usurpation," in the Appendix to the Cong. Globe, pp. 12-19.

[8] "Brief for the United States and Captors," The Prize Cases, U.S. Supreme Court, December Term, 1862, signed by R. H. Dana, Jr., p. 19; reprinted at Landmark Briefs

and Arguments of the Supreme Court of the United States: Constitutional Law (University Publications of America, 1978) (hereafter "*Landmark Briefs*"), vol. 3, p. 514.

[9] "Brief for the United States," The Prize Cases, U.S. Supreme Court, signed by William M. Evarts, p. 27; *Landmark Briefs*, vol. 3, p. 554.

[10] Ibid., pp. 31-32.

[11] The Prize Cases, 2 Black (67 U.S.) 635, 668 (1863).

[12] Ibid.

[13] Richardson, vol. 7, p. 3226.

[14] *Opinions of the Attorney General*, vol. 10, pp. 74, 81 (1861).

[15] Ibid., p. 90.

[16] Ex parte Merryman, 17 *Fed. Cases* 144, 153 (No. 9,487) (C.C. Md. 1861).

[17] 12 Stat. 755, 756, sec. 3 (1863).

[18] Steven G. Calabresi and Christopher S. Yoo, The Unitary Executive: Presidential Power from Washington to Bush (Yale University Press, 2008), pp. 428, 429, 430, 431.

[19] Black's Law Dictionary (West Publishing Co., 5th ed. 1979), p. 703.

[20] Merriam Webster's Collegiate Dictionary (Merriam-Webster Inc., 10th ed. 1993), p. 601.

[21] See Louis Fisher, "Invoking Inherent Powers: A Primer," Presidential Studies Quarterly (2007), vol. 37, p. 1, available at http://www.loc.gov/law/help/usconlaw/constitutional_law.html#agencyYoungstown Co. v. Sawyer, 343 U.S. 579 (1952).

[22] Louis Fisher, Presidential Spending Power (*Princeton University Press*, 1975), pp. 175-201.

[23] Federal Register, vol. 66, p. 57833 (2001).

[24] "Brief for Respondents," Hamdan v. Rumsfeld, on writ of certiorari to the United States Court of Appeals for the District of Columbia Circuit, U.S. Supreme Court, No. 05-184, February 2006, p. 7.

[25] Ibid., p. 8.

[26] U.S. Justice Department, "Brief for Respondents-Appellants," Hamdi v. Rumsfeld, No. 02-6895, *Fourth Circuit*, p. 14.

[27] Ibid., pp. 39-30, 31.

[28] 542 U.S. 507, 535-36 (2004).

[29] Memorandum for William J. Haynes II, General Counsel, Department of Defense, from Patrick F. Philbin, Deputy Assistant Attorney General, and John C. Yoo, Deputy Assistant Attorney General, December 28, 2001, p. 1.

[30] 339 U.S. 763 (1950).

[31] Rasul v. Bush, 215 F.Supp.2d 55 (D.D.C. 2002).

[32] U.S. Supreme Court, Rasul v. Bush, oral argument, April 20, 2004, p. 51.

[33] Ibid., p. 52.

[34] 542 U.S. 466 (2004).

[35] Memorandum from Jay Bybee, Assistant Attorney General, to Alberto Gonzales, White House Counsel, "Re: Standards of Conduct for Interrogation under 18 U.S.C. §§ 2340-2340A," August 1, 2002, p. 31.

[36] Ops. Att'y Gen. 68, 69-70 (1797); 2 Ops. Att'y Gen. 559 (1833); 3 Ops. Att'y Gen. 661 (1841); 4A Ops. O.L.C. 149 (1979).

[37] Ker v. Illinois, 119 U.S. 436 (1886); Frisbie v. Collins, 342 U.S. 519 (1952). See Louis Fisher, The Constitution and 9/11: Recurring Threats to America's Freedoms (University Press of Kansas, 2008), pp. 326-28.
[38] Dana Priest, "Ex-CIA Official Defends Detention Policies," Washington Post, October 27, 2004, p. A21.
[39] U.S. Justice Department, "Memorandum in Support of the United States' Assertion of State Secrets Privilege," Arar v. Ashcroft (E.D.N.Y.), January 18, 2005, pp. 3-4.
[40] Louis Fisher, In the Name of National Security: Unchecked Presidential Power and the *Reynolds* Case (University Press of Kansas, 2006).
[41] El-Masri v. Tenet, 437 F.Supp.2d 530, 536-37(E.D. Va. 2006).
[42] El-Masri v. United States, 479 F.3d 296 (4th Cir. 2007).
[43] Ibid., p. 304.
[44] For further information on the El-Masri case, see Fisher, The Constitution and 9/11, pp. 352-56.
[45] Ibid., p. 347.
[46] Arar v. Ashcroft, 414 F.Supp.2d 250, 281 (E.D. N.Y. 2006).
[47] Doug Struck, "Canadian Was Falsely Accused, Panel Says," Washington Post, September 19, 2006, p. A1; Ian Austen, "Canadians Fault U.S. for Its Role in Torture Case," New York Times, September 19, 2006, p. A1.
[48] "Prime Minister releases letter of apology to Maher Arar and his family and announces completion of mediation process," available at http://www.pm.gc.ca/eng/media.asp?id=1510, accessed on September 22, 2009; Doug Struck, "Tortured Man Gets Apology from Canada," Washington Post, January 27, 2007, p. A14; Ian Austen, "Canada to Pay $9.75 Million to Man Tortured in Syria," New York Times, January 27, 2007, p. A5.
[49] Arar v. Ashcroft, 532 F.3d 157, 164 (2d Cir. 2008).
[50] E.g., "State Secret Protection Act of 2009," hearing before the Subcommittee on the Constitution, Civil Rights, and Civil Liberties of the House Committee on the Judiciary, 111th Cong., 1st Sess. (June 4, 2009). For articles and testimony on the state secrets privilege, see http://www.loc.gov/law/help/usconlaw/index.php
[51] The White House, "Remarks by the President on National Security," May 21, 2009, available at http://www.whitehouse.gov/the_press_office/Remarks-by-the-President-On-National-Security
[52] U.S. Department of Justice, Office of the Attorney General, "Policies and Procedures Governing Invocation of the State Secrets Privilege," September 23, 2009, p. 1.
[53] See Charlie Savage, "Justice Dept. Planning to Limit Government's Use of State Secrets Privilege," New York Times, September 23, 2009, p. A22; Carrie Johnson, "Obama to Set Higher Bar For Keeping State Secrets," *Washington Post*, September 23, 2009, p. A1.
[54] U.S. Department of Justice, "Attorney General Establishes New State Secrets Policies and Procedures," September 23, 2009, p. 2, available at http://www.fas.org/sgp/news/2009/09/doj092309.html
[55] Statement of U.S. Senator Russ Feingold on the Obama Administration's New Policy on the State Secrets Privilege, September 23, 2009, available at http://feingold.senate.gov/record.cfm?id=318158
[56] "Bush on the Patriot Act and Eavesdropping," New York Times, December 18, 2005, p. 30.

[57] "The President's News Conference," December 19, 2005, *Weekly Compilation of Presidential Documents* , vol. 41, pp. 1885-96.
[58] Press Briefing by Attorney General Alberto Gonzales and General Michael Hayden, Principal Deputy Director for National Intelligence, December 19, 2005.
[59] "Legal Authorities Supporting the Activities of the National Security Agency Described by the President, Office of Legal Counsel, U.S. Department of Justice, January 19, 2006, pp. 1, 6-7.
[60] Ibid., p. 3.
[61] Hearing of the Senate Select Committee on Intelligence on the nomination of General Michael V. Hayden to be Director of the Central Intelligence Agency, May 18, 2006, transcript, p. 35.
[62] Ibid., p. 69.
[63] Ibid., p. 74.
[64] Ibid., p. 88.
[65] Ibid., p. 68.
[66] Pub. L. No. 110-261, 122 Stat. 2469 (2008).
[67] Youngstown Co. v. Sawyer, 343 U.S 579, 655 (1952).

In: President or King?
Editor: Meena Bose, pp. 43-61
ISBN: 978-1-61324-655-9

INSTITUTIONAL RIVALRIES IN PRESIDENTIAL WAR POWERS CASES: A POLITICAL PERSPECTIVE ON THE JURISPRUDENCE

Rebecca Curry

ABSTRACT

Presidential war powers jurisprudence is as unsettled as it is controversial.In this chapter, I argue that the Supreme Court's rulings in the field are best understood as political phenomena – that is, as evidence of institutional rivalries between different branches of the federal government. Focusing on cases involving wartime detainees, I find that the Court takes a surprising approach. Even where Justices share the president's political ideology, there is a tendency to parse constitutional language quite strictly, a reluctance to bend even in the face of important national security exigencies, and a tendency to declare the executive's actions unconstitutional. Tracing this to Justice Black's opinion in the landmark *Youngstown Sheet and Tube v. Sawyer* case, I refer to it as a kind of constitutional formalism. Moreover, I note that the Court tends to adopt the formalist approach in a predictable way, using it wherever assertions of presidential authority seem to encroach upon the Court's own institutional competences. The analysis therefore forecasts that the Court will likely continue to hold presidential powers in check where cases involve such matters as habeas corpus and military tribunals.

INTRODUCTION

In the 1952 landmark case of *Youngstown Sheet and Tube Co. v. Sawyer*,[1] the Supreme Court foreclosed an attempt by President Harry Truman to exert extraordinary powers in response to what he claimed was a critical threat to national security. In the many years since, the complex set of judicial rulings in the case have become fundamental to our thinking about presidential war powers, and these opinions – particularly Justice Jackson's concurrence – are still used to resolve presidential war powers cases to this day.

Moreover, the *Youngstown* opinions have come to represent important prototypes for very different kinds of constitutional jurisprudence in separation of powers cases generally. Justice Jackson famously took a *functionalist* view of the Constitution, arguing that the president need not be confined to the powers listed in Article II but that he could, instead, rightfully exercise additional powers where Congress had authorized him to do so. As one observer put it, the functionalist approach "allows governmental branches to share some responsibilities as long as they do not interfere with the core functions of another branch."[2] On the other end of the spectrum, Justice Black is renowned for having spelled out the *formalist* approach, requiring an explicit constitutional basis for any executive action and maintaining distinct duties for the three separate branches of government.[3] Finally, in a less well-known concurring opinion, Justice Frankfurter offered still another approach, one that may be called the *realist* view. He argued that, while it may be true that the Constitution formally bars certain presidential actions in response to national security threats, it will not do for the Supreme Court simply to point to such constitutional provisions and order the commander-in-chief to revise his policies commensurate with those constraints. Rather, where the president has already acted, perhaps with the approval of the people or of other elected officials, then the Court should not attempt to curtail his actions, constitutional limits notwithstanding. "It is an inadmissibly narrow conception of American constitutional law," Frankfurter wrote, "to confine it to the words of the Constitution and to disregard the gloss which life has written upon them."[4] Interestingly, although their reasoning differed considerably, all three approaches led to the same practical result in the *Youngstown* case, with each Justice voting to declare President Truman's action unconstitutional.

Just as the members of the *Youngstown* Court had very distinct approaches to the question of presidential war powers, lawyers, scholars and presidents still question what the constitutional rules are in this field. In fact, this area of jurisprudence is quite remarkable for the level of uncertainty that obtains here. Thus, despite Supreme Court decisions on everything from Abraham Lincoln's Civil War policies to George W. Bush's responses to the terrorist attacks of September 11, 2001, the law regarding presidential war powers is unusually unsettled. Given the high stakes associated with national security and the values with which it so often comes into conflict (checks and balances principles, civil rights, and individual liberties), there is still less consensus about what the rules should be and continuing disagreement about the proper sources for the president's wartime and national security authority.

Stepping away from traditional legal analysis and from the normative approaches with which many have treated presidential powers cases, I propose that we try to make sense of the constitutional rulings in the field as purely political phenomena, i.e. as indicators of who is likely to win the separation of powers battles at the heart of these cases and why. Looking at the cases from this perspective, I find that the three *Youngstown* approaches outlined above are not just important legal and constitutional theory, but also analytically useful keys to understanding judicial decisions in this area. In fact, I would contend that each spells out a political treatise as much as a legal rule. That is, the views expressed by Jackson, Black and Frankfurter represent three different ways the Court has navigated through the political minefield of war powers jurisprudence, with the Court taking each of these three approaches in various lines of its caselaw. As such, these prototypes offer an important way to make sense of judicial outcomes in this area, and they help to explain what may at first appear to be haphazard decisions from one era – or one administration – to the next.

These are broad claims, and space limitations will not allow me to discuss them fully here. Rather, the following article will focus on just one aspect of the larger argument, i.e., the formalist view spelled out by Justice Black in *Youngstown*. Less celebrated than Jackson's functionalism, Black's formalism has nevertheless been critical to the outcome of many presidential powers cases. As I argue below, a formalist approach has been the key to Supreme Court decisions on wartime detainees. Indeed, the approach predates the *Youngstown* controversy, with the Court taking a formalist line consistently from its first consideration of such questions during the Civil War era through its most recent review of presidential policies in the war on terror. As such, it has often ignored the functionalist's rule of allowing the executive's national security policy wherever Congress has authorized it; instead, in many important cases, the Court has acted independently of both political branches to declare executive acts unconstitutional on the strength of constitutional text alone. As we will see in Part II, below, this is the likely approach in war powers cases where the executive branch seems to be encroaching upon the Court's own institutional competences – such as when the president attempts to replace trials in the civil justice system with military tribunals. My view is therefore that case outcomes are best explained not by virtue of legal rules or in terms of general theories of constitutional adjudication. Rather, the key variable here is the struggle for power between the various branches of government, i.e., the institutional politics behind any given war powers controversy. Taking a look at the scorecard in war powers cases, we see that this political gloss helps to specify when the Court is likely to rebuff the commander-in-chief.

First, however, we should consider the more conventional understandings of war powers jurisprudence and the puzzles that they present. This is the subject of Part I.

I. An Overview of War Powers Jurisprudence

War powers cases are often viewed from the outside as simple matters. That is, there is a conventional wisdom that says the president has extensive powers in the realm of national security. Thus it is common knowledge that, while he is never completely free of constitutional limits, the executive's powers are broadest when the country is in a state of emergency or when it is at war. However, when one turns to the Supreme Court record in war powers cases, one finds that it is actually a fairly complex terrain: presidents from Abraham Lincoln to George W. Bush have met national crises with assertions of plenary power, but the Supreme Court has rebuffed these as often as it has approved them. Thus, it is more accurate to say that the president wins some and loses some, often in seemingly anomalous and unpredictable ways. Beyond the wide scope of outcomes in war powers cases, there is the problem that judicial rulings do not seem to make much difference to presidential actions. That is, even the White House's constitutional losses are not necessarily policy setbacks; instead, presidents from Lincoln to Bush have carried out the policy they wanted regardless of Supreme Court objections. Thus, the constitutional rules here are hard to track, and it is harder still to say which branch truly sets them.

Certainly, the chief executive is given wide latitude in the field of national security. In the 1936 *Curtiss-Wright* decision, the Supreme Court concluded that Franklin Roosevelt was well within his constitutional powers to prohibit the sale of arms even within the U.S., on the grounds that the sale would affect an international conflict in which the U.S. had an interest.[5] This conclusion derived not from any enumerated Article II powers, but from Justice Sutherland's view that the president enjoys, "very delicate, plenary and exclusive power . . . as the sole organ of the federal government in the field of international relations."[6] The Court went so far as to assert that the President's exclusive power "does not require as a basis for its exercise an act of Congress…."[7] Rather, he takes his plenary foreign affairs powers from the traditions that passed to the U.S. upon declaring independence from Britain.[8] The case has thus come to be seen as the high water mark in presidential war powers jurisprudence and scholars have noted its persistence as constitutional precedent well into the modern era.[9]

Even prior to the *Curtiss-Wright* ruling, however, the Court had appeared to establish foreign policy as a special area for executive branch discretion. In *Missouri v. Holland*, for example, the Court confronted the question of whether our international treaties may violate the Constitution.[10] There, the Court held that the president may establish treaties, subsequently passed into statutes by Congress, even where doing so amounted to enacting policies that defy constitutional protections.[11] (In this case, the constitutional protection at issue was state sovereignty, not the more conventional civil liberties questions we tend to see in this field). While, Justice Holmes was quick to say that the treaty-making power was not without constitutional limits,[12] his opinion for the Court maintained that the president's authority to direct American foreign policy had tipped the balance. Thus, Holmes argued that constitutional rules can and should bend when the president is acting to protect vital matters of national security. Moreover, given that the case concerned the protection of migratory geese, rather than a life-or-death emergency powers question, Justice Holmes appears to have set the bar very low for what constitutes national security. From such precedent, it would be easy to argue that constitutional rules regarding the treatment of criminal suspects could give way in the face of much more important national security issues, such as preventing or prosecuting terrorist attacks.

Subsequent cases have proceeded in the same vein, with the Court allowing executive branch officials to order the return of illegal aliens to their country of origin, despite U.S. immigration laws barring the practice where racial or political oppression was likely in the home country; permitting the president to suspend claims that American nationals held against Iran in the wake of the Iranian hostage crisis; allowing the executive branch to forego Fifth Amendment constraints when issuing diplomatic recognition to foreign states; as well as allowing the president to abridge international treaties with respect to his diplomatic recognition power.[13] Most notoriously, executive authority in national security matters has been held to trump important individual rights protections enjoyed by U.S. citizens. Thus, *Hirabayashi* and *Korematsu* authorized President Roosevelt's World War II internment of American nationals, solely on the basis of their Japanese heritage, by finding that the government's war effort presented an overriding interest that outweighed claims to racial equality.[14] Looking at these rulings, scholars have concluded that the president almost always wins in war powers cases.[15] As presidents continue to draw on these constitutional holdings to claim extensive national security authority, it has become almost commonplace to speak of an "imperial presidency."[16]

However, that is certainly not the whole story. In fact, the president is not without limits in this area. Rather, the Supreme Court has declared the President's actions unconstitutional at many different points in our nation's history. And it has done so despite White House claims that such actions were necessary in the face of grave threats to national security. For example, Abraham Lincoln's Civil War detention policies were first rebuked in *Ex parte Merryman*, where the Court held that the president could not act unilaterally to suspend the writ of habeas corpus.[17] Lincoln's claim to special national security authority was rejected yet again when he sought to maintain the detentions, this time with congressional approval. Thus, a second case, *Ex parte Milligan*, found that even when acting with Congress's blessing, a wartime president is not immune from constitutional restraints.[18] Many generations later, that rule is still the law of the land. Indeed, some of the more prominent war powers cases of our day address similar questions, with the Supreme Court applying these Civil War era rules to contemporary military detention facilities both at home and abroad. And, from *Hamdi* to *Boumediene*, the high court has maintained a relatively hard line, subjecting George W. Bush's anti-terror policies to the same kind of constitutional scrutiny Lincoln experienced, and favoring detainee rights over the power of the President.[19]

Beyond this narrower question of the executive's authority with respect to detainees in times of civil or international war, the Court has been known to block the president's actions in the broader realm of foreign policy. These cases have all centered on attention to individual rights under the Constitution. Thus, as Norman Dorsen explains, "the Court…has upheld the right to picket before foreign embassies and it has safeguarded rights of aliens, including the right to educational opportunity for 'undocumented' alien children not lawfully admitted to the country. Lower courts have issued rulings that go closer to the bone of national security. These decisions suggest that civil liberties can be protected in foreign affairs cases," notwithstanding assertions of presidential authority.[20]

So, while the conventional wisdom on emergency powers is that civil liberties take a back seat during times of national emergency, the case record seems to tell a very different story. In fact, a wide-ranging study done in the 1970s found that "the overall record of the Court was surprisingly sensitive to claims of civil liberties when juxtaposed with claims of national security."[21] Indeed, on the strength of these aspects of the case record, an alternative school in the war powers literature argues that the Constitution matters quite a lot to the Court's jurisprudence.[22]

Confusing the issue still further is the fact that much of what transpires in response to wartime emergencies is not subject to judicial review at all. On the one hand, this is because the Supreme Court has often fallen back on prudential considerations, limiting its own jurisdiction to hear claims so as to avoid deciding cases challenging the President's foreign policy activities. One finds the Court refusing war powers cases, for example, even though the constitutional bases for judicial review seem much clearer than they are in other areas where the Court has not shied away from review. Thus, just as the Court was abandoning the political question doctrine that had kept it from hearing cases on voting districts,[23] or the qualifications for federal office,[24] it insisted on a broad definition of political questions to refrain from deciding whether military action in Vietnam required Congress to exercise its Article I power to declare war.[25] And so, running right along side holdings asserting that the president has special authority in foreign policy and those that find concrete limits to his authority, we have case after case in which the Supreme Court refuses to provide an answer either way.[26]

On the other hand, what transpires in national security policy seems not to be governed by judicial interpretations of the Constitution because presidents have boldly asserted their power, not just to act, but to decide for themselves whether their actions fall within the Constitution's limits. Lincoln, for instance, responded to the Court's initial finding that it had been unconstitutional for him to suspend the writ of habeas corpus in certain parts of the country by suspending the writ *nationwide*. And, though he would eventually get legislative approval for that decision, he acted well in advance of any decision from Congress. As Gil

Gott notes, "it would not be incorrect to say that presidents [have] rather consistently pressed the apparent constitutional limits of their foreign affairs powers. From Polk's initiation of a war of conquest with Mexico, and Lincoln's suspension of habeas corpus and issuance of the Emancipation Proclamation under a broad reading of commander-in-chief powers, to Theodore Roosevelt's imperial campaigns in the Caribbean and the Pacific under his theory of the president as 'a steward of the people,'foreign affairs has been distinctly fruitful grounds for the assertion of executive prerogative."[27] This is not to say that such actions were completely legitimate constitutionally, or that they became such by virtue of the president undertaking them. Rather, it is simply to note that scholars have found even "illegitimate actions under conditions of exigency [to be] foreseeable and quasi-systematic."[28]

In the end, then, what are we to make of the jurisprudence governing the President's exercise of war powers? The foregoing indicates that it is quite a mixed bag, with few discernable rules applying across the board. Certainly, much has been said about whether these disparate rulings are legally or ethically sound. However, to date, there has been relatively little positive political science on the question of how we got here. The following analysis therefore explores the caselaw from that perspective, looking for patterns that might indicate why the Court rules differently in seemingly similar cases. It emphasizes, in particular, an apparent tendency of the Court to rebuff the president in certain cases, despite a general understanding that the commander-in-chief enjoys special authority in national security matters.

II. Formalism in the Realm of Judicial Authority

The formalism Black espoused in *Youngstown* contended that the Court, as defender of the Constitution, should declare executive acts unconstitutional on the strength of constitutional text alone, maintaining a formal separation between the powers of each branch. From what we saw in the jurisprudential history in this field, the Court certainly does not take this approach in every war powers case. However, there is an important, if somewhat overlooked, pattern in the rulings here. In fact, the Court seems to take the formalist line in predictable ways. That is, the opinions in this area tend to follow the approach when cases concern questions of *judicial* power. If the president's wartime actions encroach upon duties that have traditionally been performed by courts, then the Supreme Court will usually rebuff the chief executive even where Congress has authorized his endeavor. In this way, the Court adopts a formalist attitude to protect its own place in the federal balance of power.

As we saw in Part I, there is a school of thought that expects this type of independent judicial defense of constitutional values to arise around most civil liberties issues. Black's initial expression of the formalist view indeed came out of his concern for the private property rights at stake in the *Youngstown* case,[29] and thus the approach was first formulated as a rule whereby the Court would act to protect all civil liberties, broadly defined. However, my case analysis reveals that war powers formalism tends to have a much narrower application. It is used not in every case pertaining to civil liberties, but in those that raise issues concerning judicial practices and courtroom procedures, e.g., the right to a trial, whether to use the civilian or military justice system, which evidence is allowed and which must be excluded.

On this score, the Court appears willing to take an independent stand against the political branches, and there seem to be two core reasons for the different approach to the Constitution in these circumstances. First, this is the easiest place for the Supreme Court to invoke constitutional norms because such rulings are usually directed at members of the judicial branch. That is, when the Court rules that a detainee in military custody is entitled to a trial in the civilian justice system, it is, for all practical purposes, ordering the lower federal courts to accept the detainee's case – an order that is sure to be heeded. The same cannot be said for other types of civil liberties cases, or for other issues in war powers jurisprudence, since the political branches have much more discretion as to whether or not to comply with Supreme Court rulings. Second,since the rights protections at stake in criminal procedure controversies are some of the most important for the judiciary, institutionally speaking, the Court can hardly afford *not* to take a more independent stance on these questions. In our system, the judiciary's reason for being is to exercise its authority to try cases and to determine the guilt or innocence of a defendant. If other branches of government attempt to take over those duties in the name of public security, then the power of the civilian court system would be quite seriously curbed. Thus, as the following analysis of wartime detainee cases shows, the Court will protect that power even when doing so is not easy and even when it stands alone among federal policymaking branches.

Ex Parte Milligan

The Court's attention to its own institutional interests can be seen in war powers cases from the start. For example, the *Ex parte Milligan* Court exhibited this concern and issued a ruling that parallels Black's formalist approach in *Youngstown.* As noted above, the case concerned Lincoln's suspension of habeas corpus during the Civil War, and an initial Supreme Court ruling had held that the President could not suspend the writ independently; rather, he needed congressional approval to do so. *Milligan* came about after Lincoln had secured that legislative approval, yet the Court still rebuffed the President in a very important way. That is, *Milligan* held that, while the Constitution allows for suspension of the writ and thus for *detention,* it does not allow the detainees to be tried by military commissions, so long as the regular courts are open and available.[30] Civil rebellion may very well present a serious enough national security threat to justify suspending the Great Writ, but that is no reason for the Court to do away with its own governmental duties. The Court therefore rejected the use of a military tribunal for the trial and conviction of a citizen detained during the war.[31]

The operative factor here was not so much the necessity of the government's military action or the salience of the national security threat. In fact, the Court held that where such a threat exists, "there is then an exigency which demands that the government...should not be required to produce the persons arrested in answer to a writ of habeas corpus."[32] Instead, the critical factor was a distinction the Court drew between detentions, *per se,* and trials. While the Constitution provides specific procedures for suspending the writ of habeas corpus, the *Milligan* Court wrote, "The Constitution goes no further. It does not say after a writ of habeas corpus is denied a citizen, that he shall be tried otherwise than by the course of the common law; if it had intended this result, it was easy by the use of direct words to have accomplished it."[33] And, with that, the Court preserved the judiciary's role in this sphere: if a state of war or national emergency requires detention without habeas corpus, then so be it; but, once detained, alleged "enemy combatants" will have to be brought before regular, Article III courts to have their guilt or innocence determined.

The procedural history in *Milligan* indicates that the Court's decision may indeed have been motivated by its institutional interests. That is, Milligan had been prosecuted through both the civilian and the military justice systems, and there were stark differences between the outcomes in each venue: a civilian grand jury had failed even to indict Milligan,[34] whereas he had been tried, convicted and sentenced to be hanged by the military tribunal.[35] And the Supreme Court's intervention came as Milligan was still threatened with execution by the U.S. government, despite his having been exonerated in the civilian justice system. Mr. Milligan was therefore the subject of a fairly explicit turf war between the courts and the executive branch. When the Supreme Court ruled that the executive could not substitute the military justice system for the civilian one, it was not just striking a blow for the individual's civil liberties. It was also defending its own institution against an attempt by the executive branch to render it irrelevant to the prosecution of an American citizen on American soil.

Hamdi v. Rumsfeld

That same sense of the judiciary's institutional interests has carried over from *Milligan*, which was among the Supreme Court's first forays into war powers doctrine, into its most recent cases. For example, in the 2004 *Hamdi v. Rumsfeld* case, the staunchly Republican Rehnquist Court rejected George W. Bush's arguments regarding the availability of habeas relief for detainees in the war on terror. *Hamdi* concerned an American citizen detained by the U.S. military as an "enemy combatant"[36] who was seeking habeas relief in federal court. The Bush administration argued that it was fully within its powers to detain Mr. Hamdi and pleaded for the Court to stay out of the matter.[37] To support its view, the administration pointed to the Joint Resolution For The Authorization For Use Of Military Force (AUMF), passed by Congress soon after September 11, 2001, which authorized the president to "use all necessary and appropriate force against those nations, organizations, or persons he determines planned, authorized, committed, or aided the terrorist attacks."[38] The question before the Supreme Court in *Hamdi* was therefore very much like that of *Milligan*: whether Congress had authorized the detention and, if so, whether there was any further role for the Article III courts. And, just as in *Milligan*, the Court was inclined to take a very legalistic, almost hair-splitting approach. The Court held that the AUMF constituted congressional authorization such that it allowed Mr. Hamdi's detention.[39] However, this did not mean that the military could keep the detainees out of federal court altogether. Rather, the Court ruled that "due process demands that a citizen held in the United States as an enemy combatant be given a meaningful opportunity to contest the factual basis for that detention before a neutral decisionmaker."[40] In the absence of a formal and explicit suspension by Congress, "the writ of habeas corpus remains available to every individual detained within the United States."[41]

The question then turned to the standards for reviewing habeas petitions in such cases. The President lobbied for something of a rubber stamp rule, asking the Court to find that, where a detainee had been seized "in a combat zone, the habeas determination can be made purely as a matter of law, with no further hearing or fact-finding necessary."[42] Thus, habeas review for enemy combatants would be reduced to "investigating only whether legal authorization exists for the broader detention scheme,"[43] rather than reviewing whether the government had just cause for detaining each individual in question. Such a scheme would obviously amount to suspending the writ of habeas corpus by judicial fiat: once the Court found that Congress had authorized detentions, federal courts would cease conducting habeas review for any such detainees.

Consistent with the theory that formalism comes into play when the judiciary's own authority is threatened, the Court rejected the President's view on two grounds. First, the facts presented in Mr. Hamdi's specific circumstance indicated that the government had very little reason to hold him. Instead of alleging that Hamdi was "part of or supporting forces hostile to the United States or its coalition partners and engaged in armed conflict against the United States," the government presented the Court with no facts to justify his detention except to say that "when seized by the United States government, Mr.Hamdi resided in Afghanistan."[44] Second, the Court rejected the President's proposal because it suggested a very limited role for the judiciary in such matters. "Under the government's most extreme rendition of this argument, 'respect for separation of powers and the limited institutional capabilities of courts in matters of military decision-making in connection with an ongoing conflict' ought to eliminate entirely any individual process…."[45] Thus the Court characterized the government's argument as a contention that the judiciary either had no role at all or that it should adopt a "very deferential…standard and simply assume the accuracy of the government's articulated" reasons for detaining a given suspect.[46]

The Supreme Court sided instead with Mr. Hamdi's view that there was indeed a role for courts in the government's anti-terror policy, i.e., as the "neutral tribunal [that would] determine whether the Executive's asserted justifications for [a] detention have basis in fact and warrant in law."[47]

Because the Court specified that its reasoning rested on such facts as Hamdi being a U.S. citizen and his being detained within the United States, it appeared that the Court might rule otherwise in the case of a non-citizen or where military detentions took place off American soil, for example at Guantanamo Bay.[48] However, as in *Milligan*, the Court's defiance of the President here seems to be a matter of the judiciary's institutional interests. For example, the opinion strongly implied that the Court was insulted at the administration's suggestion that the judiciary cannot handle habeas questions arising out of wartime detentions. "We think it unlikely that this basic process will have the dire impact on the central functions of warmaking that the government forecasts…," Justice O'Connor wrote, "While we accord the greatest respect…to the judgments of military authorities in [such] matters…, *it does not infringe on the core role of the military for the courts to exercise their own time-honored and constitutionally mandated roles of reviewing and resolving claims like those presented here*."[49] Moreover, the *Hamdi* court expressed concern that the AUMF was entirely open-ended as to both the persons covered under the authorization and the time for which it would be in effect.[50] With this, the Court seemed to take note that to issue any other ruling in this case would reduce the judiciary to something less than a coequal branch for an indefinite time period and with respect to an unknown swath of potential cases.[51]

The case, decided in the final years of the Rehnquist Court, was a significant loss for President Bush. Only Justice Thomas was persuaded that the executive's powers in the national security realm warranted the Court's deference. The eight remaining Justices all sided with Mr. Hamdi.[52] Thus, rather than producing the usual split of five conservatives against four liberals, Hamdi's case found the Court's right flank arguing over how emphatically it should *reject* President Bush's arguments. Antonin Scalia authored an opinion (joined by Justice Stevens and paralleling the arguments of Justices Souter and Ginsburg) contending that the AUMF did not authorize citizen detentions at all.[53] Notably for our purposes, Scalia's reasoning from this conclusion was quite legalistic. Rather than finding a way to favor his fellow Republican, perhaps by noting that the special circumstances of the war on terror required a new look at past precedent and extraordinary deference to the executive, Scalia' opinion simply argued that the Court should follow the rule of law set forth in the Civil War era: "Absent suspension of the writ, a citizen held where the courts are open is entitled either to criminal trial or to a judicial decree requiring his release. It follows…that Hamdi is entitled to a habeas decree requiring his release unless (1) criminal proceedings are promptly brought, or (2) Congress has suspended the writ of habeas corpus."[54] Noting that Congress had not suspended the writ, Scalia advocated simply granting Hamdi's habeas petition, whereupon "the Executive may then hand him over to the criminal authorities…or else must release him."[55]

In fact, Scalia's reliance on the *Milligan* precedent demonstrated his support not only for the ruling in that case, but also for its defense of the judiciary against encroachment by the executive branch. Responding to the government's argument that it should have special wartime powers to detain suspected enemies and to dispense with civilian trials, Scalia asserted that such an exception would be both unconstitutional and unnecessary, since the civilian courts can be counted on to apply the law in such cases as reliably as they apply any other legal standards: "if the law of war cannot be applied to citizens where courts are open, then Hamdi's imprisonment without criminal trial is no less unlawful than Milligan's trial by military tribunal."[56] The civilian justice system is not simply to be overlooked wherever the government feels the defendant is especially dangerous. Rather, the "criminal process [is] the primary means – and the only means absent congressional action suspending the writ – not only to punish traitors, but to incapacitate them."[57]

With Scalia and seven other Justices rejecting arguments for executive branch autonomy over the prosecution of so-called enemy combatants, the *Hamdi* case evidences the Court's use of formalism in the interest of judicial power. There seems to be something driving the Court to rebuke presidential exercises of wartime authority where they encroach on what are normally seen as judicial activities, i.e., determining whether the government has rightfully imprisoned an individual, hearing evidence against that person in a criminal trial, applying the law to the specifics of the case, and, where the person is found guilty, issuing a sentence. The fact that the President had attempted to do away with these judicial duties in the name of national security seemed to motivate even those Justices normally sympathetic to Bush's cause to rule against him in this case.

The institutional interests of Supreme Court Justices do not always outweigh partisan affiliations and other considerations in such cases – for example, Justice Scalia sides with the government in subsequent cases. However, while the individual Justices might switch sides from one case to the next, the majority of the Court continued to affirm the institutional interests of the judiciary against executive encroachment in all the key cases that followed. The Court therefore ruled with detainees against the Bush administration even when the individual in question was not an American citizen and was not held on American soil. Further, it maintained this stance despite rather explicit congressional authorizations of both the detentions and the removal of detainee prosecutions to military tribunals.

Hamdan v. Rumsfeld

The next case to come before the Court, *Hamdan v. Rumsfeld*,[58] seemed to invite a different ruling from *Hamdi* on a number of fronts. It was brought by a non-citizen detained outside of the U.S., at Guantanamo Bay, Cuba. In addition, in the wake of the *Hamdi* decision, Congress had enacted the Detainee Treatment Act (DTA), limiting the jurisdiction with which federal courts had been considering applications for the writ of habeas corpus from Guantanamo detainees.[59] And yet, the *Hamdan* ruling was remarkably parallel to that of *Hamdi*. Again, the Court ruled in favor of the detainee against the President. And again, it did so with a very formalist view of the Constitution's separation of powers principles.

While the Court had read beyond the written text of the Constitution at many other times in its history and implied presidential powers in countless other incidences, it refused to do so here. Instead, it held fast to the Constitution's formal separation of powers. For instance, the Court noted that the President had established "penal tribunals not contemplated by Article I, section 8 and Article III, section 1 of the Constitution."[60] Thus, to persuade the Court that the executive had the power to set up military commissions, the President would have to point to "some other part of that document authoriz[ing]" the use of commissions over courts.[61] It then put up an added hurdle, namely that the President must not only find a textual basis for his exercise of special wartime powers, he must also garner congressional support for such action: "constitutional authority, if it exists, can derive only from the powers granted jointly to the President and Congress in time of war."[62]

Like Black in *Youngstown*, then, the Court was unmoved by the President's invocation of special national security threats, preferring instead to stick with the letter of the law. "There is nothing in the text or legislative history of the AUMF even hinting that Congress intended to expand or alter the authorization set forth in Article 21 of the [Uniform Code of Military Justice]" (UCMJ).[63] Even the DTA, enacted presumably in response to the *Hamdi* decision, fell short of the explicit congressional consent that the Court was looking for: "it contains no language authorizing [the military commission that tried Hamdan] or any other [tribunal] at Guantanamo Bay."[64] The Court's refusal to see authorization in the DTA was quite striking, since, except for a very limited appeals procedure to the D.C. Circuit court, the measure very directly stripped federal courts of jurisdiction to review detainees' habeas petitions.[65] As before, that reluctance to acknowledge any congressional support for, and thus constitutional validity in, the President's policy seemed to be borne out of a concern for preserving judicial authority. Jana Singer writes, for example, that "the majority's decision in *Hamdan* says as much about judicial authority as it does about the respective roles of Congress and the president in national security matters….*Hamdan* suggests that the Supreme Court views the federal judiciary as an indispensable player, not merely a passive onlooker, or even a neutral umpire."[66]

The Court maintains its indispensable position by highlighting the role of conventional legal institutions as the default venues for prosecuting offenses, even during wartime and against the government's contention that "the danger posed by international terrorism" makes either civilian or courts martial "impracticable."[67] So, though the Court was willing to consider the use of standard courts martial to try detainees, it could not find that the newly created military commissions offered the kinds of protection to defendants that are required under the UCMJ and the Geneva Conventions. This led the Court to conclude that the President had acted without congressional authorization in establishing the military commissions; according to the *Youngstown* case, this put his power in question and rendered the commissions illegitimate.[68] Several observers have noted that such a conclusion was not at all clear from the evidence in the case[69] and that the Court therefore exercised substantial discretion to reach its holding. For purposes of this analysis, it is interesting to note that, where the Court apparently had a choice to see things another way, it opted instead for the formalist style of legal interpretation[70] to order detainees to be tried either within the already clearly codified and very limited exceptions to civilian courts or within the regular Article III courts themselves. We see the full strength of the Court's formalism in the subsequent case, which clarified just how intently the Justices were interested in maintaining judicial authority in war powers matters.

Boumediene v. Bush

Boumediene v. Bush was the Court's answer to anyone who thought Hamdan's case, like Hamdi's before it, simply turned on particular facts that could easily change in the near future. For example, the most clear-cut explanation for the *Hamdan* outcome was that the Justices differed as to whether Congress had authorized precisely the sort of military commissions that were underway at Guantanamo Bay, with a four-Justice concurrence inviting the President to go back to Congress and "seek the authority he believes necessary" to continue with the military commissions.[71] Combined with the three dissenting Justices who contended that Congress had already provided such authorization under the DTA,[72] it appeared as though whatever precedent *Hamdan* established would be quickly overridden by a new congressional statute. Congress enacted just such a statute in the same year that the *Hamdan* decision issued, this time specifically stripping habeas jurisdiction from Article III courts, and authorizing both the government's detention policies and trial of detainees by military commissions. When detainees brought constitutional challenges to the Military Commissions Act (MCA), however, the Court still refused to condone the President's approach. Instead, it ruled that detainees held as enemy combatants at Guantanamo Bay were entitled to the privilege of habeas corpus to challenge the legality of their detentions, and that the provisions of MCA denying federal courts of jurisdiction to hear habeas corpus actions were unconstitutional.[73]

In holding fast to judicial participation in the criminal processes associated with the government's war on terror, the *Boumediene* Court preserved a very fundamental role for itself as a check on the executive branch. The Court therefore made the case for its institutional authority explicitly in the majority opinion:

> "The [Suspension] Clause protects the rights of the detained by a means consistent with the essential design of the Constitution. It ensures that, except during periods of formal suspension, the Judiciary will have a time-tested device, the writ, to maintain the 'delicate balance of governance' that is itself the surest safeguard of liberty...The Clause protects the rights of the detained by affirming the duty and authority of the Judiciary to call the jailer to account."[74]

The conservative Justices in the dissent also saw the holding as a play for judicial power. For example, Chief Justice Roberts advised that "this decision [was] not really about the detainees at all, but about control of federal policy regarding enemy combatants...,shift[ing] responsibility for those sensitive foreign policy and national security decisions from the elected branches to the Federal Judiciary."[75] Likewise, Justice Scalia accused his brethren of simply usurping the power that rightfully belongs to the political branches, writing, "What drives today's decision is neither the meaning of the Suspension Clause, nor the principles of our precedents, but rather an inflated notion of judicial supremacy."[76]

Given the heated disagreement between the majority and the dissent, it is fairly remarkable how little they actually differed as to the role of civilian courts in war powers issues. That is, the dissenters approved of the MCA precisely because it maintained review by an Article III court, allowing military determinations regarding detainees to be reviewed by the D.C. Circuit court.[77] Thus, neither side argued that the judiciary should be removed from the process altogether – rather the fight was over how central the courts, and especially the Supreme Court, should be in the process. It is therefore doubtful that the Supreme Court is likely to shift away from the above holdings in detainee cases anytime soon. There seems to be broad consensus that no changes are warranted with respect to U.S. citizens detained in the war on terror and even general agreement that at least one Article III court must be involved where cases concern noncitizens detained abroad.[78]

Civil Liberties or Judicial Power?

Speaking in general terms, then, the wartime detainee jurisprudence indicates that the Supreme Court will, indeed, curtail presidential authority even in wartime and even where the president arguably has received congressional approval for his foreign policy actions. Thus the operative rule does not appear to fit the conventional wisdom that the president necessarily enjoys more power and discretion when acting in the interest of national security. Rather, the cases maintain a very formalist approach to constitutional reasoning to hold that the president must comply with what the Court views as the letter of the law. This is not to say, however, that the cases support the observation noted in Part I, above, that the Court will act independently to protect against any facial violations of constitutionally protected civil liberties. *Hirabayashi* and *Korematsu* seem to be classic counter-examples to that notion. Instead, the Court appears to defy the will of the political branches in a much narrower field of issues, namely in situations where the executive has encroached upon duties that are normally the exclusive province of the Article III courts. The Court has therefore allowed the executive to institute wartime trial procedures in only a very narrow set of circumstances, and normally only when litigation concerned the law of war. Consequently, even in periods in which the Court was inclined to be exceptionally deferential to the President's wartime policies, as in FDR's internment of Japanese-Americans, we find rulings that go against the President's attempts to supersede judicial authority.

One critical example is *Ex parte Mitsuye Endo*, a 1944 case concerning the habeas petition of a Japanese-American detained during the war.[79] Here, the Court deviated completely from the approach it took in the more familiar internment cases, and as with all its detainee cases, it did so by making formalist distinctions between the powers of the various branches. That is, the wartime internments were carried out not just by the military, but also by the executive branch agency created pursuant to the policy, the War Relocation Authority. It was this authority that formally detained Ms. Endo. This fact turned the case in the petitioner's favor because the Court saw no reason that it could not hear Endo's claim against what was, technically speaking, a civilian agency. Citing the Act of March 21, 1942, which provided for civil penalties where citizens contravened internment rules, the Court maintained that the civilian courts were the proper venue for such prosecutions.[80] Finding no dispute as to whether Ms. Endo was a loyal citizen, and noting that the government's "power to detain [was] derived from the power to protect the war effort against espionage and sabotage" by the disloyal, the Court concluded that the detention served no rational purpose.[81] With that, and on the same day that it upheld the military's policy with respect to Fred Korematsu, the Court ordered Endo released from custody.[82] If the outcomes depended on raising civil liberties issues, plain and simple, then it would be hard to see why the two cases should warrant such different treatment. To the contrary, it seems to be not civil liberties *per se*, but the individual's right to ordinary civilian trial procedures that seems likely to win the day in a war powers case.

Conclusion

At the outset, I proposed that one could make sense of presidential war powers cases by considering them as political phenomena, rather than from the point of view of traditional legal analysis or constitutional theory. And our initial overview of the legal terrain here revealed that there was much to explain. For example, it seemed at first that war powers jurisprudence gave the president wide latitude in the field of foreign affairs; as such, we saw cases where the Court either downplayed or overlooked constitutional protections that would seem to bar the president's actions. However, just when it seemed that the jurisprudential rule was one of wide deference to the commander-in-chief, we found rulings that had the opposite outcome, rebuking the president for national security measures on the grounds that they offended the Constitution. Add to this the many instances in which Supreme Court rulings censuring presidential actions have gone unheeded, and it is little wonder that there is still considerable question as to what the constitutional rules are in this field. Broadly speaking, the cases do not seem to adhere to a coherent legal rationale or follow any single framework for constitutional interpretation.

By looking at a given line of cases from a more political perspective, however, one discovers that they make sense as instances of institutional rivalry. Wartime detainee cases from the Civil War era through to the present day seemed to raise concerns for Supreme Court Justices beyond the facial constitutional questions presented as to the prisoners' rights to habeas corpus or due process. They also presented the Court with situations in which the executive branch had attempted to perform duties normally thought of as the province of the judiciary – i.e., reviewing evidence against the accused, conducting formal trials, and issuing criminal sentences. In such instances, the Court has taken a hard line against executive action, being relatively unpersuaded by presidents' claims of national security exigency, and refusing to acknowledge even fairly blatant attempts by Congress to authorize executive action. Where presidents have attempted to encroach on the traditional work of legal institutions, they have been rebuffed by the Supreme Court. In fact, the institutional politics at work in these cases seem to trump party politics much of the time, and even Justices who share the president's party affiliation are sometimes reluctant to grant the power he seeks.

The cases therefore demonstrate that the Court's interest is in preserving its authority in these matters as much as in protecting individual rights. Overall, then, they seem to offer an example of what James Madison predicted would arise from our constitutional structure: a sort of equilibrium in which ambition counters ambition.[83] In the war powers situation, it is the ambition of the Court to remain relevant to an important area of national security policy that counters presidents' ambition for more discretion in the field. At the same time, however, we do not seem to enjoy the benefits that were supposed to arise from this institutional competition. Whereas Madison expected institutional rivalries to protect individual rights and to prevent the expansion of authority in any one branch of government, this study has uncovered only a very narrow area in which the judiciary has acted to preserve its own power. The Court's ambition does not seem to motivate it to protect Congress from encroachments by the Chief Executive, for example. Nor does it lead the Court to act where the president treads on individual rights in a way that does not specifically implicate the institutional powers of the judiciary. Therefore, rather than reaping the benefits of a system in which constitutional limits reign supreme, we have a system in which our high court invokes those limits primarily to guard its own authority in the government.

Whatever normative judgments one may make about that state of affairs, it does appear to be with us for the long term. That is, the Supreme Court has maintained a practice of guarding the judiciary's role in national security matters rather consistently throughout our history, with little change from one era to the next, from one military conflict to another, or from liberal to conservative Courts. Instead, the protectiveness with which the Supreme Court guards its role here seems rather ingrained. Having neither the power of the purse nor the sword, "the least dangerous branch"[84] is, understandably, also the most defensive one when it comes to encroachments on its core authority.

REFERENCES

[1] *Youngstown Sheet and Tube Co. v. Sawyer*, 343 U.S. 579 (1952).

[2] Michael J. Turner, "Fade To Black: The Formalization of Jackson's Youngstown Taxonomy by Hamdan and Medellin," American University Law Review 58 (2009), 670 (internal quotations removed).

[3] See Turner, 670-671.

[4] *Youngstown*, 610.

[5] *U.S. v. Curtiss-Wright Export Corporation*, 299 U.S. 304, 312 (1936).

[6] *Curtiss-Wright*, cited in Harold Hongju Koh, "Why the President (Almost) Always Wins in Foreign Affairs: Lessons of the Iran-Contra Affair," Yale Law Journal 97 (1988), 1307.

[7] *Id.*

[8] *Curtiss-Wright*, 299 U.S. 304, 316-317. See also Christopher A. Ford, "War Powers As We Live Them: Congressional-Executive Bargaining Under The Shadow Of The War Powers Resolution," Journal of Law and Politics 11 (1995), 613.

[9] Koh, 1255. Scholars have also been very critical of the Court's approach here; see, e.g., Louis Fisher, "The 'Sole Organ' Doctrine," in Studies on Presidential Power in Foreign Relations (The Law Library of Congress: 2006).

[10] *Missouri v. Holland*, 252 U.S. 416 (1920), 431.

[11] *Id.*, 435.

[12] *Id.*, 433. "We do not mean to imply that there are no qualifications to the treaty-making power; but they must be ascertained in a different way," Holmes wrote.

[13] See, respectively, *Sale v. Haitian Centers Council, Inc.*, 509 U.S. 155 (1993); *Dames and Moore v. Reagan*, 453 U.S. 654 (1981); *United States v. Pink*, 315 U.S. 203 (1942); and *Goldwater v. Carter*, 444 U.S. 996 (1979), all cited in Ford, 613.

[14] *Hirabayashi v. United States*, 320 U.S. 81 (1943); *Korematsu v. United States*, 323 U.S. 214 (1944).

[15] Koh, 1988. See also Louis Henkin, Foreign Affairs and the Constitution (Mineola, New York: The Foundation Press, 1972), and Harold Hongju Koh, The National Security Constitution: Sharing Power after the Iran-Contra Affair (New Haven: Yale Univ. Press, 1990).

[16] Charlie Savage, Takeover: The Return of the Imperial Presidency and the Subversion of American Democracy (Boston: Little, Brown and Company, 2007); Frederick A.O. Schwarz, Jr. and Aziz Z. Huq, Unchecked and Unbalanced: Presidential Power in a Time of Terror (New York: New Press, 2007).

[17] *Ex parte Merryman*, 17 Fed.Cas. 144 (1861).

[18] *Ex parte Milligan*, 71 U.S. 2 (1866).

[19] *Hamdi v. Rumsfeld*, 542 U.S. 507 (2004); *Boumediene v. Bush*, 128 S.Ct. 2229 (2008).

[20] Norman Dorsen, American Journal of International Law 83 (1989), 845.

[21] *Id.*, 842, citing Morton Halperin and Daniel Hoffman, Freedom vs. National Security: Secrecy And Surveillance (New York: Chelsea House Publishers, 1977), and Halperin, The National Security State: Never Question the President, in The Burger Years: Rights and Wrongs in the Supreme Court 1969-1986, 51 (Herman Schwartz ed., New York: Viking, 1987).

[22] *Id.* See also, Gil Gott, "A Tale of New Precedents: Japanese American Internment as Foreign Affairs Law," Boston College Law Review 40 (1998), 205-206. I take issue with the claims of such scholars in Part II in that I find the Court's decisions turning on a much narrower set of individual rights than those normally classified as civil liberties.

[23] See, e.g., *Baker v. Carr*, 369 U.S. 186 (1962) and *Reynolds v. Simms*, 377 U.S. 533 (1964).

[24] *Powell v. McCormack*, 395 U.S. 486 (1969).

[25] Kathleen Sullivan and Gerald Gunther, Constitutional Law, 16th edition (Eagan, MN: West), 260-261.

[26] A good summary is provided in Ford, 613, citing *Crockett v. Reagan*, 558 F. Supp. 893, 901 (D.D.C. 1982), as "finding existence of 'war' in El Salvador within meaning of U.S. Constitution to be [a] political question," *Sanchez-Espinoza v. Reagan*, 568 F. Supp. 596 (D.D.C. 1983), as "finding injusticiable [a] suit challenging U.S. aid to Nicaraguan contra rebels," and *Dellums v. Bush*, 752 F. Supp. 1141 (D.D.C. 1990), as "declaring [a] War Powers challenge to presidential deployments in Persian Gulf unripe for decision until [a] majority of Congress can be shown to disagree with President."

[27] Gott, 205, fn 118, citing Koh (1990), 89 and Arthur M. Schlesinger, Jr., The Imperial Presidency (New York: Houghton Mifflin, 1973), 41-43.

[28] *Id.*, citing Jules Lobel, "Emergency Power and the Decline of Liberalism," Yale Law Journal 98 (1989), 1392, and Gordon Silverstein, Imbalance of Powers: Constitutional Interpretation and the Making of American Foreign Policy (New York: Oxford

University Press, 1997) 62. For an earlier analysis concluding much the same thing, see also Andreas F. Lowenfeld, "Book Reviews" Harvard Law Review 87 (1973), 494. Lowenfeld writes, "it is increasingly apparent that the answers to many of the constitutional concerns of the nation are not to be found in litigated cases. Among these concerns the allocation of powers within the federal government is a prime example, and within that area the most perplexing problem has been the conduct of foreign affairs. For a variety of reasons, the judiciary has generally stayed out of this area. This has meant not that the problems are free from the need for legal analysis, but that government officials of the other two branches have had to make the legal judgments, for the most part with little guidance and on the basis of divergent and incompletely articulated premises."

[29] *Youngstown*, 585 and 588.

[30] *Milligan*, 76.

[31] *Id.*

[32] *Id.*, 79.

[33] *Id.*

[34] Sullivan and Gunther, at 266.

[35] *Milligan*, 7.

[36] *Hamdi*, 509.

[37] *Id.*, 595 (Thomas dissenting).

[38] Pub. L. No. 107-40, 15 stat. 224 sec. 2(a)(2001).

[39] *Hamdi*, 517.

[40] *Id.*, 509.

[41] *Id.*, 525.

[42] *Id.*, 526.

[43] *Id.*, 527.

[44] *Id.*, 526-527.

[45] *Id.*, 527, citing the government's "Brief for Respondents," 26.

[46] *Id.*, 527-528.

[47] *Id.*, 528.

[48] In addition, the ruling left open "the possibility that the standards [it had] articulated could be met by an appropriately authorized and properly constituted military tribunal," Sullivan and Gunther, 277.

[49] *Hamdi*, 534-535, emphasis added.

[50] *Id.*, 520-521.

[51] That factor is much less salient where the government is involved in a declared war with a conventionally-defined enemy state. This difference may explain, in part, the different approach taken in World War II, see e.g., *Ex parte Quirin*, 317 U.S. 1 (1942). The *Hamdi* Court reserved the discretion to bar detentions where the war on terrorism becomes considerably different from more conventional war efforts: "[W]e understand Congress' grant of authority for the use of 'necessary and appropriate force' to include the authority to detain for the duration of the relevant conflict, and our understanding is based on longstanding law-of-war principles. If the practical circumstances of a given conflict are entirely unlike those of the conflicts that informed the development of the law of war, that understanding may unravel" *Hamdi*, 521.

[52] There was no majority on the question of whether the AUMF truly authorized military detentions, and so the Justices divided on their reasoning, filing four separate opinions.
[53] *Hamdi*, 554 (Scalia dissenting).
[54] *Id.*, 572-573.
[55] *Id.*, 576.
[56] *Id.*, 567-568.
[57] *Id.*, 568.
[58] *Hamdan v. Rumsfeld*, 548 U.S. 557 (2006).
[59] *Sullivan and Gunther*, 282.
[60] *Hamdan*, 591.
[61] *Id.*
[62] *Id.*
[63] *Id.*, 594.
[64] *Id.*, 560-561.
[65] The statute reads, "Except as provided in section 1005..., no court, Justice, or judge shall have jurisdiction to hear or consider[] an application for a writ of habeas corpus filed by or on behalf of an alien detained by the Department of Defense at Guantanamo Bay, Cuba," Sullivan and Gunther, 282.
[66] Jana Singer, "Hamdan as an Assertion of Judicial Power," Maryland Law Review 66, 761; see also Adam Liptak, "The Court Enters The War, Loudly," *New York Times*, July 2, 2006, § 4, 1.
[67] *Hamdan*, 561.
[68] Turner, 665. A concurring opinion maintained that Bush had acted contrary to a congressional bar on the practice and thus that executive power was "at its lowest ebb," see *Singer*, 770.
[69] *Id.*
[70] "[T]he new standard resembles Justice Black's opinion more than Justice Jackson's," according to Turner, 670.
[71] *Hamdan,* 636 (Breyer concurring, joined by Kennedy, Souter, and Ginsburg).
[72] *Id.*, 655 and 670.
[73] *Boumediene*, 2272.
[74] *Id.*, 2247, citing *Hamdi*, 536.
[75] *Id.*, 2279-2280 (Roberts dissenting).
[76] *Id.*, 2302 (Scalia dissenting).
[77] See Roberts' dissent, 2293.
[78] Scalia's *Boumediene* dissent "conclude[s] that the Court's ultimate, unexpressed goal is to preserve the power to review the confinement of enemy prisoners held by the Executive anywhere in the world," 2303.
[79] *Ex parte Mitsuye Endo*, 323 U.S. 283 (1944).
[80] "Mitsuye Endo is detained by a civilian agency, the War Relocation Authority, not by the military. Moreover, the evacuation program was not left exclusively to the military; the Authority was given a large measure of responsibility for its execution and Congress made its enforcement subject to civil penalties by the Act of March 21, 1942. Accordingly, no questions of military law are involved." *Id.*, 298.
[81] *Id.*, 302.

[82] *Id.*, 304.

[83] James Madison, The Federalist no. 51, 322.

[84] Alexander M. Bickel, The Least Dangerous Branch: The Supreme Court at the Bar of Politics (New Haven: Yale University Press, 1986).

In: President or King?
Editor: Meena Bose, pp. 63-76
ISBN: 978-1-61324-655-9

REVERSE EFFECT: CONGRESSIONAL AND JUDICIAL RESTRAINTS ON PRESIDENTIAL POWER*

Nancy Kassop

ABSTRACT

Eras of excessive claims of presidential power are often followed by congressional and judicial efforts to trim back or monitor that power. This pattern occurred in response to the "imperial presidency" of the late 1960s and early 1970s, when Congress in the mid-1970s passed such laws as the War Powers Resolution of 1973 and the Foreign Intelligence Surveillance Act of 1978 and when the Supreme Court, for example, denied a president's claim of executive privilege in *U.S. v. Nixon* (1974). Three decades later, it is possible to see that many of the statutory reforms and judicial principles that were generated by those efforts to reduce executive excess have had the paradoxical effect of legitimizing the very power they sought to curb and, at times, have extended to the president even greater authority than existed previously. Reasons for this "reverse effect" are, in part, the legislative compromises accepted as the price for passage and judicial decisions that misinterpreted congressional intent or left loopholes to be exploited in future cases. The recent change of administration provides Congress and the Court, once again, with the opportunity to review executive branch overreaching by the Bush presidency over the past eight years and to determine how to scale back excessive claims of executive power. Lessons from the past offer a cautionary tale.

Why is it that congressional reform efforts and court decisions that have as their purpose the "checking" of excessive presidential power result, paradoxically, in authorizing and legitimizing the very powers they intended to curb? The examples are easy to identify: for starters, the War Powers Resolution of 1973, the Hughes-Ryan Amendment to the Foreign Assistance Act of 1974, and the Foreign Intelligence Surveillance Act of 1978 (FISA) all originated as statutory efforts to monitor and restrict presidential powers, but resulted, instead, in legitimizing actions that presidents had never before been permitted to take. Similarly, three Supreme Court decisions popularly regarded as prime examples of rejection of constitutionally excessive claims of presidential power – *Youngstown Sheet and Tube Co.*

* Presented at Hofstra University Symposium, President or King? Evaluating the Expansion of Executive Power from Abraham Lincoln to George W. Bush. November 4-5, 2009.

v. Sawyer (1952), *New York Times v. U.S.* (1971), and *U.S. v. Nixon* (1974) – actually had the reverse effect of making clear that there could, indeed, be circumstances when presidential exercise of the same powers negated in the specific conditions in those cases could be legitimate. For that matter, it could be argued that the three instances where Congress cranked up its machinery, unsuccessfully, to use its most extreme form of constitutional rebuke to a president, impeachment, may have contributed only to a reduced incentive to use that weapon in the future. [1]

How and why do such paradoxical effects occur? If the institutions upon which we depend to hold presidents in check are ineffective, and possibly, worse, what hope is there for government that depends on institutional checks and balances?

This chapter will explore some of these examples and will offer insights as to why efforts by Congress and the courts often fail to achieve their intended reform purpose and even promote the expansion, rather than the limiting, of the powers that they tried to curb. This pattern has occurred throughout history, although the focus here will be on the period of the last half of the twentieth century.

This time frame is a significant one, since it includes the era that Arthur Schlesinger, Jr. dubbed "the imperial presidency," as well as its sequel – the myriad efforts during the 1970s when Congress and the courts appeared, on the surface, to act to rein in a capacious executive, but laid the groundwork for only wider and deeper presidential power in the future, providing subsequent presidents with a permissive environment in which to exercise the very powers that the other branches tried to prevent them from using.

EXPANSION AND CONTRACTION – AND EXPANSION – OF PRESIDENTIAL POWER

It is, perhaps, a truism that power once exercised is unlikely to be relinquished – or, at the very least, will not be abandoned willingly. And so it is with presidents who, for any number of reasons or through a variety of circumstances (e.g., war, economic crisis, national disaster, popular mandate), accumulate power in the office, and, at once, become possessive and protective of it, with no thought of returning to the status quo ante. If this scenario continues, unabated, over time, its inevitable result will be an ever-growing residuum of power in the executive, leading to an increasing and entrenched imbalance among the three branches. No Framer was more sensitive to this potential than Madison, though he feared a too-powerful legislature more than an excessive executive. But his penchant for balance and for relative equilibrium among the branches was the overarching principle for the Constitution and for the new government structure it created. Presidents come and go, but the Constitution and its first principles are intended to endure.

There is nothing remarkable about changes in the relative ebb and flow of power among the three branches, over time. Strong, activist presidents have flexed their executive muscles during periods of heightened public anxiety, whether it is Lincoln during the Civil War or Teddy Roosevelt's independent antitrust initiatives and foreign policy adventures at the start of the 20th century, or FDR's actions in the lead-up to World War II. And, just as predictably, Congress and, occasionally, the courts have reacted to aggressive presidential behavior: we often find that periods of presidential supremacy are followed by eras of congressional dominance or reassertion. Madison fully expected these fluctuations to occur, and the genius of the system was that the people held in their own hands the keys to self-correction and the remedy for excessive power.

Why, then, and how did inter-branch relations reach the point under the George W. Bush presidency where it was common to hear that we were, once again, living under an "imperial presidency?" Hadn't we banished that conception of the office, once and for all, after the departure of Richard Nixon? Why was it back to haunt us once again?

Whether or not one agreed that the Bush presidency was, in fact, "imperial" was, itself, a matter of some debate. Vice-President Cheney, in his oft-stated comment that one goal of the Bush administration was to restore the power of the institution and "to leave the presidency stronger than we (they) found it" was countered by those who believed that the presidency had not been weakened at all. Andrew Rudalevige and others have argued that although Congress attempted a "resurgence" and reclaiming of its power after Watergate and Vietnam, it was clear by the time that President Bush took office that Congress's efforts had not instituted lasting restraints on executive power, and were not likely to prevent any president from exercising strong power. [2] To Rudalevige, these congressional reform efforts had not succeeded, and the office was certainly no "victim" of congressional limitations and legislative domination.

Thus, two camps or schools of thought existed: those forceful proponents of executive power, or "presidentialists," who lamented that Congress had wrongly restricted the realm of presidential actions in the post-Watergate/Vietnam era (a view best represented in the minority report, led by then-Representative Dick Cheney, of the joint congressional committee investigating the Iran-contra scandal) vs. those who concluded that there had been no appreciable or enduring restraining effect on presidential power from the 1970s reform efforts. Regardless of the existence of these opposing views, the key inquiry is to determine exactly what these efforts during the 1970s tried to accomplish, and to assess to what degree they either succeeded or failed.

Framework Legislation

Statutes that impose detailed procedures for carrying out governmental decision-making have been dubbed "framework laws" because they provide an organizational structure (thus, "framework") within which Congress and the president carry out each one's constitutional duties. Harold Koh has explained that such legislation formed "a statutory superstructure that declares in greater detail how power should be distributed among institutions" in specific policy areas. [3]

An example of a "statutory superstructure" is the War Powers Resolution of 1973, born out of Congress's frustration and inability to assert its own constitutional prerogatives and to effectively challenge a president during an unpopular war. The Constitution gives Congress in Article I and the president in Article II specific and distinct war powers responsibilities, but questions of how and when each branch was supposed to act have engendered controversy since the nation's founding. The War Powers Resolution, similar to other framework laws, may be viewed as a separate layer of law sitting on top of those constitutional articles (hence, "a statutory superstructure") as an attempt to clarify the respective duties of each institution and to provide an orderly process through a series of sequential actions by which those duties are exercised. In this sense and in the most charitable description of the resolution, although it does not change or add to the Constitution, it "facilitates" the legal authorities specified in Articles I and II. Similar descriptions would apply to other framework laws.

Koh focused exclusively on the use of these laws in foreign policy decision-making, where they were "designed not only to restrain executive discretion, but also to increase congressional input into key foreign policy decisions," [4] although this description applies as well to such laws in the domestic policy arena. As examples, in addition to the War Powers Resolution of 1973, he cites the National Emergencies Act of 1976 and the International Emergency Economic Powers Act of 1977, to which one can also add the Case-Zablocki Act of 1972 (regulating executive agreements), the Hughes Ryan Amendment to the Foreign Assistance Act of 1974 (requiring presidential reporting to Congress of covert actions), the Foreign Intelligence Surveillance Act (FISA) of 1978 (regulating national security surveillance), and the Intelligence Oversight Act of 1980 (the product of the 1976 Church and Pike congressional committee hearings on intelligence operations, establishing congressional intelligence committees and requiring presidential "findings" for covert operations). In the domestic policy field, examples include the Congressional Budget and Impoundment Control Act of 1974 (establishing new congressional budget committees and a new budget process), the Ethics in Government Act of 1978 (containing provisions to determine the need for and selection of an independent counsel), and the Presidential Records Act of 1978 (establishing governmental control of presidential records and a process for public release of them).

The intended purpose common to all of these laws is to both limit discretionary actions of presidents and to promote greater participation by Congress. This was to be accomplished by congressional monitoring and close oversight of executive actions through the imposition of procedural requirements, such as reporting and consulting provisions, legislative vetoes, findings of fact, and/or funding restrictions.

It is not difficult to see how these desired outcomes were an obvious reaction to the Watergate/Vietnam era where the exact opposite inter-branch dynamic predominated: unlimited discretion by presidents and ineffective efforts by Congress to exercise its constitutional powers.

Koh was quick to note, specifically in reference to foreign affairs but equally as true in domestic affairs, that "virtually overlooked.....was that this generation of statutes created not only procedural constraints, but also substantial fresh delegations of foreign affairs authority. By 1988, it had become clear that the executive branch had successfully tapped many of these broad new authorizations while paying only lip service to the accompanying procedural strictures." [5]

Herein, then, lies the key to why these statutes, prompted by a congressional motive to restrain the chief executive, resulted, instead, in expanding executive power because they simultaneously delegated power to that office. Additionally, the intense politics involved in the legislative process through which each of these statutes was produced ultimately led negotiators to compromise, which, thus, diluted the force and effect of the proposed legislation. In other words, presidentialists would not willingly agree to tie the hands of future chief executives: therefore, in exchange, they demanded and received some *new* delegation of power from Congress to counter-balance their grudging acceptance of *new* legislative restrictions and controls on presidential policy-making.

The War Powers Resolution of 1973

The War Powers Resolution, the quintessential framework statute, imposes a series of steps (consultation, reporting and congressional action/inaction) on Congress and the president by which they are to carry out their respective constitutional functions from Articles I and II of "declaring war" and serving as "Commander in Chief, when called into the actual Service of the United States." It began as a robust effort by Congress to reclaim its constitutional war-making role but ended in a far weaker and, ultimately, ineffective shadow of its initial proposal. Political wrangling in the conference committee watered down its most potent provisions from the Senate version, forcing its proponents to decide whether a weaker bill was better than no bill at all. [6] They opted for the weaker bill – and the rest is, as they say, "history."

The most important features of the WPR concerned consultation, reporting requirements and the effect of congressional action or inaction. Its stated purpose in Section 2 was "to fulfill the intent of the framers of the Constitution of the United States and insure that the collective judgment of both the Congress and the President will apply to the introduction of the United States Armed Forces into hostilities, or into situations where imminent involvement in hostilities is clearly indicated by the circumstances." [7] That "collective judgment" was to be achieved by directing in Section 3 that "the President in every possible instance shall consult with Congress before introducing United States Armed Forces into hostilities or into situations where imminent involvement in hostilities is clearly indicated by the circumstances." [8] The other key provisions were the limitations in Section 2 on the president's Commander in Chief powers, which could be exercised pursuant only to "1) a declaration of war, 2) specific statutory authorization, or 3) a national emergency created by an attack upon the United States…;" Section 4, requiring the president, in the absence of a declaration of war, to provide a written report to Congress within 48 hours when armed forces are introduced into hostilities; Section 5(b), providing for automatic termination by the president of the use of force within 60-90 days if Congress had neither authorized it nor declared war or was "physically unable to meet as a result of an armed attack on the United States;" and Section 5(c), permitting Congress, by a concurrent resolution (not requiring the president's signature), at any time, even within the 60-90 day period, to order the president to remove United States forces from hostilities, absent a declaration of war or specific statutory authorization. [9]

In short, Congress hoped these steps would insure its inclusion in decisions to use military force, would give it a continuing role in monitoring the president's actions, and would guarantee that any use of force longer than 60-90 days could proceed beyond that point only if Congress had affirmatively acted to authorize it. If Congress took no action, the law required the president to withdraw the troops at the close of 60-90 days.

Interpretations of the War Powers Resolution ran the gamut from a) President Nixon, who noted in his veto message that "the restrictions which this resolution would impose upon the authority of the President" were "both unconstitutional and dangerous to the best interests of our Nation," [10] to b) Senator Thomas Eagleton (D-MI), one of the original sponsors of the bill who ultimately voted against it because he believed that the final version, without the stronger, initial Senate provisions, no longer limited presidential power but, rather, now, delegated to a president, *for the first time*, the authority to use military force, without congressional authorization, for 60-90 days), [11] to c) others who believed that it served its functional purpose of providing a procedural framework or roadmap that defined the respective constitutional roles of both Congress and the president in decisions to use military force. [12] In short, some thought it unconstitutionally restricted executive power, others thought it unconstitutionally expanded presidential authority, while others thought it would provide a practical solution that more clearly designated how each branch should carry out its constitutional role.

The verdict on the War Powers Resolution, after more than 35 years of operation, is that it has been a profound disappointment to its initial supporters, and has been either ignored, circumvented or cleverly interpreted by post-1973 presidents so as to distort and subvert its intended objective. [13] At the very most, its only effect has been its symbolic value as a constant reminder to presidents that they *should* seek authorization from Congress when intending to use military force, which most have done, but claiming all the while that they are doing so for the purpose of gaining *political* support, rather than as a *constitutional* or *legal* requirement, stating that they are acting "consistent with" but not "pursuant to" the statute. Such wording confirmed that these presidents did not bring themselves under the requirements of the law, thus, managing to wiggle out of any binding effect of the legislation: in essence, then, the law means nothing.

Outcomes from Other Framework Laws

It is easy to trace the legacy of the War Powers Resolution, since it has maintained a high public profile, and it surfaces each time a president contemplates the use of military force. The follow-up from other framework statutes and reform efforts is less obvious, but some identifiable patterns have emerged. Consider a few examples:

1. The 1972 Case-Zablocki Act, aimed at monitoring the proliferation of executive agreements at the expense of treaties, was watered down in the legislative process. Its initial, strict requirement of congressional review of executive agreements morphed into a mere "notification" requirement to Congress by the president of any international agreement. Presidents have used even more subtle efforts through treaty "re-interpretation" and by characterizing some agreements as "non-agreement agreements" to circumvent the treaty ratification and congressional notification processes altogether; [14]
2. The International Emergency Economic Powers Act of 1977, passed by Congress as an effort to impose controls on executive discretion to declare national emergencies, has been undermined by three Supreme Court decisions that interpreted the delegations of power in the statute to the president much more generously than Congress intended [15] and by other Court decisions that declared challenges to the statute non-justiciable political questions, [16] thus, leaving unresolved complaints that the executive branch was misusing the power delegated to it by the statute;
3. The effect of the Hughes-Ryan Amendment, enacted in 1974 to create accountability for covert operations by requiring the president to report through an explicit "finding" that each covert operation is "important to the national security of the

> United States," has dwindled over time. Even this requirement is a diminished version of its initially proposed mandate, and is an example of the inter-branch bargaining endemic to such laws. In the pre-Vietnam era, presidents had denied responsibility for covert actions: with the Hughes-Ryan Amendment, the "price" for permitting presidents to engage in covert actions was compliance with Congress's statutory reporting requirement. Yet, even these requirements were gradually loosened so much as to rob them of any effective control. The Intelligence Authorization Act of 1980 began by ostensibly strengthening the reporting requirement, mandating the president to give *prior notice* to intelligence committees in Congress of any "significant anticipated intelligence activity." To sweeten the deal, Congress relaxed the number of committees to which the president must give notice from eight to two, and furthermore, where the president determined the existence of "extraordinary circumstances affecting vital interests of the United States," he was required only to report "in a timely fashion," and, thus, without prior notice, to the "Gang of Eight" (congressional leaders). [17] Koh concludes that the 1980 act "did little more than codify the executive practice followed by the Carter administration over the previous four years….." and that "the act's effectiveness therefore hinged upon informal congressional-executive accords and the president's willingness to issue and enforce the executive orders and national security decision directives necessary to discharge his statutory responsibilities." [18]

This last example set the stage for the massive presidential circumvention of congressional restrictions that occurred when Reagan administration officials engaged in covert actions in the late-1980s Iran-contra scandal and failed to comply with a series of legislative enactments prohibiting aid to the contra rebels in Nicaragua. In addition to violation of substantive policy, the executive branch offered an aggressive legal position that illustrates the futility of congressional efforts to control executives determined to act in disregard of congressional limitations.

The Office of Legal Counsel in the Department of Justice issued an opinion by Charles Cooper on December 17, 1986 that laid out the legal justification for President Reagan's decision to postpone for several months notifying Congress about the administration's secret overture to Iran in the "arms-for-hostages" deal. [19] The Intelligence Oversight Act of 1980 amended Section 501 (B) of the National Security Act of 1947, and was the operative statute requiring the president to notify congressional intelligence committees "in a timely fashion" of intelligence operations "for which prior notice was not given…" (50 U.S.C. Sec. 413 [b]) Cooper's legal analysis interpreted the "timely fashion" notice requirement in these circumstances as "to leave the President with virtually unfettered discretion to choose the right moment for making the required notification. The word 'timely' is inherently vague: in *any* statute, it would ordinarily be read to give the party charged with abiding by a timeliness requirement the latitude to interpret it in a reasonable manner. Congress apparently thought that the notification requirement was meant to limit the President's exercise of his inherent authority, while at the same time Congress acknowledged the existence and validity of that authority." [20]

This opinion argues 1) that the president has "inherent and plenary constitutional authority in the field of international relations," with the requisite homage to *U.S. v. Curtiss-Wright*, [21] and 2) that Congress may not, by statute, infringe on the president's inherent authority to conduct foreign policy. [22] Cooper asserts that 1) "decisions and actions by the President and his immediate staff in the conduct of foreign policy are not subject to direct review by Congress;" 2) "Congress may not attach conditions to Executive Branch appropriations that require the President to relinquish any of his constitutional discretion in foreign affairs;" and 3) "any statute that touches on the President's inherent authority in foreign policy must be interpreted to leave the President as much discretion as the language of the statute will allow..... Because the president's constitutional authority in international relations is by its very nature virtually as broad as the national interest and as indefinable as the exigencies of unpredictable events, almost *any* congressional attempt to curtail his discretion raises questions of constitutional dimension." [23] (emphasis in original) He then finishes by noting that any questions of "statutory ambiguity" must be resolved "in accord with the presumption that recognizes the President's constitutional independence in international affairs." [24]

Patterns of Congressional Response and Presidential Implementation and Congressional Response

From the examples above, it is possible to suggest some explanations for why congressional efforts to require accountability from presidents have proven so elusive. The cycle begins with the discovery of presidential excess, usually brought to light either by scandal, as in Iran-contra, or by eventual congressional recognition of its own abdication of its authority, as with intelligence operations and war powers. Congress launches internal inquiries, exposes executive branch wrongdoing or use of constitutionally questionable authority, and vows to take action to forestall such abuses in the future. Well-meaning intentions give way to political reality, as legislative compromises produce not only weaker results than initially promised, but Congress also a) acknowledges *new* power in the president that had not previously been understood to reside in the office (as in the Hughes-Ryan Amendment), or b) delegates away its own constitutional authority to the president (as in the War Powers Resolution), or c) uses ambiguous legislative language (as in the "timely fashion" notification requirement in the Intelligence Oversight Act) that presidents can interpret to fit their purposes. Additionally, the courts can play a role by interpreting legislative language inconsistent with Congress's intent or by abdicating a judicial role entirely and, thus, wiping out challenges to the president's actions (as in the International Emergency Economic Powers Act). Ultimately, presidents maintain their own arsenal of unilateral tools (e.g., presidential directives, executive orders, executive agreements or signing statements that direct non-enforcement or selective enforcement of statutes) by which to implement legislation in ways that accommodate their political purposes and broaden their constitutional authority (as in the Case-Zablocki Act).

The examples offered here – and the accompanying analysis – are just the tip of the iceberg in an inquiry as to why efforts to restrain executive power so often fail to meet that objective. It seems that whenever we talk about how to contain expansive presidential power, what we really end up discussing is Congress. The source of efforts to keep presidential power within bounds certainly lies in all three branches, to some degree, but more often than not, it falls to Congress to monitor and enforce constitutional limits on the chief executive.

The efforts of the 1970s present a cautionary tale of how not to do this, and one hopes that wiser legislative drafters in the future will learn from past failures.

The country is poised at a point in history where, similar to the post-Watergate/Vietnam era, dynamics are in place to suggest that this may be a time when Congress may choose, once again, to take stock of "the state of the presidency," as bequeathed to Barack Obama from George W. Bush. After the Bush presidency where the powers of the office were pushed to their outermost limits, with invocations of "national security" as the frequent justification, there may well be good cause to examine the confines of the powers of the presidency, as they existed at the time of the transfer of power just one year ago. It is also useful to study past failures of efforts to constrain presidential power, as this essay does, in order to avoid the very same mistakes again.

Only after the 2006 midterm elections brought a Democratic majority to power did Congress start to crank up the machinery of inquiry, with a bevy of hearings on many of the most controversial aspects of the Bush antiterrorism policies, such as domestic warrantless wiretapping, use of the state secrets privilege, coercive interrogations, detention of terrorist suspects, and military commissions. Passage of the National Defense Authorization Act of 2010 in October 2009 (P.L. 111-84) included provisions modifying Bush administration policies on the treatment and status of terrorist suspects and on procedures for military commissions. The State Secret Protection Act of 2009 (H.R. 984) was reported out of the House Judiciary Committee on November 5, 2009, but has languished in the Senate Judiciary Committee. Congress passed the Department of Defense Appropriations Act 2010 (P.L. 111-118) and the president signed it on December 19, 2009, which contains provisions to extend the sunset of the "library," "lone wolf," and "roving wiretaps" provisions of the USA PATRIOT Act.

Thus, it seems, from a cursory overview, that current legislative efforts are aimed more at changing substantive policies than providing procedural frameworks for future legislation. If so, then, this may be an early signal that Congress is moving beyond the failed approach of the 1970s reforms, and that it is, instead, honing in directly to change past policies that had been supported by and depended upon excessive executive power. It is, then, *indirectly* modifying claims of presidential power, through White House support of revised policies that are marked by slightly narrower use of executive power. This contrasts with the 1970s efforts that *directly* targeted for "down-sizing" the president's constitutional authority, which, as this essay notes, have been spectacularly unsuccessful, in the long term.

THE JUDICIAL RESPONSE

Cases from the 1970s Era

Some examples of Supreme Court decisions during the 1970s (or those that ruled on claims of expansive executive power stemming from circumstances arising during that era) are *New York Times v. U.S.* (the Pentagon Papers case) (1971), *U.S. v. Nixon* (1974), *Nixon v. Administrator of General Services* (1977), and *Morrison v. Olson* (1988). [25] The general understanding is that the Supreme Court struck down presidential claims to power in each of these cases. It rejected claims of inherent executive authority in *New York Times v. U.S.*

(denying the administration's request for an injunction to prevent newspaper publication of material that the executive deemed damaging to national security) and in *U.S. v. Nixon* (denying the president's generalized and absolute claim to executive privilege, but concluding that the office possessed a qualified right); it rejected former President Nixon's five separate challenges to the Presidential Recordings and Materials Preservation Act of 1974 (the forerunner to the Presidential Records Act of 1978) in the *Nixon v. GSA* case, ruling that although a president's qualified right to executive privilege "survived the individual President's tenure," that right of former presidents diminished over time; and it ruled in *Morrison* against the arguments of the executive branch that a) the independent counsel provisions of the Ethics in Government Act of 1978 violated the president's Article II powers under the Appointments Clause, b) interfered impermissibly with the president's power to control the removal of inferior executive branch officials, and c) violated the principle of separation of powers by reducing the president's control over prosecutorial authority.

Yet, there is room to argue that at least three of these decisions, viewed generally as unfavorable to the president's claims, left some "wiggle room" for later presidents to salvage some authority. Presidents could convince some future Court a) to grant a requested injunction against publication, where there is sufficient evidence that publication of certain information threatens to cause "grave and irreparable" injury to the public interest (an element that was *not* present in *N.Y. Times v. U.S.*); b) that a president's qualified right to protect confidentiality of his presidential communications meets the standard set in *U.S. v. Nixon*, especially, where those communications involve "a claim of need to protect military, diplomatic or sensitive national security secrets" (again, conditions that did *not* exist in *U.S. v. Nixon*); and c) to grant a former president's claim to executive privilege of his official records when such claim is close in time to the end of his term of office (and, when a president's papers were *not* likely to be needed for future criminal proceedings, as was still possible with Nixon's papers). The aftermath of *Morrison* is, perhaps, distinct among these cases, since the specific statutory provisions upheld in that decision were allowed to lapse, due to mutual agreement by both political branches to refrain from renewing the statute in the 1990s. Thus, the exact issue in the case was unlikely to arise again in a similar context for future presidents: however, the legal principles articulated in the Court's decision have endured.

Although these four cases constitute a small sample, the larger point is that even where judicial decisions deny presidential claims in the immediate case, there is often sufficient discretion in the standards imposed in these rulings to permit later chief executives to "exploit" the openings left in prior decisions.

Recent Cases

Can we begin to compare judicial decisions from the 1970s era that addressed claims of presidential power with any from the Bush era where the president urged the Court to support expansive interpretations of his constitutional power?

The policy arena in which so many of the Bush-era executive power cases developed was national security and, more specifically, antiterrorism policy, in response to challenges to claims of expansive presidential power arising under the administration's actions after the September 11, 2001 attacks. The lower federal courts entered this field as early as 2002, and the Supreme Court began issuing decisions in 2004, starting with the trilogy of *Hamdi v.*

Rumsfeld, *Padilla v. Rumsfeld*, and *Rasul v. Bush*, and followed later by *Hamdan v. Rumsfeld* in 2006. [26] These decisions contained some mixed results for the executive branch, but, largely, they repudiated claims of presidential power, based on the Commander-in-Chief clause, the executive power clause of Article II, or inherent executive power, or, at times, based on delegations from Congress. The Supreme Court ruled in *Hamdi* that the president has authority from the 2001 Authorization to Use Military Force (AUMF) to detain U.S. citizens on the battlefield, but that detainees have due process rights; it dismissed *Padilla* for lack of jurisdiction, but the defendant was later prosecuted and convicted in criminal court for conspiracy; it ruled, contrary to the government's argument, in *Rasul* that Guantanamo detainees are entitled, under statute, to federal court review of their executive detention; and in *Hamdan*, it declared unconstitutional the establishment of military commissions, based on either the president's inherent power or the 2001 AUMF, as a violation of the Uniform Code of Military Justice (UCMJ) and Common Article Three of the Geneva Conventions.

Although these decisions addressed highly technical and focused arguments about the scope of government authority to act during wartime, still, the unmistakable, cumulative message from them to the president about the scope of his powers, even in "extraordinary times," [27] was that the Court, not the president, would be the judge of that scope. The legacy from the 1970s-era cases was no different, although there were more opportunities in those earlier decisions that offered "cues" to future presidents about how to slip through loopholes. There were no similar "winks and nods" from the Court in the Bush-era cases, where the language of the majority opinions was infused with the seriousness of the liberty vs. security dilemma, and where there was no doubt as to the side of that debate on which the Court majority found itself.

Perhaps, the 1971 Pentagon Papers case offers the closest comparison to the Bush-era decisions, not only because national security concerns dominated all of these cases but, also, because the president relied, in part, on the claim of inherent power in all of them. That claim was soundly rejected by three justices (Black, Douglas and Brennan) in *New York Times v. U.S.*, but of the remaining six justices (three concurring and three dissenting), at least four (excluding Marshall and White) gave varying degrees of support to an inherent executive power argument, where, in the future, the circumstances might be more dire than those presented by the publication of the Pentagon Papers in 1971.

That same claim of inherent executive power was presented in the Bush-era cases, although here it was the alternative or "even if" argument rather than the primary one, since the government was able to rest on the AUMF for authority in these cases, and only threw in the "inherent power" argument as a back-up. The Court declined to rule on the inherent power claim when it did not need to reach that argument.

Conclusions

What conclusions can we draw here about congressional and judicial responses to constitutionally questionable claims of executive power in times of an "imperial presidency," and are there lessons from history that can be useful today? With Congress, the lesson from the 1970s was that forcing procedural requirements on presidents in order to monitor their actions more closely resulted only in creative ways by the executive to either bypass or undermine those devices imposed to, ultimately, restrain or monitor presidential power. By the advent of the next "generation" of the imperial presidency after 2001, congressional efforts to push back went from procedural to substantive. It is too early to tell if the changed approach will produce the results Congress intended.

With the Court, the two sets of cases examined here are representative of their two respective eras in history, but are not parallel in key respects. It seems unlikely that claims of executive privilege and appointment and removal powers are on the same level of importance with claims of the president in his wartime role as Commander-in-Chief (however, some may readily argue that, in fact, there is no reason to presume a lack of equivalency – in that there is no hierarchy or ranking of powers under Article II). The Court's 1970s-era decisions denied the president's expansive claims in the immediate cases, but left the door open for potential rulings in the future in the president's favor (i.e., the *president* may have lost the battle but the *presidency* may have won the war in these cases), while the Bush-era cases were of a different magnitude, dealing with claims of inherent power that, if upheld, could have changed the nature and structure of government in the most fundamental ways. The Court chose not to address those claims, to neither affirm nor reject them, leaving their status unanswered and uncertain, while finding other ways to pull back presidential power that had ventured too far.

Two different decades spawning separate approaches by two different branches to two different "imperial presidencies:" we witnessed the ineffective attempts of Congress and the Court in the 1970s to achieve their intended results, and we have the chance now to still determine whether precautions are needed to insure that Bush-era excesses do not become institutionalized. All eyes should be on Congress and the Court going forward, with work still to do, while learning from the past.

REFERENCES

[1] Impeachment efforts against Andrew Johnson, Richard Nixon, and Bill Clinton proceeded to varying stages, but none of these culminated in a successful Senate vote of removal from office.

[2] Andrew Rudalevige, *The New Imperial Presidency: Renewing Presidential Power After Watergate* (Ann Arbor: University of Michigan Press, 2005).

[3] Harold Hongju Koh, *The National Security Constitution: Sharing Power After the Iran-Contra Affair* (New Haven: Yale University Press, 1990), pp. 69-70.

[4] Harold Hongju Koh, "Why the President (Almost) Always Wins in Foreign Affairs," *Yale Law Journal*, 1988, p. 1300.

[5] Koh, 1988, p. 1264.

[6] See testimony by Louis Fisher, "War Powers for the 21st Century: The Constitutional Perspective," in HJ Res 53, Hearing before Subcommittee on International Organizations, Human Rights and Oversight of the Committee on Foreign Affairs, House of Representatives, 110th Congress, 2nd sess., April 10, 2008. Fisher details the initial Senate version of the WPR, which contained clear limits on the few, narrowly defined circumstances for which presidents could initiate military action. The Senate report included the powers "to take necessary and appropriate retaliatory actions in the

event of [an armed attack upon the U.S., its territories or possessions]," "to forestall the direct and imminent threat of [an attack against the armed forces of the United States located outside the United States, its territories and possessions]," and "to protect while evacuating citizens and nationals of the United States, as rapidly as possible, from [certain situations] involving a direct and imminent threat to [their] lives." S. 440, 93rd Cong. Sec. 3 (1973), as quoted in Dycus, Berney, Banks and Raven-Hansen, *National Security Law*, 4th ed. (Aspen Publishers, 2007), p. 246.

[7] P.L. 93-148, 87 Stat. 555 (1973), 50 U.S.C. Sec 1541-48 (2000).

[8] Ibid.

[9] Ibid.

[10] H. Doc. 171, 93rd Cong., 1st Sess. (1973).

[11] Prepared Statement of Senator Eagleton – July 13, 1988 in "The War Power After 200 Years: Congress and the President at a Constitutional Impasse," Hearings before the Special Subcommittee on War Powers of the Committee on Foreign Relations, U.S. Senate, 100th Cong., 2nd Sess., July 13, 1988, 364-370. Senator Eagleton described the "compromise" that emerged from the Senate-House conference as "a totally illogical, illegitimate child."

[12] Michael Glennon, professor of law at The Fletcher School of Law and Diplomacy and former general counsel on the Senate Foreign Relations Committee in 1973 who participated in drafting the War Powers Resolution, concedes that it contains flaws, but appears to believe that it can be revised, rather than repealed. See, for example, Michael Glennon, "The War Powers Resolution, Once Again," http://ssrn.com/abstract=1340622.

[13] Walter Dellinger, "Deployment of United States Armed Forces into Haiti," 18 Op. O.L.C. No. 34 (September 27, 1994), reprinted in H. Jefferson Powell, *The Constitution and the Attorneys General* (Durham, NC: Carolina Academic Press, 1999), pp. 572-577.

[14] Koh, 1990, pp. 42-44.

[15] Ibid., pp. 46-47; See *Dames and Moore v. Regan*, 453 U.S. 654 (1981); *INS v. Chadha*, 462 U.S. 919 (1983); *Regan v. Wald*, 468 U.S. 222 (1984).

[16] Ibid., pp.; See *Beacon Products Corp. v. Reagan*, 633 F. Supp. 1191 (D. Mass.1986), aff'd, 841 F. 2d 1 (1st Cir. 1987).

[17] Ibid., p. 58.

[18] Ibid., p. 58.

[19] Charles J. Cooper, "The President's Compliance with the "Timely Notification" Requirement of Section 501 (B) of the National Security Act," 10 Op. O.L.C. 159 (December 17, 1986), reprinted in H. Jefferson Powell, *The Constitution and the Attorneys General* (Durham, NC: Carolina Academic Press, 1999), pp. 483-498.

[20] Ibid., p. 497.

[21] *U.S. v. Curtiss-Wright Export Corp.*, 299 U.S. 304 (1936).

[22] Cooper, 1986.

[23] Ibid.

[24] Ibid., pp. 493-494.

[25] *New York Times Co. v. U.S.*, 403 U.S. 670 (1971); *U.S. v. Nixon*, 418 U.S. 683 (1974); *Nixon v. Administrator of General Services*, 433 U.S. 425 (1977); and *Morrison v. Olson*, 487 U.S. 654 (1988).

[26] *Hamdi v. Rumsfeld*, 542 U.S. 507 (2004); *Padilla v. Rumsfeld*, 542 U.S. 426 (2004); *Rasul v. Bush,* 542 U.S. 466 (2004); and *Hamdan v. Rumsfeld*, 548 U.S. __ (2006). The Court also ruled in *Boumediene v. Bush*, 553 U.S. __ (2008), that Guantanamo detainees have a constitutionally guaranteed right to the writ of habeas corpus, for which the Detainee Treatment Act passed by Congress in 2005 was an inadequate substitute for federal court review. The Court's decision did not reach claims of executive power, although Solicitor General Paul Clement's brief for the government included them, arguing that "Even apart from the AUMF, petitioners' detention is independently justified by the President's constitutional authority" from "the executive power" and Commander-in-Chief clauses of Article II. (http://www.wilmerhale.com/files/upload/boumediene_061195bs.pdf)

[27] *Boumediene v. Bush*, 553 U.S. __ (2008).

Part II:

Examining the Use of Presidential Power in the George W. Bush Administration

In: President or King?
Editor: Meena Bose, pp. 79-97
ISBN: 978-1-61324-655-9

Congressional Abdication and the Cult of the Presidency

Gene Healy

Abstract

James Madison believed that the constitutional separation of powers would be self-executing. Ambition would counteract ambition, with each branch fighting to preserve its proper place in the constitutional order. That scheme has worked well with regard to the presidency: no president wants to leave the office weaker than he found it. But congressional abdication has been an increasing problem throughout the era of the modern presidency. Congress has been all too eager to punt to the president, leaving the hard decisions to the nation's chief executive, and reserving the right to lambaste him when he gets it wrong. Anyone who hoped that the Obama administration would de-imperialize the presidency has had major grounds for disappointment. But expecting a president to voluntarily reduce his own powers is among the most audacious of hopes. The constitutional separation of powers has always depended upon Congress and the courts defending their own prerogatives and keeping the executive branch in check.

There was a revealing moment in the first presidential debate in September 2008, when moderator Jim Lehrer asked the candidates, "Are you willing to acknowledge, both of you, that this financial crisis is going to affect the way you *rule the country* as president of the United States?" [1] Neither John McCain nor Barack Obama thought to quibble with Lehrer's phrasing. Both, it seemed, were comfortable with the idea that what the president does, essentially, is "rule the country."

That's a disturbing notion in a country born through rejection of monarchy. But you could see how the candidates might get the idea that ruling the country was the president's job. Despite the bitterness of our current ideological battles, liberals and conservatives largely agree on the boundless nature of presidential responsibility. Neither Left nor Right sees the president as the Framers saw him: a constitutionally constrained chief executive with important, but limited, responsibilities. Today, for conservatives as well as liberals, it is the president's job to protect us from harm, to grow the economy, spread American ideals abroad, and even to heal spiritual malaise.

Worse still, the irrational expectations Americans invest in the office drive the growth of presidential power. Asked to perform miracles, modern presidents have often sought powers to match that responsibility — and all too often Congress has obliged. Indeed, by the time both major parties had settled on their nominees for the 2008 race, it had become clear that whoever won would, as Yale Law professor Jack Balkin observed, "inherit more constitutional and legal power than any president in U.S. history." [2]

When questioned about the Bush administration's aggressive approach toward presidential power, Vice President Dick Cheney often commented that he and President Bush aimed to leave the office as strong as they'd found it. And though Bush ended his second term as one of the most reviled presidents of the modern era, that was one charge he'd managed to keep.

To the modern president's already enormous powers — vast discretion over warmaking, the ability to shape large areas of domestic policy via executive order — George W. Bush had added a host of new powers hardly dreamt of before the twin crises that bookended his presidency. The September 11th attacks gave the president greatly enhanced surveillance authority and new powers over the disposition and treatment of "enemy combatants." And the intensifying financial meltdown of late 2008 gave him what amounted to a presidential power of the purse: so broad was the authority Congress delegated in the law that established the $700 billion Troubled Assets Relief Program, that Bush used it to lend billions of dollars to Chrysler and GM a week after Congress voted down legislation authorizing the auto bailout.

Throughout the Twentieth Century, America drifted far from the Framers' comparatively modest vision of the president's purpose and powers, as more and more Americans looked to the central government — and, increasingly, to the president — to deal with highly visible public problems, from labor disputes to crime waves to natural disasters. And as responsibility flowed to the center, presidential power grew accordingly. In the Twenty-first Century, that trend seems to be accelerating.

If we're disturbed by the growth of presidential power — and we should be — we'd do well to explore how we got here. It won't do, obviously, to curse our bad luck and blame a succession of aggrandizing presidents. Most analysts of the "Imperial Presidency" have concluded, as Arthur Schlesinger Jr. did, that the growth of presidential power over the course of the Twentieth Century "was as much a matter of congressional abdication as of presidential usurpation." [3]

Our experience in the first decade of the Twenty-first Century gives us little reason to amend that assessment. Nearly every recent advance in presidential power has its roots in Congress's willing abandonment of the powers the Constitution grants it.

This essay will explore the growth of executive power in the Bush and Obama years and the key role congressional abdication has played in that growth. I'll begin with a brief discussion of Congress's dominant role in the Framers' original design and James Madison's vision of a self-reinforcing constitutional order in which individual ambition could be properly channeled to preserve the interbranch balance of powers. From there, we'll look at how Madison's plan has worked out in foreign and domestic affairs, focusing chiefly on the last two administrations. Given the presidency's increasing dominance at home and abroad, the answer is, not very well. Finally, I'll suggest some reasons for the failure of the Madisonian vision and ask what, if anything, can be done about it.

Congress's Role in the Original Design

"In a government where numerous and extensive prerogatives are placed in the hands of a hereditary monarch," Madison wrote, the gravest threats to liberty would naturally be expected to come from the executive. But the American situation would be fundamentally different: in our Constitution, "where the executive magistracy is carefully limited, both in the extent and the duration of its power," *legislative* encroachment was more to be feared. [4]

We often hear it said that we have a government of "co-equal" branches. As Garry Wills points out, though, given the relative powers each branch has under the Constitution, "co-equal" is a misnomer:

> Congress can remove officers from the other two branches — President, agency heads, judges in district or supreme courts. Neither of the other two branches can touch a member of the Congress. Congress sets the pay for the other two and also for itself. It decides on the structure of the other two departments, creating or abolishing agencies and courts. [5]

Indeed, in virtually every important area of governance, the Constitution gives Congress the last word. Any treaty the president negotiates is invalid without the Senate's ratification. The president can, through use of the veto, impede the passage of legislation, but Congress can override that obstruction. Congress has the power to propose constitutional amendments, which become the law of the land when ratified by three-quarters of the states; the president has no role in the amendment process. Moreover, Article I, sec. 8, cl. 18, the so-called "Sweeping Clause," gives Congress the power to "make all laws which shall be necessary and proper to carry into execution... all other Powers vested by this Constitution in the Government of the United States, or in any Department or Officer thereof" — and thus, allows Congress to restrict any authority claimed by the executive "beyond that core of powers that are literally indispensable, rather than merely appropriate or helpful, to the performance of [its] express duties" under Article II of the Constitution. [6] As Wills puts it, "where two [branches] are dominated by a predominating third, there can be no co-equality." [7]

The enumeration of congressional powers in Article I, sec. 8 clearly demonstrates that it was *Congress's* job, not the president's, to set the national direction in terms of policy. Even in foreign affairs, where the chief executive's powers are thought to be broadest, the authority granted in the national charter is largely managerial and defensive. Just as the president will command the militia to suppress rebellions, should it be "called into the actual Service of the United States," he can command the Army and the Navy, should Congress pass the necessary appropriations, and he can lead the Army and Navy into battle, should Congress choose to declare war. As "first General" of the United States, in Hamilton's phrase, the president has an important role, but generals do not have the power to decide whether and when we go to war. [8] "In no part of the constitution is more wisdom to be found," Madison wrote, "than in the clause which confides the question of war or peace to the legislature, and not to the executive department. Beside the objection to such a mixture of heterogeneous powers: the trust and the temptation would be too great for any one man". [9]

America's experience under the Articles of Confederation revealed the danger of "the legislative department... drawing all power into its impetuous vortex".[10] And, as Madison recognized, given the dominant role the Constitution gave the Congress, there was reason to fear similar encroachments at the federal level as well. "In republican government the legislative authority necessarily predominates," he wrote in *Federalist* 51, and "this inconveniency" had to be guarded against, lest the legislature appropriate powers properly belonging to the other two branches. [11]

Mere parchment barriers wouldn't be enough to maintain the interbranch balance of power. Instead, Madison thought we could count on the constitutional architecture itself to channel man's lust for power in a manner that preserved individual liberty and limited government. "The great security against a gradual concentration of the several powers in the same department," he wrote, "consists in giving to those who administer each department the necessary constitutional means and personal motives to resist encroachments of the others. … Ambition must be made to counteract ambition." [12]

In the Madisonian vision, then, separation of powers was supposed to be largely self-executing. The members of each branch would have adequate incentive to fight any diminution of their branch's authority. "The interest of the man" — that is, the ambitions of individual representatives, judges, and presidents — would lead each to defend "the constitutional rights of the place": the authority of the particular branch each occupied. And *that*, not the fond hope that political actors would forever respect the formal limits written into the national charter, would prevent any one branch from commandeering powers belonging to the others.

Things haven't quite worked out as planned. At home and abroad, the modern president has absorbed powers that properly belong to the legislative branch. At times, he's seized those powers; but more often than not, he's received them as gifts from a Congress all too eager to hand them over.

Congressional Abdication in Foreign Affairs

The Twentieth Century collapse of congressional authority over foreign affairs is a familiar story. We haven't lacked for aggrandizing presidents, but on the Madisonian battlefield of ambition, they've rarely encountered a Congress willing to protect its institutional prerogatives.

That pattern repeated itself during the congressional debate — if you can call it that — over the Iraq War in 2003. Though Bush administration lawyers denied that they needed congressional authorization for the use of force, the administration eventually sought, and secured a resolution granting that authority. It did so despite the fact that Congress, in the main, did not want to be burdened with the vast responsibility the Constitution places on its shoulders.

Indeed, even in authorizing the president to use force, Congress attempted to shirk its responsibility to decide on war. The Iraq War resolution Congress passed in October 2002 is heavy with boilerplate about exhausting other options, but its key clause reads:

> The President is authorized to use the Armed Forces of the United States as he determines to be necessary and appropriate in order to (1) defend the national security of the United States against the continuing threat posed by Iraq; and (2) enforce all relevant United Nations Security Council resolutions regarding Iraq. [13]

Even so, prominent members of Congress insisted they hadn't really voted to use force. As then-Senate Majority Leader Tom Daschle (D.-S.D.) put it: "Regardless of how one may have voted on the resolution last night, I think there is an overwhelming consensus... that while [war] may be necessary, we're not there yet." [14] But the Constitution leaves it to Congress, not the president, to decide whether we are "there yet."

In the rush to get the Iraq War debate behind them, most members couldn't even be bothered to do due diligence on the alleged threat. For weeks prior to the October vote, copies of the 92-page National Intelligence Estimate on Iraq were kept in two guarded vaults on Capitol Hill — available to any member of the House or Senate who wanted to review them. In March 2004, the *Washington Post* revealed that only six senators and a handful of congressmen found it worth the effort to go and read the whole document. Senator Jay Rockefeller explained that, when you're a senator, "everyone in the world wants to come see you" in your office and getting away to the secure room — across the Capitol grounds at the Hart Senate Office building — is "not easy to do." He added that intelligence briefings tend to be "extremely dense reading." [15]

Congressional scholar Louis Fisher compares the Iraq vote to the Gulf of Tonkin resolution that authorized the Vietnam War. As with the Iraq War resolution, the Gulf of Tonkin resolution was worded broadly enough to allow the president to make the final decision about war all by himself. Lyndon Johnson compared the resolution to "grandma's nightshirt" because it "covered everything." [16] And, as with Iraq, the president waited for several months and an intervening election before using the authority granted him. In each case, it was easier for Congress to dodge the issue than to take responsibility.

In the 2004 and 2008 presidential campaigns, a number of prominent Democratic senators who'd voted for the Iraq war vehemently denied they'd done any such thing. Senator John Kerry, the Democrats' 2004 candidate for president, complained on the campaign trail that he hadn't meant to authorize *this* kind of war; "The president bum-rushed the thing" without building a legitimate coalition or getting the UN on board. [17] In 2007, Senator Hillary Clinton's campaign chairman explained that Senator Clinton hadn't voted for war, just "to give the president the authority to negotiate and to have a stick to go over there and negotiate with Saddam Hussein." [18] Senator Joseph Biden, a 2008 candidate for the presidency and our current vice president, offered similar post-hoc rationalizations for his war vote. "If I had known this administration would be so incompetent," he told interviewer Charlie Rose in 2004, "I never would have given them the authority to try to avoid the war," which was an interesting way to describe a resolution titled *"Authorization for Use of Military Force Against Iraq." [19]*

When it came to the fight against Al Qaeda, congressional behavior revealed a similar lack of Madisonian ambition. In areas ranging from detention of terrorist suspects to anti-terror surveillance, from the very beginning of the conflict, the president made clear that he, not Congress, would set the rules. And when Congress found itself compelled to legislate on those topics, it usually ratified unilateral actions already taken by the president.

In November 2001, President Bush issued a military order allowing him to detain any noncitizen he suspected of terrorist involvement, and, even if that citizen was a legal resident of the United States, he or she would be barred from American courts and tried before a military tribunal with rules determined at the executive's discretion and subject to unilateral alteration at any time. [20] Even in the vast civilizational conflict of World War II, Congress had enacted articles of war and set out procedures to ensure that the executive branch would not write the laws it was charged with executing. But post-September 11 Congresses showed little interest in asserting their constitutional authority to formulate the rules for Twenty-first Century warfare. [21]

By early 2004, President Bush's job approval numbers dipped below 50 percent for the first time, and after April 2005, he never again rose above that mark. [22] Yet time and again, during his presidency's long decline, Congress gave Bush new powers, or placed its seal of approval on powers he'd already seized. As one of its last major acts, in October 2006, the 109th Congress responded to the Supreme Court's June 2006 decision striking down the president's military tribunals order with legislation reinstating most of the powers he'd claimed. [23]

A month after the MCA's passage, the voters gave Congress back to the Democrats, but the new majority proved utterly unable to prevent the president from sending more troops to fight a war that most Americans by then considered a disaster. In August 2007, eager to leave town for summer recess, Congress passed the "Protect America Act," which effectively legalized the NSA surveillance program. [24] In the summer of 2008, after that law expired, Congress passed the FISA Amendments Act, which left very little of the original Foreign Intelligence Surveillance Act standing. Like the PAA, the FISA Amendments Act removed the requirement for individualized warrants, allowing FISA Court judges to approve the parameters of executive surveillance programs, without access to information about the targets to be observed, or the factual basis for observing them. [25]

In his seminal book *Presidential Power and the Modern Presidents,* Richard Neustadt argued that the presidency is an inherently weak office, and to grow its powers, the president needed to build up political capital and spend it wisely. [26] Oddly enough, though, despite the fact that Bush's political capital had utterly evaporated early in his second term, he continued to secure broad new grants of authority from Congress. Thanks largely to congressional abdication, in the first decade of the Twenty-first Century, the Imperial Presidency is alive, well, and menacing as ever.

CONGRESSIONAL ABDICATION IN DOMESTIC AFFAIRS

In 1966, political scientist Aaron Wildavsky posited that there were really "Two Presidencies": one with broad discretion over foreign affairs, and another with comparatively limited ability to work its will on the home front. "Since World War II," Wildavsky observed, "Presidents have had much greater success in controlling the nation's defense and foreign policies than in dominating its domestic policies." [27]

That remains the case, but two caveats are in order. First, Congress's eagerness to delegate lawmaking authority to executive branch agencies has given modern presidents considerable power to reshape the law via executive fiat. Second, over the last year, the ongoing financial crisis has driven Congress toward new frontiers in delegation. [28]

Delegation of lawmaking authority is nothing new, of course. Since the New Deal era, the legislative branch has only intermittently fulfilled the central duty the Constitution imposes on it: making the law. The first sentence of that document's first article makes clear that "all legislative Powers herein granted" are vested in Congress. The Supreme Court once took that language seriously, as when, in 1935, it struck down a key New Deal program for delegating legislative power to the executive. [29]

But the Court eventually made its peace with statutes that allow the executive branch to both make and enforce the law. Its post-1937 refusal to strike down broad delegations of legislative authority helped give us what Theodore Lowi has called the “Second Republic” of the United States, in which Congress routinely passes statutes with ambitious, noble — and underspecified — goals, leaving it to the relevant executive branch agencies to issue and enforce the regulations governing individual behavior. [30]

True, the president’s control over administrative agencies is nowhere near as extensive as partisans of unitary executive theory would like. The Supreme Court has never endorsed the proposition that the Constitution’s grant of “the executive power” to the president means that Congress cannot limit his control over the administrative state. Even so, as Elena Kagan, now President Obama’s Solicitor General, proclaimed in a 2001 *Harvard Law Review* article, “we live today in an era of presidential administration.” [31] The president’s ability to manipulate the executive branch bureaucracy has expanded greatly in recent years, “making the regulatory activity of the executive branch agencies more and more an extension of the President’s own policy and political agenda.” [32] Though the “unitarians” originally saw presidential control as a way to rein in aggressive regulatory agencies, Kagan argues that there’s little reason to think that “presidential supervision of administration inherently cuts in a deregulatory direction.” [33]

President Obama’s recent move to regulate greenhouse gas emissions via executive fiat is a case in point. Though legislation to impose a nationwide cap and trade program remains stalled in Congress, the Obama administration recently moved ahead with plans to limit emissions from power plants and large industrial facilities. [34] That decision flowed inexorably from *Massachusetts v. EPA,* in which the 2007 Supreme Court ruled that the 1970 Clean Air Act's definition of air pollutant was broad enough to allow regulation of CO2 emissions. [35]

The proposed rule doesn’t cut as deeply as it might, but the authority Congress delegated in the Clean Air Act could allow the Obama administration to go much further in imposing emission restrictions. According to a comprehensive legal analysis issued by NYU Law School’s Center for Policy Integrity, *“if Congress fails to act, President Obama has the power under the Clean Air Act to adopt a cap-and-trade system.” [36] Even staunch supporters of cap and trade ought* to be discomfited by the notion that, in a democratic country, the president could contemplate such a move without specific authority from Congress.

In a political climate where even green-leaning representatives periodically rail against rising gas prices, President Obama may be reluctant to stretch his authority as far as the law will allow. But the more immediate threat represented by the financial meltdown of 2008-2009 has led to a dramatic expansion of presidential power at home.

On the campaign trail in 2008, then-presidential candidate Hillary Clinton declared, "we need a president who is ready on day one to be commander in chief of our economy." [37] There’s no hint of such a role for the president in the Constitution’s second article, but Clinton’s description might well fit a president who can appoint a “czar” to set executive pay at major companies and summarily fire the CEO of GM.

In “The Two Presidencies,” Wildavsky noted that “great crises” could enhance the president’s domestic policy powers, periodically allowing him to shape policy on the home front as thoroughly he dominates affairs abroad. Earlier this year, the president's chief of staff, Rahm Emanuel, raised Republican ire with his statement that "You never want a serious crisis to go to waste.... [it] provides the opportunity for us to do things that you could not do before." [38]

That sentiment transcends party lines, however. George W. Bush's lame-duck period repeated the pattern that had prevailed throughout his two terms: the announcement of an unprecedented crisis, demands for new presidential powers to meet that crisis, and — after some perfunctory grumbling — Congress's capitulation to those demands.

Treasury Secretary Henry Paulson's original three-page proposal for a bank bailout demanded unchecked power over some $700 billion in taxpayer assets: "Decisions by the Secretary pursuant to the authority of this Act are non-reviewable and committed to agency discretion, and may not be reviewed by any court of law or any administrative agency." [39] Congress rejected that language, and, on October 3, 2008, passed a much longer bill: some 18,000 words, compared to 849 in Paulson's original draft. The Emergency Economic Stabilization Act of 2008 (EESA) allowed the executive branch to set up the Troubled Assets Relief Program (TARP) to purchase toxic mortgage-backed securities, and the act contained what looked like restraints on the executive branch's discretion. [40] Nonetheless, by the end of 2008, Paulson looked a lot like the modern equivalent of a Roman dictator for economic affairs, using a broad delegation of authority from Congress to decide which financial institutions would live and which would die.

In December 2008, American automakers General Motors and Chrysler tottered on the brink of bankruptcy, while Congress debated legislation to provide some $15 billion to keep two of the "Big Three" alive. On December 11, the auto bailout bill failed to pass a key procedural vote in the Senate. But a week later, President Bush announced that, despite the bill's failure, he had decided to lend the car companies $17.4 billion. White House spokesman Tony Fratto explained:

> Congress lost its opportunity to be a partner because they couldn't get their job done.... This is not the way we wanted to deal with this issue. We wanted to deal with it in partnership. What Congress said is ... "We can't get it done, so it's up to the White House to get it done." [41]

As the Bush administration saw it, then, by not giving the president the power to bail out the automakers, Congress "lost its opportunity to be a partner," and the president had every right to order the bailout anyway.

Some commentators saw that decision as yet another example of Bush administration lawlessness. [42] The president claimed that he had the power to act under EESA, the operative clause of which gave the treasury secretary the power to buy "troubled assets" from "financial institutions." From the start, the Bush administration interpreted that authority broadly, abandoning the original plan almost immediately, and using EESA to buy shares in banks — some of which, such as Wells Fargo, weren't "troubled." But invoking the legislation to bail out car companies seemed a bridge too far. How could a statute empowering the executive branch to buy mortgage-backed securities from banks be used to lend money to automakers, which surely couldn't qualify as "financial institutions"? Having repeatedly insisted that he could not be bound by validly enacted statutes in matters related to national security, it seemed that President Bush had decided he couldn't be bound by clear statutory language when it came to addressing the nation's economic woes.

The truth was even more disturbing. A closer look at the TARP statute reveals that Congress wrote legislative language so irresponsibly broad that the administration actually had a colorable argument that it could reshape the bailout as it saw fit. [43] Though Congress recoiled from Secretary Paulson's September demand for a "non-reviewable" TARP, at the end of the day, as my colleague John Samples pointed out in a recent study, they "delegated more power to Secretary Paulson than he sought originally":

> Paulson's original draft proposed giving the Secretary the power to purchase only "mortgage-related assets from any financial institution having its headquarters in the United States." EESA… gives the Secretary the power to buy both mortgage-related assets and "any other financial instrument that the Secretary, after consultation with the Chairman of the Board of Governors of the Federal Reserve System, determines the purchase of which is necessary to promote financial market stability." [44]

Thus, under the law, the treasury secretary has virtually unlimited discretion to decide what counts as a "troubled asset." The definition of "financial institution" is equally broad. It includes "*any institution*, including, *but not limited to*, any bank, savings association, credit union, security broker or dealer, or insurance company, established and regulated under the laws of the United States or any State, territory, or possession of the United States" (emphasis added). [45]

Various members of Congress angrily protested that the president had gone from buying toxic assets to recapitalizing banks to bailing out carmakers — shifting priorities almost daily, regardless of what the people's representatives believed they'd authorized. But after ceding such vast authority to the president, their outrage was more than a day late and $700 billion short. Congress, Samples concludes, "showed itself to be a bit player in a multi-hundred billion dollar drama that appeared to implicate the economic future of the nation." [46]. Once again, on a core issue of governance, Congress had abdicated its legislative responsibilities, leaving the hard choices to the president. The buck stops *there*.

THE FAILURE OF THE MADISONIAN VISION

In the Madisonian design, recall, the ambition of presidents was to be met and checked by the ambition of legislators. Clearly, when it comes to Congress, that incentive structure has failed. That failure is, in large part, a result of the divergence between the interests of individual legislators and the interests of Congress as a whole in maintaining its constitutional prerogatives. "Congress" is an abstraction. Congressmen are not, and their most basic interest is in getting reelected. [47]

Federalist 51 envisions a constitutional balance of power reinforced by the connection between "the interests of the man" and "the constitutional rights of the place." Yet, as NYU's Daryl Levinson notes, "beyond the vague suggestion of a psychological identification between official and institution, Madison failed to offer any mechanism by which this connection would take hold." [48] Congress retains a few institutionalists (Sen. Russell Feingold (D.-WI) comes to mind) [49], but, for most members, the psychological identification with party appears greatly to outweigh loyalty to the institution. Levinson notes that when one party holds both branches, presidential vetoes greatly decrease, and delegation skyrockets. Under unified government, "the shared policy goals of, or common sources of political reward for, officials in the legislative and executive branches create cross-cutting, cooperative political dynamics rather than conflictual ones." [50]

For all that, Congress formally retains the powers it has ceded, and could begin using them to reassert its authority at any time. As Professor Charles Black put it in 1974:

> My classes think I am trying to be funny when I say that, by simple majorities, Congress could, at the start of any fiscal biennium, reduce the president's staff to one secretary for answering social correspondence, and that, by two-thirds majorities, Congress could put the White House up at auction. But I am not trying to be funny; these things are literally true, and the illustrations are useful for making [clear] the limits — or the practical lack of limits — on the power of Congress over the president. [51]

If Congress has the power to sell the White House, surely it has the ability to, for example, wind down the Iraq War. No less an advocate of broad presidential power than John Yoo points out that Congress could legally "require scheduled troop withdrawals," and "shrink or eliminate units," deployed to Iraq. [52] On *Meet the Press* in January 2007, then-Senator Joe Biden offered the typical rejoinder to such suggestions: hey, don't look at us, we're just Congress. When host Tim Russert asked Biden, "Why not cut off funding for the war?," Biden replied, "I've been there, Tim. You can't do it." [53]

Actually, you can. In the early 1970s, Congress successfully used strings attached to spending bills to help wind down our involvement in Vietnam. [54] But it seems to take an enormous waste of blood and treasure before voters provide Congress with sufficient incentive to reclaim its powers over war and peace.

If members' constituents regularly chose to punish them for failing to defend Congress's institutional turf, then we'd expect to see that turf defended. But when the president pushes the envelope of his authority via unilateral action, members tend to object only when that action injures vocal constituents: "the fact that [an] executive order might well be seen as usurping Congress's lawmaking powers, or that it has the effect of expanding presidential power, will for most legislators be quite beside the point." [55] Nor do voters often (ever?) object to laws ceding vast authority to the president.

In fact, in both domestic affairs and foreign policy, delegation holds distinct advantages for individual members of Congress, allowing them to position themselves on both sides of any given issue. At home, they can take credit for reform when they pass a high-minded, broadly worded bill, and they can please their constituents by railing against executive branch agencies that use that broad language to impose unpopular costs. Delegation is a "political shell game," says New York Law School's David Schoenbrod: by passing a vague, expansive statement in favor of environmental protection, such as the Endangered Species Act, Congress curries favor with the majority of Americans who favor conservation. Then, when the Fish and Wildlife Service restricts logging throughout the Pacific Northwest to preserve habitat for the Spotted Owl, congressmen get to rail against the bureaucracy for abuse of the authority delegated to it. [56] Members derive similar benefits when, through delegation or inaction, they leave to the president the final decision to go to war — they get to take credit if the war goes well, and blame the president if things go badly.

Delegation's "shell game" works for Congress in large part because the public, conditioned by the media's relentless focus on presidential action, views the president as "our perennial main character, occupying center stage during almost all dramas in national political life." [57] The fact that the federal chief executive is front and center on the nightly news whenever there's a significant economic downturn, a hurricane, or a terrorist attack reinforces the view that he is the man in charge — responsible for, and capable of, dealing with the emergency of the week, whatever it may be. [58] All things considered, as Professor Levinson observes, the current environment of assertive presidents and "stubbornly passive Congresses bears only a very partial resemblance to the mutually rivalrous self-aggrandizing branches imagined by separation of powers law and theory." [59]

WHAT IS TO BE DONE?

In the post-Watergate era, Congress passed a number of laws designed to relimit presidential power. The failure of those reforms has in turn inspired new proposals to address the problem of congressional abdication at home and abroad. [60]

In 1999, disturbed by President Clinton's late-term flurry of executive orders, Representative Ron Paul (R-TX) introduced the Separation of Powers Restoration Act. That act would have required presidents to identify the specific constitutional or statutory provisions they're relying on to justify any given executive order and allowed congressmen who believed a particular directive was illegal to challenge it in court. [61]

Others have suggested means by which Congress might bind itself before the fact, restraining its tendency toward overbroad delegations of authority. Post-Watergate Congresses frequently used so-called "legislative vetoes" to retain checks on statutes granting power to administrative agencies. [62] Such provisions, inserted into statutes delegating power, allowed Congress to nullify regulations issued pursuant to the authority delegated; but in 1983 case of *INS v. Chadha,* the Supreme Court took that tool away. [63]

Shortly after the *Chadha* decision, then-judge, now-Justice Stephen Breyer suggested replacing the legislative veto with statutory language stating that "the agency's exercise of the authority to which the veto is attached is ineffective unless Congress enacts a confirmatory law within, say, sixty days." Agencies could recommend particular courses of action, but their recommendations would not have the effect of law until they passed through the normal constitutional channels. [64]

After the GOP takeover of Congress in 1994, some enterprising Republican freshmen introduced a measure based on Breyer's idea. The "Congressional Responsibility Act" went further than Breyer did, applying his confirmatory law requirement to *all* executive branch regulations. The act's sponsors hoped to ensure "that Federal regulations will not take effect unless passed by a majority of the members of the Senate and House of Representatives." [65]

The Separation of Powers Restoration Act and the Congressional Responsibility Act were laudable attempts to rein in executive-branch lawmaking, but each had serious flaws. By giving aggrieved congressmen the right to sue, the Separation of Powers Restoration Act aimed to dragoon the courts into the fight over executive orders. But the judiciary would almost certainly resist such a move. [66] Likewise, forcing Congress to vote on significant federal rules is a noble idea, but the Congressional Responsibility Act presupposes a Congress that's interested in taking responsibility for the law. That is not the Congress we have, or are likely to have, anytime soon. [67]

Similar problems have bedeviled congressional attempts to rein in executive warmaking. The 1973 War Powers Resolution has proved an abject failure: in the 35 years since the resolution's passage, presidents have put troops in harm's way over 100 times without letting the WPR cramp their style. [68] Attempts to enforce the WPR through litigation haven't worked either, as judges are unendingly creative in finding ways to avoid policing interbranch fights.

Various scholars and legislators have considered ways to give the toothless WPR real bite. In his landmark study of congressional abdication of war powers, *War and Responsibility,* Stanford's John Hart Ely proposed a "Combat Authorization Act" that would shorten the WPR's current 60-day "free pass" to 20 days and command the courts to hear suits by congressmen seeking to start the clock — automatically cutting off funding if a judge found that Congress did not authorize the intervention. [69] In 2007, Republican congressman Walter Jones introduced a bill similar to Ely's proposal. Jones's "Constitutional War Powers Resolution" would allow the president to use force unilaterally only in cases involving an attack on the United States or U.S. forces, or to protect and evacuate U.S. citizens. As with Ely's "Combat Authorization Act," the CWPR would give congressmen standing to "start the clock," and would cut off funding should Congress refuse to authorize military action. [70]

In 2005, foreign-policy luminaries Leslie H. Gelb and Anne-Marie Slaughter proposed an even simpler solution to the problem of presidential warmaking: "A new law that would restore the Framers' intent by requiring a congressional declaration of war in advance of any commitment of troops that promises sustained combat." Under the Gelb/Slaughter proposal, any prolonged military engagement would require a declaration, otherwise "funding for troops in the field would be cut off automatically." [71]

Each of these proposals has the merit of demanding that Congress carry the burden the Constitution places upon it: responsibility for the decision to go to war. And it's worth thinking about how best to tie Ulysses to the mast. But the problem with legislative schemes designed to force Congress to "do the right thing" is that Congress seems always to have one hand free. Even if any of these measures became law, Congress would remain free to avoid the pinch: ducking responsibility for new regulations and presidential wars. Statutory schemes designed to precommit legislators to particular procedures have a terrible track record. No mere statute can truly bind a future Congress. In areas ranging from agricultural policy to balanced budgets, Congress has rarely hesitated to undo previously enacted limitations when short-term political advantage beckons. [72]

In *War and Responsibility,* Professor Ely noted that the usual solution offered by those of us who rue congressional abdication is an ineffectual "halftime pep-talk imploring [Congress] to pull up its socks and reclaim its rightful authority." [73] Legislators have little incentive to reclaim that authority unless and until their constituents demand that they do so.

The proper target of that "pep-talk" is really the American people themselves — but there's little reason to expect better results there. Like congressmen, voters face their own collective action problem. The chances that any one person can effect the outcome of national political deliberations are so vanishingly small that voters lack the incentive to gather basic information about politics, much less inform themselves about the political pathologies that accompany overbroad delegation. [74] Anyone with the laudable aim of encouraging a "constitutional culture" among the general public faces daunting obstacles, and we shouldn't expect such efforts to solve our current dilemma anytime soon.

THE AUDACITY OF HOPE?

Where does that leave us? After our century-long drift away from the Framers' vision, are we doomed to spiral down through successive cycles of crisis and centralization?

Rather than closing on a note of despair, let me suggest that there are two long-term trends, at least, that could improve our chances of "right-sizing" the presidency.

The first trend is America's waning dominance abroad. One major factor that led to the growth of the Imperial Presidency was America's increasing global role in the Twentieth Century, and its unrivaled supremacy after the collapse of the USSR. As neoconservative commentator Charles Krauthammer wrote in 1987,

> Superpower responsibilities inevitably encourage the centralization and militarization of authority.... And politically, imperial responsibility demands imperial government, which naturally encourages an imperial presidency, the executive being (in principle) a more coherent and decisive instrument than its legislative rival. [75]

As the Twenty-first Century progresses, the United States is likely to distance itself from those responsibilities — and, perhaps, from the presidential powers they enabled.

Fareed Zakaria predicts that China and India's rise, along with waning US power, will, in this century, usher in "the Post-American World." [76] A recent report from the National Intelligence Council, the government agency that advises the US intelligence community supports Zakaria's thesis. That report notes that "Shrinking economic and military capabilities may force the US into a difficult set of tradeoffs between domestic versus foreign policy priorities." [77] Fifteen years from now, the United States will retain enormous military power, but economic and technological advances by other nations, coupled with "expanded adoption of irregular warfare tactics by both state and nonstate actors... increasingly will constrict US freedom of action." [78]

It's possible, then, that shrinking American power, and the emergence of new superpowers, will result in the United States behaving more like a normal country in the international sphere. That in turn could help enable a shift to a "normalized" presidency.

The second long-term trend that may reduce the presidency's power and importance in American life is growing distrust of government, or what I'd prefer to call "skepticism toward power." That trend is one of the most important political developments of the last half-century. In the late 1950s, when pollsters started tracking trust, nearly three quarters of Americans said they trusted the federal government to do what is right "most of the time or just about always" — and most of all they trusted the president. Those numbers collapsed after Vietnam and Watergate. [79]

One of the leading experts on this phenomenon is Vanderbilt political scientist Marc Hetherington. Professor Hetherington leans left, so he takes no joy in reporting what the data have convinced him: that the rise in distrust is going to make it very difficult for any future president to have another FDR- or LBJ-style 100 days. Indeed, supporters of national health care discovered over the last year that distrust's rise made it very difficult for them to achieve that goal. [80] But burgeoning skepticism toward power has also made it somewhat more difficult than it was 60 years ago for presidents to permanently evade legal and political checks when it comes to civil liberties in wartime. [81]

Hetherington notes that in the four presidential elections following the largest decline in political trust (1968, 1972, 1976, and 1992) the party that held the presidency lost it three times. [82] A skeptical public tends to vote for divided government, which in turn leads to greater policing of the executive branch. William G. Howell and Jon C. Pevehouse have found that when the public rewards the opposition party, the result is more vigorous policing of the incumbent administration's conduct, including many more congressional oversight hearings. [83]

In our public discourse — especially in Washington, D.C. — we tend to view distrust as a political pathology. But should we? Skepticism toward power lies at the heart of our constitutional culture, and if it makes it harder for presidents to do great works, it also makes it harder for them to abuse power.

References

[1] First Presidential Debate," *New York Times,* September 26, 2008.

[2] Jack Balkin, "Obama and the Imperial Presidency," *The Guardian*, November 12, 2008, www.guardian.co.uk/commentisfree/cifamerica/2008/nov/12/obama-white-house-barackobama.

[3] Schlesinger, Arthur. *Imperial Presidency*. Boston: Houghton Mifflin, 1973.

[4] *Federalist* No. 48, in George W. Carey and James McClellan, ed.s, *The Federalist,* (Indianapolis, IN: Liberty Fund, 2001), p. 257.

[5] Wills, Gary. *A Necessary Evil: A History of American Distrust of Government.* New York: Simon and Schuster, 2002.

[6] William Van Alstyne, "The Role of Congress in Determining Incidental Powers of the President and of the Federal Courts: A Comment on the Horizontal Effect of the 'Sweeping Clause,'" 36 *Ohio L.J.* 788, 794 (1975).

[7] Wills, Gary. *A Necessary Evil: A History of American Distrust of Government.* New York: Simon and Schuster, 2002.

[8] *Federalist* No. 69, p. 357.

[9] James Madison, "Helvidius No. IV," in *The Letters of Pacificus and Helvidius (1845) with The Letters of Americanus,* A Facsimile Reproduction, New York: Scholars' Facsimiles and Reprints, 1976, pp. pp. 89-90.

[10] *Federalist* No. 48, pp. 256-57.

[11] *Federalist* No. 51, p. 269.

[12] *Federalist* No. 51, p. 268.

[13] P.L. 107-243, Sec. 3(a).

[14] Elisabeth Bumiller and Carl Hulse, "Threats and Responses: The Overview; Bush Will Use Congress Vote to Press U.N.," *New York Times*, October 12, 2002.

[15] Dana Priest, "Congressional Oversight of Intelligence Criticized," *Washington Post,* March 27, 2004.

[16] Jack Beatty, "The One-Term Tradition," *Atlantic Monthly,* September 2003.

[17] Ceci Connoly, "Kerry Defends Votes on Military Action," *Washington Post,* January 26, 2004.
[18] Maggie Haberman, "Hillary Does Iraq Flip," *New York Post,* January 23, 2007.
[19] Healy, Gene. "A Profile in Cowardice," *National Review Online.* September 25, 2008. http://article.nationalreview.com/?q=MmJjNzk5YTRmNDA5OWQxZDBiZWI5ODdmMzI0ZTliOTk=#
[20] Section 7(b)(2) of the Military Order provides, "the individual shall not be privileged to seek any remedy or maintain any proceeding, directly or indirectly, or to have any such remedy or proceeding sought on the individual's behalf, in (i) any court of the United States, or any State thereof." That order has been superseded by the Military Commissions Act (P.L. 109-366) passed on October 17, 2006.
[21] By holding that the president had exceeded his constitutional and statutory authority in the November 2001 military order the Supreme Court's 2006 *Hamdan* decision forced Congress to act, at which point Congress, in the Military Commissions Act of 2006, codified most of what the president had ordered unilaterally five years before.
[22] Gallup presidential approval polls, available at http://www.pollingreport.com/BushJob1.htm;
[23] Among other things, the Military Commissions Act of 2006 declared that the Geneva Convention did not apply to non-citizen detainees, and that terrorist suspects could not challenge their detention in American courts. *Military Commissions Act of 2006,* Public Law 109-366, *U.S. Statutes at Large* 109(2006): sec. 948(b)(g) "No alien unlawful enemy combatant subject to trial by military commission under this chapter may invoke the Geneva Conventions as a source of rights.", sec. 7(a) "No court, justice, or judge shall have jurisdiction to hear or consider an application for a writ of habeas corpus filed by or on behalf of an alien detained by the United States who has been determined by the United States to have been properly detained as an enemy combatant or is awaiting such determination." However, in *Al-Marri v. Wright*, 487 F.3d 160, (4th Cir. 2007), a case involving a legal resident of the United States picked up on American soil and subjected to military detention, the Fourth Circuit Court of Appeals recently held that, "the MCA was not intended to, and does not, apply to aliens like al-Marri, who have legally entered, and are seized while legally residing in, the United States."
[24] The PAA removed the FISA court from individualized review of wiretaps of Americans' phone calls and emails when the government "reasonably believe[s]" that the targeted person on the other end is outside the United States. *Protect America Act of 2007*, Public Law 110-55, U.S. Statutes at Large 110 (2007).
[25] *FISA Amendments Act of 2008*, Public Law 110-261, U.S. Statutes at Large 110 (2008).
[26] Richard E. Neustadt, *Presidential Power and the Modern Presidents: The Politics of Leadership from Roosevelt to Reagan*, (New York: Free Press, 1990).
[27] Aaron Wildavsky, "The Two Presidencies," *Trans-Action,* December 1966.
[28] Perhaps a third caveat is necessary as well: the war on terror has blurred whatever line once separated foreign and domestic policies; many of the powers that President Bush accrued, and President Obama retains, apply on the home front as well. *See, e.g.,* Jack Balkin, "The Constitution in the National Surveillance State," 93 *Minnesota Law Review* 1 (November 2008).
[29] *A.L.A. Schechter Poultry Corp. v. United States*, 295 U.S. 495 (1935).

[30] Theodore J. Lowi, *The Personal President: Power Invested, Promise Unfulfilled* (Ithaca, NY: Cornell University Press, 1985), p. 52.
[31] Elena Kagan, "Presidential Administration," 114 *Harvard L.R.* 2246, 2246 (June 2001).
[32] Kagan, p. 2248.
[33] Kagan, p. 2249.
[34] Broder, John M. "E.P.A. Moves to Curtail Greenhouse Gass Emissions," *New York Times*, September 30, 2009, http://www.nytimes.com/2009/10/01/science/earth/01epa.html?_r=3andref=todayspaper
[35] *Massachusetts v. EPA, 549 U.S. 497 (2007)*
[36] Chettiar, Inimai M., and Jason A. Schwartz. *The Road Ahead: EPA's Options and Obligations For Regulating Greenhouse Gases.* Rep no. 3. New York: Institute for Policy Integrity, 2009 http://www.policyintegrity.org/publications/documents/TheRoadAhead.pdf
[37] Healy, Patrick. "Clinton Calls for Action on Housing," *New York Times*, March 24, 2008.http://www.nytimes.com/2008/03/24/us/politics/24cnd-campaign.html?pagewanted=print
[38] Rauch, Jonathan. "Is Obama Repeating Bush's Mistakes?" *National Journal Magazine,* March 28, 2009 http://www.nationaljournal.com/njmagazine/st_20090328_6609.php
[39] "Text of Draft Proposal for Bailout Plan," *New York Times*, September 20, 2008, www.nytimes.com/2008/09/21/business/21draftcnd.html?_r=1andref=business.
[40] *Emergency Economic Stabilization Act of 2008*, Public Law 110-343, *U.S. Statutes at Large* 110 (2008).
[41] David Cho and Zachary A. Goldfarb, "UAW Vows to Fight Wage Concessions," *Washington Post,* December 24, 2008.
[42] *See, e.g.,* Jacob Sullum, "Illegal Lending Practices," *Reason Online*, December 17, 2008, http://reason.com/news/show/130600.html.
[43] Under the law, a "troubled asset" is "any … financial instrument" the secretary of the treasury "determines the purchase of which is necessary to promote financial market stability," and "financial institution" is defined as "*any institution*, including, *but not limited to*, any bank, savings association, credit union, security broker or dealer, or insurance company, established and regulated under the laws of the United States or any State, territory, or possession of the United States" (emphasis added). *Emergency Economic Stabilization Act of 2008*, Public Law 110-343, *U.S. Statutes at Large* 110 (2008).
[44] "Lawless Policy: TARP as Congressional Failure," Cato Institute Policy Analysis no. 660, February 4, 2010.
[45] *Emergency Economic Stabilization Act of 2008*, Public Law 110-343, *U.S. Statutes at Large*, 110 (2008).
[46] Samples.
[47] *See* David R. Mayhew, *Congress: The Electoral Connection,* (New Haven: Yale University Press, 1974).
[48] Levinson, p. 952.
[49] Phillips, Kate. "Feingold Plans Hearing on Czars." *The Caucus: The Politics and Government Blog of The* Times. New York Times, September 29, 2009 http://thecaucus.blogs.nytimes.com/2009/09/29/feingold-plans-hearing-on-czars/
[50] Levinson, p. 953.

[51] Quoted in Van Alstyne, p. 824.

[52] Chu, Lynn, and John Yoo. "Why Are the Pacifics So Passive?" *New York Times,* February 12, 2007http://www.nytimes.com/2007/02/12/opinion/12yoochu.html

[53] *Meet the Press.* NBC. New York, NY, January 7, 2007 http://www.msnbc.msn.com/id/16456248/page/3/

[54] Grimmett, Richard F. "Congressional Use of Funding Cutoffs Since 1970 Involving U.S. Military Forces and Overseas Deployments," *Congressional Research Service,* January 10, 2001. http://www.fas.org/man/crs/RS20775.pdf

[55] Terry M. Moe and William G. Howell, "The Presidential Power of Unilateral Action," 15 *J.L. Econ and Org.,* 132, 144 (1999).

[56] David Schoenbrod and Jerry Taylor, "The Delegation of Legislative Powers," *Cato Handbook for the 108th Congress*, Cato Institute (2002). *See also* David Schoenbrod, *Power without Responsibility: How Congress Abuses the People through Delegation,* (New Haven, CT: Yale University Press, 1993).

[57] Bruce Miroff, "Monopolizing the Public Space: The President as a Problem for Democratic Politics," in Thomas E. Cronin, ed., *Rethinking the Presidency,* (Boston: Little, Brown and Company, 1982), p. 220.

[58] Michael A. Fitts suggests that the public's overestimation of the president's responsibility for the fate of the nation reflects the "availability heuristic" studied by social psychologists. The public has a "heuristic bias toward overestimating the causal significance of readily accessible factors" widely discussed in the media. Fitts, Michael. "The Paradox of Power in the Modern State: Why a Unitary, Centralized Presidency May Not Exhibit Effective or Legitimate Leadership." *University of Pennsylvania Law Review,* p. 886.

[59] Levinson, 957.

[60] *See* Andrew Rudalevige, *The New Imperial Presidency: Renewing Presidential Power after Watergate,* (Ann Arbor: University of Michigan Press, 2005) Chapters IV and V for a discussion of Watergate reforms and their unraveling.

[61] H.R. 2655, 106th Congress.

[62] *See* Andrew Rudalevige, *The New Imperial Presidency: Renewing Presidential Power after Watergate,* (Ann Arbor: University of Michigan Press, 2005) p. 115: "While they varied in form and stringency, legislative vetoes enabled all or part of Congress to review the executive branch's use of a given power statutorily delegated to it before the executive decision took final effect.... Often the action could be vetoed—sometimes merely by a committee, sometimes by one chamber, sometimes by both." Rudalevege cites a study showing that 423 such provisions were passed in the 1970s.

[63] *INS v. Chadha*, 462 U.S. 919 (1983). Specifically, the Court struck down a one-House veto provision in the Immigration and Nationality Act that allowed either House to veto the attorney general's decision, pursuant to authority Congress had delegated, to allow a legally deportable alien to remain in the United States. According to the Court, the veto provision at issue violated the Constitution's requirements of Bicameralism and Presentment embodied in the lawmaking procedure outlined in Article I, section 7.

[64] Stephen Breyer, "The Thomas F. Ryan Lecture: The Legislative Veto After *Chadha,*" *Georgetown Law Journal* 72 (February 1984) 785-99.

[65] H.R. 2727 (104th Congress)

[66] Federal courts rarely welcome the opportunity to sort out fights between the other two branches, and they've generally denied standing to congressmen alleging an injury to Congress's institutional interests. *See Raines v. Byrd,* 521 U.S. 811 (1997), *see also* Ryan McManus, "Note: Sitting in Congress and Standing in Court: How Presidential Signing Statements Opened the Door to Legislator Lawsuits," *Boston College Law Review* 48 (May 2007): 739-80.

[67] It's often argued that abandoning delegation would be impossible because Congress simply would not have the time to make the laws we live under. There's some force to that objection, though it ignores the fact that, as David Schoenbrod and Jerry Taylor write,

> delegation forces Congress to spend a large chunk of its time constructing the legislative architecture—sometimes over a thousand pages of it—detailing exactly how various agencies are to decide important matters of policy. Once that architecture is in place, members of Congress find that a large part of their job entails navigating through those bureaucratic mazes for special interests jockeying to influence the final nature of the law. Writing such instructions and performing agency oversight to ensure that they are carried out would be unnecessary if Congress made the rules in the first place.

David Schoenbrod and Jerry Taylor, "The Delegation of Legislative Powers," *Cato Handbook for Policy,* (Washington DC: Cato Institute, 2005) p. 157. But an end to delegation—whether piecemeal (as with the Breyer proposal) or wholesale (as per the Congressional Responsibility Act)—would force Congress to prioritize. That might mean a return to prescriptive laws, a new respect for federalism, and a renewed appreciation of the Framers' view that the chief danger to republican government lies in legislative overzealousness, not legislative inaction. A Congress that wanted to reclaim control of the law would have to do less, do it constitutionally, and be held accountable for the results. For most legislators, that's hardly an attractive proposition.

[68] The WPR's time limit is supposed to kick in when the president reports that he has sent American forces into hostilities or situations where hostilities are imminent. However, the statute is ambiguous enough to allow the president to "report" without starting the clock, and presidents have exploited that ambiguity. Of 111 reports submitted from 1975 to 2003, only one president deliberately triggered the time limit, and that was in a case where the fighting had ended before the report was made. That occurred in the 1975 Mayaguez affair. *See* Richard F. Grimmett, "The War Powers Resolution After Thirty Years," *CRS Report for Congress,* RL 32267, March 11, 2004.

[69] John Hart Ely, *War and Responsibility: Constitutional Lessons of Vietnam and Its Aftermath,*(Princeton University Press: 1993), p. 138.

[70] "Constitutional War Powers Amendments of 2007," H.J. Res. 53.

[71] Leslie H. Gelb and Anne Marie Slaughter, "Declare War: it's time to stop slipping into armed conflict," *Atlantic Monthly*, November 2005.

[72] David Orden and Robert Paarlberg, "The Withering of Farm Policy Reform," *Cato.org,* April 16, 2002, http://www.cato.org/pub_display.php?pub_id=3446; Louis Fisher, *Constitutional Conflicts Between Congress and the President,* 4th ed., (Lawrence: University Press of Kansas, 2007) pp. 207-11.

[73] John Hart Ely, *War and Responsibility,* (Princeton University Press, 1993), p. 52.

[74] *See* http://www.cato.org/pubs/pas/pa594.pdf; http://www.cato.org/pubs/pas/pa525.pdf
[75] Charles Krauthammer, "The Price of Power," *The New Republic,* February 9, 1987.
[76] Fareed Zakaria, *The Post-American World,* (New York: W.W. Norton and Co.) 2008.
[77] National Intelligence Council, *Global Trends 2025: A Transformed World,* (2008) p. iv.
[78] National Intelligence Council, p. xi
[79] Table 5A.1 "Trust the Federal Government 1958-2004," *ANES Guide to Public Opinion and Electoral Behavior*, http://www.electionstudies.org/nesguide/toptable/tab5a_1.htm
[80] Kohut, Andrew. "Would Americans Welsome Medicare if it Were Being Proposed in 2009?" *Pew Research* Center, August 19, 2009. http://pewresearch.org/pubs/1317/would-americans-welcome-medicare-if-proposed-in-2009
[81] Jack Goldsmith and Cass R. Sunstein, "Military Tribunals and Legal Culture: What a Difference Sixty Years Makes," *Constitutional Commentary* 19 (Spring 2002): 282, 289.
[82] Marc J. Hetherington, "The Effect of Political Trust on the Presidential Vote, 1968-96," *The American Political Science Review* 93 (June 1999): 312. Hetherington's article was written before the post-9/11 spike and decline; George W. Bush's reelection would make it three out of five.
[83] William G. Howell and Jon C. Pevehouse, "When Congress Stops Wars: Partisan Politics and Presidential Power," *Foreign Affairs* (September/October 2007).

Prepared for the Hofstra University Symposium "President or King?" November 5, 2009

In: President or King?
Editor: Meena Bose, pp. 99-121

ISBN: 978-1-61324-655-9

To Be (Unitarian) or Not to Be (Unitarian): Presidential Power in the George W. Bush Administration

Christopher S. Kelley

Abstract

President George W. Bush pushed the envelope on presidential power while defending many controversial actions in the name of the *unitary executive* theory of presidential power. This left many in the public, including those in Congress, with the mistaken belief that 1) the theory originated there and 2) that its behavior is actually condoned by the theory itself. This chapter seeks to dispel that opinion in the following ways: First, I will examine the theory's core values, where it originated, and how it evolved to negate the opinion that it is a 21st century phenomena; Second, I will compare the actions of the Bush administration, particularly in its use of the *presidential signing statement*, to determine whether there was congruence or conflict; and third, I will look at whether the theory had been so damaged that it did not make it out of the Bush administration by examining, briefly, the actions of the Obama administration, and in particular how it has used the signing statement. I make the following conclusions: First, the Bush administration's behavior violated the tenets of the unitary executive theory and his actions were admonished by many of its adherents, and second, so far the Obama administration has behaved consistent with the values of the theory, which was embraced by Presidents Reagan, Bush I, and Clinton, though there are some troubling signs in its use of the signing statement.

In the 2008 Presidential Election, an obscure theory of presidential power was front and center. The theory, the *unitary executive theory* of presidential power, had heretofore been relegated to law journals and conferences held by and for conservative legal scholars. Now, because of the administration of George W. Bush (hereafter, the Bush II administration), the theory had reached the level of popular consciousness—"*would the next president depend on it to justify controversial actions?*" The theory would be discussed not just in newspapers and magazines, but also on the blogosphere.

The Bush II administration had been both a blessing and curse to the theory's adherents — the blessing in the popular attention brought to it and the curse a general lack of context regarding it's origins. Many were led to believe that the theory began and ended with the presidency of George W. Bush. The fact of the matter is that the theory extends well before the Bush administration. The unitary executive theory was constructed in the Reagan administration, though some of its defenders claim that it has been a part of every administration since Washington. [1]

The purpose of this chapter is two-fold: First, to examine whether Bush's exercise of power conformed to the unitary executive theory. And second, to determine whether Bush's abuse of the theory has rendered it useless to the Obama, and succeeding, administrations.

To address these two points, I will discuss the following: First, I will provide a brief overview of the unitary executive theory and discuss its origins/evolution. Second, I will explain how and why the actions of the Bush administration were not consistent with the tenets, and even practices, of the unitary executive theory. To illustrate this, I will look at the way in which the Bush administration used the signing statement to deal with provisions of law it did not like. Then third, I will wrap up by looking at the behavior of the Obama administration, and in particular its use of the signing statement, to determine whether the unitary executive is long gone or alive and well.

I. The Unitary Executive: Theory, Origins, and Evolution

The unitary executive is a product of the post-Watergate 1970s, where the presidency underwent an assault upon its prerogatives and privileges from the public, the media, and especially the Congress. For instance, the president's law enforcement powers were challenged in the Church Committee hearings, his foreign policy prerogatives were limited by the passage of the Clark and Boland Amendments as well as the establishment of the Foreign Intelligence Surveillance Courts, and his control over executive branch officers and information was severely curtailed by the creation of an independent counsel and expansion of the Freedom of Information Act provisions as well as the creation of the Presidential Records Act.[2] It was during this period that President Ford remarked that the "imperial" presidency had become an "imperiled" presidency.[3]

During this period, presidents were forced to play defense in protecting the constitutional powers of the office so that future presidents would be in a better position to govern, and at the same time these presidents were expected to lead—but to do so without the traditional avenues opened to them. That is, presidents ran on ambitious agendas and found, once elected, a Congress that was not receptive to work with them (especially since this period saw persistent divided and polarized government). Thus if the president was expected to not only bequeath to a successor an office in better shape than he found it and if he hoped to be reelected, it meant figuring out how to navigate these hostile political waters. It is here that the unitary executive theory of presidential power was born.

As noted above, the unitary executive theory is the creation of conservative legal scholars, many of whom served in the Reagan Justice Department and were charged by their bosses for figuring how to restore the powers of the presidency. Despite its conservative origins, however, Democrats and Republicans have embraced the unitary executive because it offers a pathway to success—success in protecting the Office and success in advancing policy.

The unitary executive theory is primarily a defensive theory of presidential power, viewing the president's place and role in our constitutional system much the same way as the

Founders viewed it, where each institution is afforded the requisite power to keep the other institutions in their place while preserving and protecting the Constitution itself. This defensive power is known as *coordinate construction* or *departmentalism*, and James Madison in *Federalist #49* described it as: "The several departments being perfectly co-ordinate by the terms of their common commission, none of them, it is evident, can pretend to an exclusive or superior right of settling the boundaries between their respective powers."[4]

To most, the power over constitutional interpretation belongs exclusively to the judiciary since most of us have been taught that the power of *judicial review* gives the courts *final say* over constitutional meaning. But if we accept that interpretation, then we offend the design of the Founders, who created the system as co-equal branches and not one of *primus inter pares*.[5]

The unitary executive theory finds three important constitutional sources of power for the president—The *vesting* power, the *take care* power, and the *oath* power. The vesting power comes from the Vesting Clause of Article Two, Section One of the Constitution. For unitarians, it gives to the president all executive power, which includes all the powers found in Article II and those powers that "....go beyond those specifically enumerated in Article Two, Sections Two and Three, and includes at least some implied, residual executive powers."[6] Unitarians make a great deal out of the difference in wording between the Vesting Clause of Article One and Three, and the Vesting Clause of Article Two. In Articles One and Three, the Vesting Clause is either limited or divided, while in Article Two there are no qualifications. The Vesting Clause gives the president the power to remove, for example, anyone who exercises executive power.

The second tenet of the unitary executive theory comes from the Take Care clause of Article Two, Section Three. It directs the president, with advice and assistance of his inferior officers, to make sure that the laws are "faithfully executed." This gives the president authority over inferior officers to insure they are not pursuing an "independent policy goal" to the benefit of Congress or some special interest.[7] As Elena Kagan, a former domestic policy advisor in the Clinton administration, and now solicitor general in the Obama administration, argued: "When Congress delegates discretionary authority to an agency official, because that official is a subordinate of the President, it is so granting discretionary authority [unless otherwise specified) to the President."[8]

The power to direct inferior officers is the best way to insure democratic accountability because the president is the only nationally elected figure, and inferior officers (with the exception of the vice-president) are not elected and thus not directly accountable. If a bureaucrat takes actions that are controversial, then the public needs to know who to hold accountable. Thus unitarians invoke Harry Truman's famous statement that the "buck stops" at his office.

The third and final tenet of the unitary executive theory involves the power to refuse defense or enforcement of laws that the president believes violate the oath he took to protect and defend his office and the Constitution.

This power, which derives from the Oath Clause of Article Two, Section One, demands that the president defend against any unconstitutional action taken by the other branches of government. It is this tenet that serves as the justification for challenges made in the president's signing statement, which will be discussed below. While this is a power given to each branch of government, its legitimate exercise only happens when the challenge is transparent. The president must announce what he sees as a constitutional violation, which part of the Constitution is being violated, and what he intends to do about it (recommend changes for next time, refuse defense, or refuse enforcement). This gives the other branches of government the opportunity to challenge the action in whatever way they see fit. The transparency of the action is what preserves democracy and the Constitution since a challenge would almost always elicit the support of the other branches and the American public. Thus when a president refuses enforcement of a provision of the law and is secret in his challenge, there is not anything that separates his action from the actions of dictators or absolute monarchs.

Origins and Evolution

According to Calabresi and Yoo, the unitary executive theory dates to the Constitutional Convention in 1789, where the "framers set up a strongly unitary executive and that they meant to give, and did give, the president the power to remove any policymaking subordinate official in the executive branch and the power to direct the actions of executive branch subordinates exercising the executive power."[9]

Both admit to approaching their subject as "constitutional lawyers and not as legal historians," which is obvious given the selectivity in their evidence.[10] The two defend the existence of the unitary executive not by looking at how all three of its tenets have been in play, but instead defending its existence on just the strength of one—the removal power. To those who know better, this is akin to fitting round pegs into square holes.

It is the Reagan administration that is responsible for creating the unitary executive theory. There, inside the Office of Legal Counsel (OLC) inside the Department of Justice were a group of mostly young, bright, and conservative attorneys that were committed to restoring the powers and prestige of the presidency. Since Nixon resigned, the presidency had seen two different occupants in a span of six years. The presidencies of Ford and Carter were consumed by the domestic distrust of presidential power. In order to keep Reagan from suffering the same fate, these attorneys set upon a path that would allow the president to govern unilaterally in the event that compromise broke down.

Reagan successfully used executive orders to empower the Office of Management and Budget (OMB) with the task of bringing the executive branch into line with the preferences of the White House, and he developed the signing statement into a useful device to instruct bureaucrats on how to implement the law.

The presidential signing statement—a written or verbal statement the president makes after signing a bill into law—had been used sporadically by Presidents since James Monroe to praise or condemn the Congress for work done on a bill (a "rhetorical" signing statement) and from time to time to challenge defective provisions of law or to interpret provisions left vague during the legislative battles to get it to the president (a "constitutional" signing statement). Reagan's legal team, in 1985 and 1986, held a series of meetings where they elevated the signing statement from relative obscurity to becoming part of the president's cache of devices designed to control how laws were implemented. These meetings were designed to incorporate the signing statement into the unitary executive theory of power—in particular, into the second and third tenets of the theory.

In the second tenet, the signing statement was used to direct the way subordinates exercised executive power by replacing bureaucratic discretion with presidential interpretation, and in the third tenet by using the signing statement to challenge any law that violated the prerogatives of the presidency or that violated the Constitution.[11]

In the first Bush presidency (Bush 41), the president extended unitarian practices, including the use of the signing statement, that begun in the Reagan administration. In his first year, the Department of Justice issued a memo for the White House and all executive branch agencies, disclosing the dangers of congressional intrusions into the prerogatives of the presidency. The memo, which read like a top ten list, was titled "Common Legislative Encroachments on Executive Branch Constitutional Authority," and it outlined ten common types of legislative encroachments to be aware of .[12]

The memo was in line with the principles of the unitary executive. It warned against "hybrid commissions" which blended the executive and legislative functions, thus diluting the executive power. It warned against attempts by Congress to interfere with the deliberative and supervisory processes in the executive branch, thus interfering with the president's sole authority to direct and supervise inferior executive officers. And it warned against congressional interference to the power over appointments, the power to recommend legislation to Congress, which the memo described as a "plenary power," and against attempts to interfere with the foreign affair power. [13]

President Bush used the signing statement to defend the core powers of the presidency as well as to accomplish some political goals. In fact, President Bush's use of the signing statement to challenge the constitutionality of provisions of law very much mirror the pattern of challenges by his son, President George W. Bush.

President Bush spoke in 1991 at Princeton University, and he underscored just how committed he was to protecting the powers of the presidency. He told his audience that a president has "an obligation to 'preserve, protect, and defend' a constitutional government. The most common challenge to Presidential powers comes from a predictable source, "—the Congress. [14]

Both Reagan and Bush I were committed to the principles of the unitary executive, which is not surprising since it was advanced by conservative attorneys working in their administrations. Not only were they committed to unitarian principles in practice, but they also were vocal in defending certain actions according to the unitary executive. For example, President Reagan defended a challenge in a bill signing statement by citing his "authority as head of a unitary executive branch,"[15] and President George H.W. Bush defended six different actions—from signing statements to executive orders—by citing the unitary executive. [16]

When President Bush lost to Governor Clinton in the 1992 election, there was a great deal of talk about governing in a different way. And while there were some differences—what you would expect after a change in party control—President Clinton supported and advanced the core values of the unitary executive, though he would never defend his actions as such.

Clinton often does not get considered when discussion turns to expansive presidential unilateralism,[17] and he often gets overlooked in popular analysis regarding the unitary executive. The fact is that Clinton was every bit as unitarian as his predecessors, and like his successor, he advanced unitarian ideals even when his Party controlled the Congress.

At the outset, Clinton defended the use of the signing statement to defend the prerogatives of the presidency as well as to advance presidential preferences. The first year Clinton was in office he asked his head at the OLC to issue an opinion defending the signing statement. Walter Dellinger, the person in charge at the OLC, connected the signing statement to the president's right to challenge law he believes violates the Constitution. He wrote:

> ...a signing statement that challenges what the President determines to be an unconstitutional encroachment on his power, or that announces the President's unwillingness to enforce (or willingness to litigate) such a provision, can be a valid and reasonable exercise of Presidential authority (Dellinger 1993).[18]

A year later President Clinton asked Dellinger to provide him with a defense to challenge any law he determines is unconstitutional with a refusal to defend or enforce it. It was a significant action not just that Clinton was very publicly aligning himself with the beliefs of his Republican predecessors, but also because it signaled a belief—even though his Party controlled the Congress—that he would need to use it in the future.

The opinion is interesting for a couple of reasons. First, Dellinger argued that the president should attempt to comply with the law as often as possible. But he also has a responsibility to protect his office "unless he is convinced that the Court would disagree with his assessment."[19] But since clashes between the Congress and the president rarely end up in Court, the president "must shoulder the responsibility of protecting the constitutional role of the presidency… [based]… on his understanding of the Constitution."[20]

Second, and important to the unitary executive theory, if a president takes the extraordinary step to refuse enforcement, he must make public his intention: The President "may properly *announce* to Congress and to the public that he will not enforce a provision of an enactment he is signing." Only then can it be a "reasonable exercise of Presidential authority."[21] For example, in 1996, the Congress sent President Clinton an important defense authorizations bill[22] they knew he had to sign, but contained an amendment designed to box him in politically. Representative Bob Dornan (R. CA) added a provision to that bill that banned HIV-positive military personnel from continued service. In a signing statement to the bill, President Clinton told Congress that he would not abide by the provision and would not defend a lawsuit if one were brought against it.[23] This gave the Congress the ability to respond, which it did by passing follow-up legislation that repealed Dornan's provision.

II. President George W. Bush: Unitarian or Not?

Now that the historical lineage of the unitary executive has been fully reviewed (and a lineage pre-dating George W. Bush), I turn next to an examination of George W. Bush's administration to determine whether its actions were unitarian or motivated by something different all together.

President Bush was vigorous in his defense of the unitary executive. In fact he publicly referred to the "unitary executive theory" in signing statements, executive orders, and other proclamation a total of 148 times over the course of his eight years in office.

President Bush advanced unitarian principles from the moment he took office in 2001. He protected executive branch communications involving meetings regarding the vice-president's energy task force. He issued an executive order creating the Office of Faith-Based Initiatives. He unilaterally removed the US from the ABM Treaty with Russia. And he issued an unprecedented number of challenges to various provisions of bills for the purpose of protecting the powers of the presidency. And it is clear that he and his immediate subordinates were hyper-concerned with not just protecting presidential power, but also in restoring it to its pristine state pre-Watergate. They were so concerned about power that White House Counsel Alberto Gonzales, on his first day of work, informed his staff that the order from the President was to "…leave the presidency better off than [they] found it."[24]

It appears that most of the concern with presidential power came not from the Oval Office, but instead from the Office of the Vice President. Dick Cheney, it seems, had been scarred psychologically from the effects of Watergate on the presidency. He was Chief of Staff to President Ford, and saw first hand just how perilous it was for a president without power. Cheney's actions from the 1970s through his tenure as Vice-President — even during his time as a member of the House of Representatives — was to try to increase presidential power wherever possible. As Jane Mayer described it, this zest for power meant that Cheney, and his lieutenant David Addington, had a "tin ear" for the design of our political system, and in particular for its careful system of checks and balance. Checks and balances means an institution's power is limited by what the other institutions — and the American public — are willing to accept. Instead, Cheney and Addington "viewed power as the absence of restraint." [25]

Cheney and Addington understood the power of political precedent — that when an action by one institution goes unquestioned, it becomes a legitimate action for all future circumstances. For example, when the Supreme Court struck down the legislative veto[26] in 1983, they referred to a history of presidential objections to the device that dated back to the Wilson administration. Thus for both Cheney and Addington there was a tremendous effort to push the envelope on executive power while simultaneously hiding those very actions. There is no truer incident of this than the Bush administration's use of the presidential signing statement.

The bill signing statement, prior to the George W. Bush administration, had received limited coverage — most of which was relegated to law journals. Even though the device received more attention from the Reagan administration forward, its use was so minimal that it drew very little attention from anyone — in particular, from the Congress. The second Bush administration changed all of that — not in the number of signing statements issued, but in the number of laws that were challenged.

By the time he left office in 2009, President Bush had issued just 167 signing statements — far fewer than any of his three predecessors and almost half fewer than President Clinton (167 to 316) — something the administration was quick to point out to its critics. Yet the deception is the devil in the details. The real concern is not in the signing statements per se, but rather in the details contained in the signing statement. Of the 167 signing statements, President Bush issued 1,161 challenges — far more than all previous presidents combined. Even though the administration had surpassed the challenges of all previous presidents combined by the end of its first term, the public did not notice until President Bush's second term.

In 2005, the Bush administration had pushed a military spending bill that contained language that some considered would allow US military interrogators to torture those detained as part of the Global War on Terror. Pushing back was Senator John McCain (R. AZ), who sustained intense pressure from the administration inside the Congress and in the public arena to move him away from his position to remove the torture provision from the bill, which he did not budge. By December 2005, the administration raised a white flag and agreed to the McCain position to remove the torture provision. However, on New Years Eve, 2005, President Bush signed the bill and seemingly took back his compromise with Senator McCain over the use of torture.

President Bush challenged 26 different provisions in the bill, but the one that merited special attention was his challenge to Title X, the detainee treatment provision. There, President Bush claimed he would “construe” this section “in a manner consistent with the constitutional authority of the President to supervise the unitary executive branch…”[27] There was an immediate rebuke from all quarters of the country since it seemed as if President Bush was reneging on his deal with Senator McCain. In the end, Bush would be forced to make a public statement reasserting his agreement with McCain, but the damage was done. The public interest in this once obscure device would soar such that the moment that Bush issued a signing statement, there would be intense scrutiny over its meaning. By their overreach, the administration limited the effectiveness of his device.

There are a couple of questions regarding the administration’s aggressive use of the signing statement that I wish to explore next. First, why did they issue so many challenges? From 1981 to 2001, the single greatest challenge in any single year was 96 in 1992. President George W. Bush would often beat that number in just one signing statement. Second, what can we surmise about the administration’s commitment to the unitary executive by its use of the signing statement?

It seems clear now that the reason why the Bush administration had so many challenges in their signing statements was because of the influence from Vice-President Cheney’s Office. In previous administrations, there was a process that all bill signing statements followed: When an enrolled bill came to the White House, it was sent to the OMB and the OLC for scrutiny and comments. Most of the constitutional challenges came from the OLC, and other objections emerged from the various agencies that were asked to comment on the bill. Once the comments were made, the OMB gathered them and sent them to the Oval Office for the president’s consideration. The president was free to add to or remove any of the comments assembled for his consideration.

It seems that this process was convoluted in the Bush administration. After the OMB and OLC commented on the bill, but before it was sent for White House consideration, it went to the Office of the Vice President, where Cheney’s loyal assistant, David Addington, scrutinized the bill for any infringement upon the president’s prerogatives. Brad Berenson, a lawyer in the White House Counselor’s office said that Addington would “dive into a 200 page bill like it was a four-course meal.” [28]

A different attorney in the White House, according to Jane Mayer, claimed that Addington would “…single-handedly rewrite the entire [suggested signing statement] even though it had already been vetted by the interagency process. He’d slash a red line straight through it and start from scratch, making it read the way he wanted. Only then would he send it to the President.” [29]

This apparently is what happened in the case of Bush’s signing of the detainee treatment provision discussed above. It seems that Addington intercepted the signing statement language that was carefully negotiated with McCain’s staff and drew a red line through it. He then added the language above that seemingly negated the agreement with McCain because it violated the unitary executive, among other things. What is especially egregious is that

President Bush, reportedly, was unaware that this change had happened, and was thus "blindsided" by the public uproar that ensued. [30]

Thus it seems as if Addington and Cheney — and their zest to protect the presidency at all cost — may have been too cute by half. By their actions, they not only embarrassed President Bush, but they also cost the presidency of a useful presidential device as a result of the intense public scrutiny that ensued over the use of the signing statement. As Terry Moe and William Howell have argued, the president's ability to act is at its greatest up to the point that the collective will of Congress is created, thus presidents should always attempt to act just below the radar of the Congress. [31]

The way in which the Bush administration used the signing statement to challenge provisions believed unconstitutional is also illustrative of their commitment to unitarian principles.

As I discussed above, the Founders committed the institutions to defending both the prerogatives of their own branch and the Constitution of the United States by requiring each to commit to an oath to protect and defend. This means that each branch can decide for itself the meaning of the Constitution. But with this power comes a responsibility to be open or transparent about its actions so that the branches — including the people — have the ability to respond.

If you look at the constitutional challenges from Reagan through Clinton, you find that their signing statements contain a few challenges each, and those challenges that are issued explain what the constitutional infraction is and what the president intends to do about it. This is not the way that Bush II statements read. The Bush II signing statements often contained dozens upon dozens of challenges, leaving some bills with well over a hundred separate and distinct challenges. For instance, in signing the "Consolidated Appropriations Act, 2005,"[32] President Bush issued 116 objections to nearly every provision of the bill, and many of his objections contained multiple reasons for the challenge. For example, he wrote:

> Many provisions of the Consolidated Appropriations act are inconsistent with the constitutional authority of the President to conduct foreign affairs, command the Armed Forces, protect sensitive information, supervise the unitary executive branch, make appointments, and make recommendations to the Congress. Many other provisions unconstitutionally condition execution of the laws by the executive branch upon approval by congressional committees. [33]

As you can see, it is difficult to understand just how many provisions of the bill are problematic and which problems are creating what constitutional problems. There would be numerous challenges just like this, which became even more problematic in Bush's second term. For example, in Bush's signing statement to the "Science, State, Justice, Commerce, and Related Agencies Appropriations Act, 2006"[34], he made a challenge that is typical of the vague and non-specific challenges in many of the hundreds of challenges he issued. Bush wrote:

> The executive branch shall construe as advisory the provisions of the Act that purport to direct or burden the Executive's conduct of foreign relations, including the authority to recognize foreign states and negotiate international agreements on behalf of the United States, or limit the President's authority as Commander in Chief. [35]

Similar is this challenge in the "Departments of Labor, Health and Human Services, and Education, and Related Appropriations Act, 2006," [36] Bush wrote:

> The executive branch shall construe provisions in the Act that purport to mandate or regulate submission of information to the Congress in a manner consistent with the President's constitutional authority to withhold information that could impair foreign relations, national security, the deliberative processes of the Executive, or the performance of the Executive's constitutional duties. [37]

And by the last two years in office, the challenges went from obscure to incoherent. For instance, in signing the "Consolidated Appropriations Act of 2008," [38] Bush wrote:

> Finally, this legislation contains certain provisions similar to those found in prior appropriations bills passed by the Congress that might be construed to be inconsistent with my Constitutional responsibilities. To avoid such potential infirmities, the executive branch will interpret and construe such provisions in the same manner as I have previously stated in regard to similar provisions. [39]

It is hard to think of this as anything different than what it is—a direct provocation of the Congress by folks inside the Bush White House, and given how contemptuous both Cheney and Addington were towards the Congress, it is hard to think of this statement originating anywhere other than in their office.[40] This was not lost on the Congress. Representative Sheila Jackson Lee (D. TX) laid the problem out thusly:

> In general, President Bush's signing statements do not contain specific refusals to enforce provisions or analysis of specific legal objections, but instead are broad and conclusory assertions that the president will enforce a particular law or provision consistent with his constitutional authority, making their true intentions and scope unclear and rendering them difficult to challenge. [41]

None of this is consistent with the unitary executive theory, but instead is designed to overwhelm any oversight into the manner into how the laws are executed while also building up a body of precedent whereby challenges are made without objection from those outside the executive branch. In the end, it is designed to advance power for power's sake. And it was all done out of the Vice-President's Office. Charlie Savage explains:

> Cheney was determined to expand the power of the presidency. He wanted to reduce the authority of the courts and to expand the ability of the Commander in Chief and his top advisers to govern with maximum flexibility and minimum oversight. He hoped to enlarge the zone of secrecy around the executive branch to reduce the power of Congress to restrict presidential action, to undermine limits imposed by international treaties, to nominate judges who favored a stronger presidency, and to impose greater White House control over the permanent workings of government. And Cheney's vision of expanded executive powers was not limited to his and Bush's tenure in office. Rather, Cheney wanted to permanently alter the constitutional balance of American government, establish powers that future presidents would be able to wield as well. [42]

It is clear that the behavior of the Bush administration was antithetical to the tenets of the unitary executive no matter how often the theory was evoked. As I have argued, the unitary executive is primarily a defensive theory of presidential power designed for the purposes of protecting the president's powers and place in the constitutional system. The theory is designed to insure democratic accountability by making the President of the United States — nationally elected — responsible for the decisions taken by inferior executive officers, including the vice-president. It is also designed to maintain the sanctity of executive power by insuring that certain prerogatives of the president are not shared — foreign policy, for instance. And it is designed to insure democratic responsibility by allowing the institutions to fight over the meaning of the Constitution in the realm of public opinion.

In the Bush administration, secrecy was tantamount, and many actions were taken not by the president but by the vice president and his staff. There were several examples of actions taken by the vice president that were undertaken without President Bush's knowledge — the detainee treatment provision discussed above, for one, and a second example, not discussed here, but involving an attempt to pressure an acting-attorney general to sign off on treatment of enemy detainees that violated domestic and international law.

President Bush learned of this effort only after facing mass resignations by most of the Department of Justice as well as the Director of the FBI. [43] In addition, the challenges contained in the signing statements were rarely specific, which also violated unitarian beliefs. If a challenge is legitimate, then the president should not worry about losing the battle to the Congress, the most likely agent to offer a rebuke. The Bush administration challenges were deliberately designed to make a challenge difficult if not impossible. Because they were general in their declarations of the constitutional problem and because they often threw together several different parts of the Constitution that was violated, it became a hopeless task to try determine what was violated and why. What the Bush administration did was to cloak itself in the unitary executive theory while pushing naked unilateralism all in the name of politics and at the expense of the presidency. As Harold Krent correctly notes, "President Bush has confused a unitary ideal for a unilateral one" and this unilateralism "may end up as dangerous to the nation as unilateralism in foreign affairs."[44] In support of this is Steven Calabresi, one of the young conservative attorneys in the Reagan administration and a founding father of the unitary executive, who I discussed above. Calabresi stated that he "does not recognize the unitary executive theory as Bush is using it" and that the administration has taken "leaps in legal logic" in its attempts to justify unilateralism in the name of the unitary executive. [45]

"Invasion of the Body Snatchers": Obama and the Unitary Executive

There are many who believed that the election of Barack Obama spelled an end to the unitary executive because it was an election that turned on the public repudiation of the Bush presidency. The problem with this belief is equating the unitary executive and the Bush administration as one in the same. As I have shown above, President Bush was not a unitarian, and the theory was well in place before he came to power. The unitary executive ideals and practices were supported by three administrations prior to Bush II, and thus it became *institutionalized* inside and throughout the Executive Branch. And so far it seems that President Obama has been embracing his inner-*unitarian*.

It is of course difficult to conclude much about the Obama administration since it has been in office just a short time, but what he has done so far says a great deal about his views on the unitary executive theory.

President Obama campaigned on *change* — a break from the past, in particular a promise to be more transparent in the government's actions. For years, government watchdog groups like the Project on Government Secrecy with the Federation of American Scientists and OMBWatch had released report after report on how zealous the Bush administration was with protecting information and maintaining secrecy, even when it did not make much sense to do. For instance, there were reports that showed the Bush administration had been re-classifying information that had for years had been declassified, and doing so at a startling rate.[46] Candidate Obama suggested on the campaign trail that things would be different once he became president.

It is clear that Candidate Obama did not repudiate either the unitary executive or the use of the signing statement, though some on the Left believe that he stood firm on opposing both. In both cases, Candidate Obama distorted where he stood on the question of the unitary executive and the signing statement. For instance, on the question of the signing statement, Candidate Obama claimed a valid use for them, but opposed the way they had been used by President Bush. Thus by being careful not to be pinned down on the unitary question, it made it easier for him to embrace many of its core tenets after he became President Obama.

What is clear is we probably will never hear him utter the words, unitary executive, as a justification for actions. Like President Clinton, he will likely push forward its tenets without speaking its name. Because when it gets down to brass tacks, it is inviting failure not to rely upon the advantages that the unitary executive provides to the Chief Executive. Clinton realized this right away and so has Obama.

Since Obama has taken Office, he has: continued the practice of extraordinary rendition and has legally defended the State Secrets privilege; refused to release photographs of prisoner abuse related to enemy detainees as part of the Global War on Terror; claimed the right to use military tribunals in place of the federal courts; initially refused to release the White House visitor logs, and only released them when threatened with a lawsuit; asked for extensions on some of the expiring provisions of the PATRIOT Act, the bane of civil libertarian organizations in the United States; and he has put in place individuals at the Justice Department who themselves are proponents of the unitary executive. For instance, Elena Kagan, the solicitor general, penned a 2001 *Harvard Law Review* article defending the Clinton administration's embrace of unitarian values, though she called it *Presidential Administration*.[47] In fact, so comfortable has the Obama administration been with unilateralism that one critic has claimed it is like "invasion of the body snatchers" among political appointees in the executive branch. [48]

Obama moved quickly to embrace an important component of the unitary executive — exerting White House influence over the ways in which inferior executive officers carry out executive power. He did this by reaffirming an important executive order that had first been created in the Reagan administration, modified in the Clinton administration, and then re-modified by the Bush II administration.

On January 30, 2009, President Obama issued Executive Order 13497 [49] that revoked, most importantly, Executive Order 13422 [50], issued in January 2007 shortly after the

Democrats took control of the Congress, and re-established Executive Order 12866 [51], issued by President Clinton in September, 1993. The Clinton Executive Order absorbed two Reagan Orders—12291 [52] and 12498. [53]

The Reagan administration, in an effort to bring the Executive Branch agencies into line with the White House, issued Executive Order 12291 that empowered the Office of Information and Regulatory Affairs (OIRA) inside the OMB to oversee how regulations were formulated, and to impose a *cost-benefit* calculus on any regulation that cost the economy $100 million annually. This order was designed to bring democratic accountability into the executive branch by giving the President a say on how regulations were formulated and executed. Executive Order 12498 piggy-backed on 12291 requiring all the regulatory agencies to provide OMB in an advance with a list of regulations they would be working on for any giving year. This gave the White House the ability to slow down or stop regulations it did not like while speeding along those it did.

President Clinton, when he came into Office in 1993, made a great deal about ending the secretive process of the Reagan-Bush years where regulations were formulated behind closed doors, and where certain groups, like business organizations, were allowed access to regulatory development, while others, like the public, were kept out. But instead of throwing out the Reagan orders, the Clinton administration simply incorporated them under a new order — 12866. Executive Order 12866 modified the cost-benefit calculus in the previous orders to add certain qualitative indicators into the calculation, and it aided the Clinton administration, after they lost the Congress in 1994, in advancing their social agenda through the executive branch agencies. And most importantly, 12866 brought the *independent* regulatory agencies and commissions into the pre-planning process — something that was denied to the Reagan and Bush I administrations.

President George W. Bush kept the Clinton order in place, with some slight modifications in 2002 [54], until 2007, when he issued Executive Order 13422. He did this in response to losing control of the Congress, and thus sought to insure as much control over the regulatory process as possible in case, like Clinton, he would need to ride out his final days by passing his policies administratively rather than legislatively. This order was controversial in that it re-imposed the rigid cost-benefit calculation on all regulations, but also placed White House minders inside the agencies themselves. These minders, referred to as "Regulatory Policy Officers," or RPOs, were picked by the White House and would be needed to approve any new rules formulated by the agency.

Thus when President Obama issued his order revoking the Bush order and restoring the Clinton order, it was seen as a positive move forward. Furthermore, the Obama administration opened the process to allow for public comment [55] on a new order establishing their regulatory approach, but the framework thus far retains many of the features of the Reagan-Clinton orders allowing for White House influence, and remains fully in line with the unitary executive theory.

In addition to the Obama administration's regulatory approach, a second example of President Obama's embrace of the unitary executive is his use of the presidential signing statement to challenge provisions of law he believes violates the Constitution. Since he has taken Office, President Barack Obama has issued 19 signing statements (through January 1, 2010), with seven I refer to as constitutional signing statements — signing statements that contain constitutional challenges or interpretations.[56] And within those seven constitutional signing statements are dozens upon dozens of challenges, some of which have provoked outrage both in the Congress and the country at large.

With less than two months in office, President Obama announced where he stood on the constitutionality of the signing statement. On March 9, 2009, President Obama issued a memorandum [57] outlining how his administration would use the constitutional signing statement all the while making clear that he would not abuse the privilege as his predecessor, George W. Bush, had done ("In recent years, there has been considerable public discussion and criticism of the use of signing statements to raise constitutional objections to statutory provisions. There is no doubt that the practice of issuing such statements can be abused"). [58]

What is important to underline about this memo is Obama's acceptance of the principle of coordinate construction — an important tenet of the unitary executive. He outlines four principles by which he promises to adhere, and yet all four lead to the prerogative of coordinate construction. The first principle promises to work with Congress during the legislative process to head off any constitutional problems in the legislation. The second principle promises to use his challenges sparingly, and only on "interpretations of the Constitution that are well-founded" (a clear jab at the Bush administration).[59] The third principle is a promise that if he does challenge a provision in the law, it will be clear precisely what he is challenging and why, while the fourth principle promises that the challenge will be based on constitutional problems, and not political problems.

In addition to his defense of the constitutional signing statement, Obama's solicitor general gave a speech to a meeting of lawyers and judges of the Ninth Circuit Court of Appeals where she defended the constitutional signing statement. What is interesting about the speech — which got little notice — is that she contradicted herself. Solicitor Kagan was asked whether she would refuse defense of the law, as had been done in the past, if she or the president believed the law was unconstitutional? Her answer seemed to send a conciliatory note to the Congress that Obama was different from his predecessor. She said: "I owe clear obligations to Congress…one of the most important parts of the solicitor general's job is to defend" the law.[60] What was not included in the article is her answer to a question regarding the constitutional signing statement. At the web log *dag blog*, one blogger in attendance reported that Kagan was asked whether she believed that the president has the right to refuse enforcement of the law, and she answered: "when in conflict between the legislative goal of affirming the validity of legislation, and protection of the authority of the Executive, the Executive prevails in her office."[61] The importance in the comment is to note how the executive branch agents have internalized some of the values of the unitary executive. Within the Justice Department is the belief that the president may refuse enforcement or defense of the law if the law violates the Constitution.

Back to Obama's memo, it was clear the moment that this document was released that a constitutional signing statement would shortly follow, which is precisely what happened. Just two days later, Obama issued his first constitutional signing statement to an omnibus spending bill [62] where he challenged 12 different provisions of the bill, ranging from protection of his foreign policy prerogatives and his right to control information and supervise executive branch employees, to defense against the legislative veto.[63] Since he issued that first constitutional signing statement in March 2009, President Obama would proceed to issue four more constitutional signing statements, challenging a total (including the first) of *at least* 30 provisions of law by the time 2009 came to a close.

There are a couple of questions that remain: What can Barack Obama's use of the constitutional signing statement tell us about 1) his opinion of the unitary executive; 2) his commitment to use it different from the Bush administration; and 3) the utility of the device going forward?

First, President Obama has used the constitutional signing statement to defend the prerogatives of his office, just as the unitary executive theory demands — challenges to the constitutionality of the law should be for defensive purposes. So far the challenges have come in the following areas: *Foreign Policy/Commander in Chief, Separation of Powers* (defense against hybrid commissions that mix executive and legislative functions, protection of his power to recommend legislation, protection of his power to appoint, and defense against the legislative veto), and the *prerogative to supervise inferior officers.* In fact, to give his challenges added legitimacy, in his signing statement to the "Ronald Reagan Centennial Commission Act,"[64] President Obama evoked a similar challenge to a hybrid commission made by President Reagan in the early 1980s. Obama wrote: "In accord with President Reagan's Signing Statement made upon signing similar commemorative legislation in 1983, I understand, and my Administration has so advised the Congress, that the members of Congress 'will be able to participate only in ceremonial or advisory functions…'"[65]

Charlie Savage argues, in part, that Obama has not embraced the unitary executive theory because he has not evoked its name as justification for his actions like President Bush II had: "…unlike Mr. Bush, Mr. Obama has not mentioned the Unitary Executive Theory, an expansive view of power that conflicts with Supreme Court precedent…"[66] This argument is misleading for two reasons. First, as I have argued above, President Bush II was not a unitarian. Instead, his administration justified its quest for power by hiding behind the unitary executive theory. And second, just because the administration does not proclaim that it is acting in accord with the theory does not mean that it is not there. Recall that the Clinton administration did not once speak the theory's name, yet many of its actions were consistent with the theory's core tenets. As Shakespeare said, "A rose by any other name is still a rose." It is still early, but so far Obama's actions, like Clinton's, are perfectly congruous with the theory.

Second, even though President Obama has not abused the constitutional signing statement in the manner of the Bush II administration, there are some worrisome trends that merit attention. First, he has used the constitutional signing statement earlier than any previous president. As I noted above, he has issued five constitutional signing statements with dozens of challenges, with two constitutional statements coming after just two months in office. By comparison, President Reagan did not issue his first constitutional signing statement until October 1981. President Bush I did issue one constitutional signing statement in April 1989, but then not another one until November 1989. President Clinton issued his first constitutional signing statement in October 1993 at about the same time his head at OLC issued the legal opinion defending the use of the constitutional signing statement. And finally President Bush II issued his first constitutional signing statement in May 2001, but not a second one until November 2001. There is a caveat to this: we currently live in extraordinary times, and Congress sent the White House some massive bills to deal with the economic crisis right after he was inaugurated, so in that vein Obama's first year is different from his predecessors.

A second worrisome trend has been an attempt by the Obama administration to hide the constitutional signing statements from public view. Up to this point, every bill signing statement since 1965 has been published in the *Weekly Compilation of Presidential Documents*. So far the *Weekly Compilation* has not caught up to the date of the first constitutional signing statements, and its companion, the *Public Papers of the President* only extend through the previous Bush administration. Interestingly, the *Daily Compilation of Presidential Documents* does have an up to date accounting of Obama's signing statements, which is a break from the way they were recorded in the past. And there is the White House website. Up to Obama, the signing statement could be found under the "News" section of the website.

The Obama administration decided to redesign the website when it came to office, which is not unusual, and in the redesign it got rid of the "News" section. Now, in one prominent location half way down on the frontpage of the White House website is a section titled "Featured Legislation" that originally was titled "Signed Legislation." There you will find a complete listing of all the bills President Obama has signed into law as well as a link to his public signing statements. The public signing statements are rhetorical in purpose, where the president assembles a group of prominent individuals who flank him sitting at a desk and signing the bill into law. Now try as you might, you will not find the constitutional signing statements here. Instead, you have to navigate to the bottom of the frontpage of the White House website, and there, in tiny letters, is a section titled "The Briefing Room."[67] Under that section heading is a link for "Statements and Releases."[68] If you click this link, you will find a list of all the statements released by the Obama administration. If you want to find the constitutional signing statements, you would think that looking for the name of the signed bill would be sufficient, but it is not. The Obama administration does not put the name of the bill on those that have a constitutional signing statement attached to it. Instead, all they put is the bill's number.

For instance, if you looked at President Obama's action to the "Fraud Enforcement and Recovery Act,"[69] you could click the link under the "Signed Legislation" section, and there you find President Obama's public signing statement to guests assembled in the East Room of the White House.[70] Nowhere in that statement do you find a constitutional challenge. Instead you would have to go to the link under the "Speeches and Remarks" section, and navigate to a non-descript link titled: "Statement by the President on S. 386."[71] Only if you knew that the "Fraud Enforcement and Recovery Act" was S. 386 would you click. There you find a two-paragraph statement, where one paragraph contains a challenge to Section 5(d) of the bill, which requires executive branch agents to furnish information to a congressional commission, which violates the president's prerogative to supervise those who work in the executive branch. Even the Bush II administration did not engage in this type of subterfuge. Every signing statement — constitutional or rhetorical — could easily be found in just one section of the White House website. The Obama administration has created a "bait and switch" system that is designed to keep prying eyes distracted. This is doubly frustrating because Candidate Obama promised openness and transparency, and this website design is anything but.

The third and final troubling way that Obama has used the constitutional signing statement is that he has not been true to his promise per his March 2009 memo.

For example, one part of his memo was a promise to keep the Congress informed whenever the administration believed that a provision of a bill was unconstitutional. Normally this communication occurs formally in a "Statement of Administration Policy," or SAP, but there is also a great deal of informal communication that occurs between the president and the

Congress. So if Congress was informed of a constitutional problem, why the outrage over two different constitutional signing statements?

For instance, in his first constitutional signing statement discussed above, he challenged two sections of the law that directed communications between the executive branch and the Congress. In response, Senator Charles Grassley (R.IA) wrote to President Obama, and complained that one of the two provisions was designed to protect whistleblowers, and his challenge seemed to undermine this. Grassley wrote:

> I am deeply concerned that the signing statement you issued will undermine this important whistleblower protection included in the Omnibus Appropriations Bill. Not only is your signing statement contrary to your campaign statements [72], it also goes beyond the traditional broad signing statements authored by previous Presidents. In specifically singling out this provision, you have gutted the legislative intent of this provision [by the challenge]. This is a *shocking statement* (emphasis added) that acknowledges that you will be willing to give an order preventing employee whistleblowers from making disclosures to Congress. I do not see how this statement can be reconciled with your campaign promise to protect whistleblowers. In fact, it is even more egregious than simply breaking a promise, because it actually *restricts* current and previously existing whistleblower protections.[73]

The Obama administration responded that their challenge was to a provision that, if taken literally, "…would prevent the Executive Branch from taking steps to prevent or address employee communications with Congress even where such communications are unlawful or…legitimately classified. The president's signing statement does not purport to control or limit legitimate whistle-blowing activities. Nor is it intended to break new ground on this issue."[74]

The Obama administration is on strong ground — going back to the Reagan administration, any attempt by the Congress to add a provision that tries to force executive branch officials to report to Members of Congress without first getting approval of the president has been subject to challenge. But that is not the point. There was no SAP for this provision in the bill, and it is clear, given the nature of the back and forth between Grassley and the Obama administration, that there was no discussion informally that might have avoided the challenge.

A second, and more contentious example of where Obama clearly did not communicate with the Congress is his signing of the "Supplemental Appropriations Act, 2009." In the statement, President Obama uses the last paragraph of the bill to make his challenge. He writes:

> …provisions of this bill within sections 1110 to 1112 of title XI, and sections 1403 and 1404 of title XIV, would interfere with my constitutional authority to conduct foreign relations by directing the Executive to take certain positions in negotiations or discussions with international organizations and foreign governments, or by requiring consultation with the Congress prior to such negotiations or discussions. I will not treat these provisions as limiting my ability to engage in foreign diplomacy or negotiations. [75]

The response from the Congress — which included a sizeable number of Democrats — was immediate. Despite the fact that it is almost automatic that any congressional meddling in the area of foreign policy is a certainty to draw a challenge, what remains important here is, if

President Obama had communicated his concerns to the Congress beforehand, the Congress should not have been surprised to hear of the challenge. Yet in this case, it was—not just surprised, but also outraged.

It appears that President Obama's challenges had to do with funding to international institutions like the International Monetary Fund (IMF) and the World Bank, and the Obama administration had to twist a lot of arms to get the funding it asked for. The trade-off to the funding was to allow the Congress to set conditions on how the money would be spent and reports it would receive from the executive branch. It was those conditions that were challenged, leaving the Congress to believe that, after they made a good faith compromise, President Obama got what he needed and then used the signing statement to renege on the deal.

Congressman Barney Frank (D.MA) sent President Obama a terse letter blasting the signing statement challenges and demanding that Obama publicly repudiate the challenges. If not, Frank argued, it would "make it virtually impossible to provide further allocations for these institutions."[76] The Republicans took it further. Representative Kay Granger (R. TX) added an amendment to a 2010 appropriations bill for the Department of State and Foreign Operations [77] that would withhold funds to carry out Obama's challenges. The amendment was no partisan thing — it passed the House 429-2. [78]

It is hard to make conclusions or generalizations about the role that the constitutional signing statement will play in the success or failure of the Obama administration — only time will enable us to decide that. But there are tentative conclusions that we can make with the limited evidence so far. First, Obama, like his predecessors dating to the Reagan administration, has recognized that governing will take more than just working with the Congress. If he hopes to win a second term, he will need to act unilaterally. Second, so far Obama's use of the constitutional signing statement has been in the vein of Presidents Reagan-Clinton in that they do not make sweeping claims about executive power, but instead make pointed challenges (though he could be more specific) based on the Constitution. And third, since Obama is living in the shadow of the Bush administration, it means that the effectiveness of the signing statement is muted by a heightened public (and particularly congressional) awareness to it. It is apparent the administration is keenly aware of this given how much of an effort it has made to hide the constitutional signing statement in plain sight. If it becomes too much of a problem, the administration should be prepared to abandon it in favor of a different device that accomplishes the same objectives.

CONCLUSION

From what I have seen in the months that Obama has been in office leads me to believe that the unitary executive remains alive and well, and the Obama administration will do itself — and its successor — well to continue to nurture it and advance its presence throughout the executive branch.

As I have shown, the unitary executive was somewhat damaged in name because of its abuse at the hands of the Bush II administration, which tried to justify its power grab in the name of theory. It is my belief that naming the theory was done, in part, in order to buy the support of conservative legal scholars, who have long written about it in theory and were eager to see it in practice — officially and above the board. This strategy seemed to work at the beginning, but by the last two or three years of the Bush II administration, even these supporters had opposed what the administration was doing in the theory's name.

The unitary executive theory is primarily about defense — protecting the core prerogatives of the presidency and protecting the Constitution while advancing the president's preferences in a political environment that is poisonous. It gives the president space to work unilaterally, but at the end of the day, the president cannot supersede the Constitution. It seems clear that many of the Bush administration's actions were designed to enhance the power of the presidency to the detriment of the other institutions — which is clearly not unitarian.

So far the Obama administration has seemed to embrace the theory in practice, though not in name. The Obama administration has moved to protect the president's prerogatives both domestically and internationally. It quickly spelled out the president's right to refuse enforcement or defense of the law by embracing the presidential signing statement despite the controversial nature of the device. And so far it has used the signing statement much the same way as Presidents Reagan-Clinton. President Obama has also quickly moved to exert influence over the executive branch by reinstituting a Clinton executive order empowering the OMB to monitor and influence the issuance of regulations. While it is still too early to categorically suggest that President Obama is a unitarian, what we have seen so far provides some promising actions for those who defend the unitary executive theory.

REFERENCES

[1] See Calabresi, Steven and Christopher Yoo. 2008. The Unitary Executive: Presidential Power from Washington to Bush. New Haven: Yale University Press.

[2] Gellman, Barton. 2008. Angler: The Cheney Vice Presidency. NY: Penguin Press.

[3] Stone, Marvin. 1979. "Presidency: Imperial or Imperiled." U.S. News and World Report. January 15. p. 88.

[4] Hamilton, Alexander, John Jay, and James Madison. 2009. "Federalist Paper #49." The Federalist Papers. http://www.foundingfathers.info/federalistpapers/fed49.htm. Accessed September.

[5] For an interesting discussion, see Adler, David and Louis Fisher. 2007. "Rally Round the Constitution." *Legal Times*. 30:31. July 30.

[6] Calabresi and Yoo. p.4.

[7] Herz, Michael. 1993. "Imposing Unified Executive Branch Statutory Interpretation." *Cardozo Law Review*. 15, 1-2. October. pp. 252-53.

[8] Kagan, Elena. 2001. "Presidential Administration." *Harvard Law Review*. 114:8. June. p. 2327.

[9] Calabresi and Yoo. pp. 14-15.

[10] Ibid. p.18.

[11] See Kelley, Christopher S. 2007. "A Matter of Mere Directions: The Reagan Administration, the Signing Statement, and the 1986 Westlaw Decision." *William and Mary Bill of Rights Journal*. 16:1. October.

[12] Barr, William P. 1989. "Common Legislative Encroachments on Executive Branch Constitutional Authority." Opinion of the Office of Legal Counsel. 13 Op. O.L.C. 299. July 27.
[13] Ibid. 256.
[14] Bush, George H.W. 1991. "Remarks of President George Bush at Building Dedication at Princeton University." *Federal News Service*. May 10.
[15] Reagan, Ronald. 1987. "Statement on Signing the Bill to Increase the Federal Debt Ceiling." Public Papers of the President. Book II. September 29. p. 1096.
[16] See Bravin, Jess. 2006. "Judge Alito's View of the Presidency: Expansive Powers." *Wall Street Journal.* January 5. p. A1.
[17] In Andrew Rudalevige's 2005 book, when discussing "new imperial" presidents, he looks at Reagan, Bush I, and skips right over Clinton to Bush II. See Rudalevige, Andrew. 2005. The New Imperial Presidency: Renewing Presidential Power after Watergate. Ann Arbor: University of Michigan Press.
[18] Dellinger, Walter. 1993. "The Legal Significance of Presidential Signing Statements." U.S. Op. Off. Legal Counsel. http://www.usdoj.gov/olc/signing.htm. November 3.
[19] Dellinger, Walter. 1994. "Presidential Authority to Decline to Execute Unconstitutional Statutes." http://www.usdoj.gov/olc/nonexcut.htm. November 2, 1994. Accessed September 3, 2009.
[20] Ibid.
[21] Ibid.
[22] "National Defense Authorization Act for Fiscal Year 1996." P.L. 104-106. February 10, 1996
[23] Clinton, William J. 1996. "Statement on Signing the National Defense Authorization Act for Fiscal Year 1996." Weekly Compilation of Presidential Documents. 32:7. February 10.
[24] Quoted in Angler. p. 99.
[25] Mayer, Jane. 2008. The Dark Side. NY: Doubleday. p.61.
[26] I.N.S. v Chadha. 462 U.S. 919. 1983.
[27] Bush, George W. 2005a. "Statement on Signing the Department of Defense, Emergency Supplemental Appropriations to Address Hurricanes in the Gulf of Mexico, and Pandemic Influenza Act, 2006." Weekly Compilation of Presidential Documents. December 30. pp. 1918-1919.
[28] Mayer. p. 63.
[29] Ibid. p. 63.
[30] Gellman. p. 354.
[31] Moe, Terry M. and William G. Howell. 1999. "Unilateral Action and Presidential Power: A Theory." *Presidential Studies Quarterly*. 29:4. December.
[32] Public Law No. 108-447.
[33] Bush, George W. 2004. "Statement on Signing the Consolidated Appropriations Act, 2005." *Weekly Compilation of Presidential Documents*. December 10. p. 2924
[34] P.L. 109-108. 2005.
[35] Bush, George W. 2005b. "Statement on Signing the Science, State, Justice, Commerce, and Related Agencies Appropriations Act, 2006." *Weekly Compilation of Presidential Documents.* November 25. p. 1764.
[36] P.L.109-149. 2005.

[37] Bush, George W. 2005c. "Statement on Signing the Departments of Labor, Health and Human Services, and Education, and Related Agencies Appropriations Act, 2006." *Weekly Compilation of Presidential Documents*. December 30. pp. 1920-21.

[38] P.L. 110-161. 2007.

[39] Bush, George W. 2007a. "Statement on Signing the Consolidated Appropriations Act, 2008." Weekly Compilation of Presidential Documents. December 26. p. 1638.

[40] For a description of just how contemptuous Addington is, see Milbank, Dana. 2008. "When Anonymity Fails, Be Nasty, Brutish, and Short." Washington Post. Friday, June 27. http://www.washingtonpost.com/wp-dyn/content/article/2008/06/26/AR2008062603456.html?sid=ST2008062603517ands_pos= Accessed September 30, 2009.

[41] Lee, Sheila Jackson. 2007. "Presidential Signing Statements Under the Bush Administration: A Threat to Checks and Balances and the Rule of Law?" Prepared Remarks, House Judiciary Committee. 110th Congress, 1st Session. Serial No. 110-6. January 31. p. 106.

[42] Savage, Charlie. 2007a. Takeover: The Return of the Imperial Presidency and the Subversion of American Democracy. NY: Little, Brown. pp. 8-9.

[43] See Goldsmith, Jack. 2007. The Terror Presidency: Law and Judgment inside the Bush Administration. NY: W.W. Norton and Co. Goldsmith was an attorney inside the Justice Department when this mass resignation almost took place.

[44] Krent, Howard J. 2008. "From a Unitary to a Unilateral Presidency." *Boston University Law Review*. 88:2. p. 50.

[45] Savage, Charlie. 2007b. "Reaganites Reconsider." The Nation. 285:8. September 6. http://www.thenation.com/doc/20070924/savage.

[46] For example, see the "Government Secrecy Report Card" at Openthegovernment.org. A consortium of organizations began compiling a report card, starting in 2004, that documented the Bush administration's classification program, use of executive orders, signing statements, and other unilateral devices, and the assertion of the State Secrets privilege, among other things.

[47] *See* Kagan, Elena. 2001.

[48] *See* Wills, Garry. 2009. "Entangled Giant." The New York Review of Books 56:15. October 8.

[49] Obama, Barack. 2009a. "Revocation of Certain Executive Orders Concerning Regulatory Planning and Review." *Federal Register*. 74:6113. Wednesday, February 4.

[50] Bush, George W. 2007b. "Further Amendment to Executive Order 12866 on Regulatory Planning and Review." *Federal Register*. 72:2763. Tuesday, January 23.

[51] Clinton, William J. 1993. "Regulatory Planning and Review." Federal Register. 58:190. Monday, October 4.

[52] Reagan, Ronald. 1981. "Federal Regulation." Federal Register. 46:13193. February 17.

[53] Reagan, Ronald. 1985. "Regulatory Planning Process." *Federal Register* 50:1036.

[54] See Bush, George W. 2007c. "Executive Order 13258—Amending Executive Order 12866 on Regulatory Planning and Review." *Federal Register*. 67:9385. February 28.

[55] Obama, Barack. 2009b. "Memorandum for the Heads of Executive Departments and Agencies—Regulatory Review." Federal Register. 74:21; See also, "Obama Begins Regulatory Reform" OMBWatch. February 10, 2009. http://www.ombwatch.org/node/9689. Accessed September 13, 2009.

[56] For a general discussion, see Kelley, Christopher S. 2007. "The Law: Contextualizing the Signing Statement." *Presidential Studies Quarterly*. 37:4. December.

[57] Obama, Barack. 2009c. "Memorandum for the Heads of Executive Departments and Agencies. Subject: Presidential Signing Statements." Office of the Press Secretary. March 9. http://www.whitehouse.gov/the_press_office/Memorandum-on-Presidential-Signing-Statements/. Accessed 9/12/09.

[58] Ibid.

[59] Ibid.

[60] Egelko, Bob. 2009. "Kagan Vows to Defend Some Laws Obama Dislikes." San Francisco Chronicle. Friday, July 24. http://www.sfgate.com/cgi-bin/article.cgi?f=/c/a/2009/07/24/MNV918U8MP.DTL. Accessed August 10, 2009.

[61] "The Ninth Circuit Judicial Conference: Chief Judge Kozinski Chats with Solicitor General Elena Kagan." 2009. dag blog. http://dagblog.com/politics/ninth-circuit-judicial-conference-chief-judge-kozinski-chats-solicitor-general-elena-kagan-. July 23, 2009. Accessed August 15.

[62] H.R. 1105. "The Omnibus Appropriations Act, 2009." P.L. 111-8.

[63] Obama, Barack. 2009d. "Statement on Signing the Omnibus Appropriations Act, 2009." Office of the Press Secretary. http://www.whitehouse.gov/the_press_office/Statement-from-the-President-on-the-signing-of-HR-1105/ March 11. Accessed June 3, 2009.

[64] H.R. 131. P.L. 111-25. June 2, 2009.

[65] Obama, Barack. 2009e. "Statement on Signing the Ronald Reagan Centennial Commission." Office of the Press Secretary. http://www.whitehouse.gov/the_press_office/Statement-by-the-President-on-the-Signing-of-the-Ronald-Reagan-Centennial-Commission-Act/ June 2. Accessed August 20, 2009.

[66] Savage, Charlie. 2009. "Obama's Embrace of a Bush Tactic Riles Congress." New York Times. August 8. http://www.nytimes.com/2009/08/09/us/politics/09signing.html?_r=1andhpw Accessed September 12, 2009.

[67] http://www.whitehouse.gov/briefing_room/

[68] http://www.whitehouse.gov/briefing_room/PressReleases/

[69] P.L 111-21. May 20, 2009.

[70] See Obama, Barack. 2009f. "Remarks by the President at the Signing of the Helping Families Save their Homes Act and the Fraud Enforcement and Recovery Act." May 20, 2009. http://www.whitehouse.gov/the_press_office/Remarks-by-the-President-at-Signing-of-the-Helping-Families-Save-Their-Homes-Act-and-the-Fraud-Enforcement-and-Recovery-Act/ Accessed September 15.

[71] Obama, Barack. 2009g. "Statement on Signing S. 386." May 20. http://www.whitehouse.gov/the_press_office/STATEMENT-BY-THE-PRESIDENT-ON-S-386/ Accessed September 15, 2009.

[72] This is not the case. It appears that Grassley was attempting to make political hay from the short-term memory of the public and a hunch that the press would not return to check its records. The only major candidate that foreswore the use of signing statements was Senator John McCain.

[73] Grassley, Charles. 2009. "Grassley Holds President Accountable for Promises to Make Government Transparent." Press Release. March 13. http://grassley.senate.gov/news/Article.cfm?customel_dataPageID_1502=19801# Accessed September 13, 2009.

[74] Obama, Barack. 2009h. "Statement on Signing H.R. 2346." June 26. http://www.white house.gov/the_press_office/Statement-from-the-President-upon-signing-HR-2346/. Accessed September 15, 2009.
[75] Marks, Alexandra. 2009. "Obama Gets Mixed Reviews on Government 'Openness.'" Christian Science Monitor. March 19. http://features.csmonitor.com/politics/2009/03/19/obama-gets-mixed-reviews-on-government-openness/ Accessed September 13, 2009.
[76] Frank, Barney, David Obey, et. al. 2009. "Letter to Barack Obama Re: Signing Statements." July 21. http://www.house.gov/frank/pressreleases/2009/07-21-09-signing-statements-letter-obama.html. Accessed September 13, 2009.
[77] See "H.R. 3081, Department of State, Foreign Operations, and Related Programs Appropriations Act, 2010."
[78] Alarkon, Walter. 2009. "House Overwhelmingly Rejects Signing Statement." The Hill. July 9. http://thehill.com/homenews/house/49864-house-overwhelmingly-rejects-signing-statement. Accessed September 15, 2009.

In: President or King?
Editor: Meena Bose, pp. 123-140
ISBN: 978-1-61324-655-9

BUREAUCRATIC CONTROL AND THE FUTURE OF PRESIDENTIAL POWER

Andrew Rudalevige

ABSTRACT

The theory of the unitary executive is sometimes used to suggest that Article II's "executive power" extends to complete control of the executive branch. While presidents have rarely come close to that ideal, for some decades administrative strategies have been key to how presidents have exercised control over governmental outcomes -- and thus, to how they have exercised power. In thinking about the future of presidential power, this essay traces how recent developments in presidential administrative strategies have tilted the bureaucratic playing field in favor of the executive branch. It stresses the role of appointments, regulatory review, managerial directives, and the theoretic underpinning of these through the invocation of presidential "rights" that lead from the Nixon, Reagan, and George W. Bush administrations to the choices facing Barack Obama.

"Whose bureaucracy is this, anyway?": a seemingly simple question, but one with immense practical import. [1]

Not surprisingly, presidents have a preferred answer: it's theirs. And in recent years they have sought to impose that answer on the political system in increasingly systematic, even aggressive, ways. Article II of the Constitution leads off by vesting "the executive Power" in the president: that "does not mean *some* of the executive power," Supreme Court Justice Antonin Scalia noted in 1988, "but *all* of it." [2] President George W. Bush extended that conclusion to conceiving a "unitary executive branch" completely under presidential direction. Pushed to its logical extreme, such a model denied the ability of other political actors to constrain presidential preferences, even their legitimacy in so attempting. Talking of the controversial administrative initiatives taken after the September 11 attacks, for instance, a former Bush administration attorney observed that "It's not that they think they're skirting the law. They think that this *is* the law." [3]

La loi, c'est moi?: to be sure, presidents have rarely come close to that ideal. Indeed, despite its recent invocations, the academic theory of the unitary executive does not designate *which* powers belong exclusively to the president. [4] Bureaucrats have multiple principals, including legislators, judges, and statute. [5] While the Constitution vests the executive power in the president, it does not define what that power is, or how far it extends, or where that extension meets the powers of other political actors. Instead, the long annals of inter-institutional contestation have done most of the defining. A "page of history," as Justice Oliver Wendell Holmes put it, "is worth a volume of logic." [6]

Still, history has played out in a certain overall direction. The American national state has expanded dramatically – urged on by Depression, war, civil rights, and regulatory zeal. Divided government and partisan polarization have made achieving legislative action more difficult, and what Elena Kagan called asserting "directive authority" over the bureaucracy more appealing. [7] As a result, presidents have had both enhanced opportunity and motive to seek to influence bureaucratic action and policy implementation – that is, governmental outcomes. Such influence is the very definition of presidential power. [8]

The present essay, then, assesses the development of bureaucratic control as a mechanism for the expression of presidential power. George W. Bush attracted much attention for his aggressive use of executive unilateralism; but his efforts extended principles and precedents established by his predecessors. This intellectual and political lineage, tracing what Richard Nathan called "the administrative presidency," [9] is the central topic here. The empirics focus on the Nixon and Reagan administrations' development of the theoretic and practical tools that underwrote Bush's variation on the theme.

For Nixon, as Nathan wrote, this was the "plot that failed." [10] But Nixon's successors tinkered with his script, with real success. Will Barack Obama, to whom these administrative strategies have been passed down, rewrite the plot? A page of history suggests that the answer is 'no.'

Creating a "Zone of Autonomy"

The Constitution lays out only the bare bones of the relationship between president and bureaucracy. After the vesting clause, Article II goes on to assign the responsibility of the president to "take Care that the Laws be faithfully executed" and lays out his power to make appointments (subject to the advice and consent of the Senate), fill vacant posts, and "require the Opinion, in writing, of the principal Officer in each of the executive Departments, upon any Subject relating to the Duties of their respective Offices." This last clearly contemplates both executive departments and a managerial hierarchy topped by the president. Nor does the Constitution create a plural executive, as some would have preferred. [11] The framers instead heeded the argument represented by James Iredell's remarks to the North Carolina ratifying convention in July 1788 (which themselves reflect Hamilton's better-known endorsement in *Federalist* #70 of the accountability that flows from "unity"): Iredell noted that "had [the president] a council by whose advice he was bound to act, his responsibility, in all such cases, must be destroyed." [12]

As noted above, the "executive power" itself is left undefined. As a result, arguments over what it might constitute started with the Washington administration and have continued ever since. Did the executive power allow presidents to do more or less anything, so long as it was not expressly forbidden them in the constitution or the laws? Supreme Court Justice James McReynolds sarcastically commented in 1926 that if such "illimitable" power existed, it seemed rather odd that the framers should have bothered to haggle over the need to grant that executive the authority to ask for memos from his subordinates. [13] Even James Wilson of Pennsylvania, an early advocate of a strong presidency, declared that "the only powers he conceived strictly Executive were those of executing the laws, and appointing officers." [14]

As time went on, the balance of power between the branches has ebbed and flowed. Those developments are chronicled in depth elsewhere. [15] But one notable shift, especially since the 1970s, has been the rise in importance of exactly what Wilson sought to downplay: the power inherent in "executing the laws and appointing officers."

Taking the second first, the executive departments and agencies now house some 3.3 million civilian and military personnel who report to the president. That figure does not include postal workers, workers paid for by government grants, or those contracted as third parties to do public sector work. If included these would bring what Paul Light calls "the true size of government" to an astounding 14.6 million persons. [16]

Clearly no one person can do anything like manage this mass of personnel. Presidents have reacted in two ways. On the one hand, they have increased the size of their own, centralized staff: the Executive Office of the President (EOP) has grown to around fifteen hundred staff in its own right. On the other, they have paid increased attention to the wide range of political positions within their control, seeking to (as one aide to George W. Bush put it) "implant their DNA throughout the government." [17] This meant looking for direct loyalty even in the lower-level appointments once frequently delegated to Cabinet secretaries.

The growing number of political, and politicized, officers reflected the growth in the size and scope of the U.S. government generally. The sheer number of laws and the institutionalization of a regulatory state enhanced the discretion bureaucrats had to shape policy at the most tangible level. "In a complex, technologically advanced society in which the role of government is pervasive," Nathan pointed out in 1983, "much of what we would define as policymaking is done through the execution of laws in the management process." [18] Indeed, the most salient events of recent years have been basically administrative in nature, from the handling of Hurricane Katrina and post-war Iraq to the implementation of environmental regulation and financial bailouts. That implies real advantage to the use of unilateral administrative tools as a mechanism for policy change. Directing bureaus to implement the law in a certain way – whether through executive orders, signing statements, regulatory review, or simple directive memoranda – may do as much to shape "real" policy as does legislative action. Even if Congress objects to the presidential interpretation, presidents (as unitary actors) have a structural edge over their collective co-equal branch. As Alexander Hamilton shrewdly predicted, "the Executive in the exercise of its constitutional powers, may establish an antecedent state of things" which shapes the policy terrain other political actors must cross. Congress may be the first branch, but it doesn't usually get the first move.

Relatedly, presidents have taken to heart the claims of the theory of the "unitary executive," at least its aggressively exegetic interpretation. This means asserting expansive boundaries to the office's prerogative authority, leading to broad claims about secrecy, war powers, and the unilateral abilities of the president to act in the absence of legislative authorization (or even in the face of legislative disapproval.)

Such stratagems may bring with them their own costs. [19] Nonetheless, efforts to control bureaucratic preferences and thus policy implementation – through people, and through processes – have become a crucial part of how presidents sought to fortify their office's powers vis-à-vis other political actors. Presidents have sought to place such tactics within what George W. Bush's administration called the president's "zone of autonomy" [20] – a zone whose boundaries would be determined by the president himself, and which clearly lay in newly occupied interbranch territory.

NIXON'S "PLOT THAT FAILED"

To understand these developments, we must first look back to the administration of Richard Nixon. Nixon set an administrative template still utilized today. The vocabulary of "rights" he used in justifying his aggressive managerial tactics set the tone for his successors. And the anvil against which subsequent presidents have hammered out their expanded power is the legislative resurgence against Watergate and the "imperial presidency." [21]

Nixon sought sequentially to shift policymaking resources to the EOP and to politicize the wider bureaucracy. Early on the plan to rein in the wider executive branch, whose policy preferences Nixon distrusted, involved centralized control: as a 1972 staff memo reminded the president, "To ... attempt to gain control, we attempted to manage the government by establishing a bureaucracy to deal with the existing bureaucracy." [22] The so-called Responsiveness Project of the first term likewise sought to ensure the "use of the available federal machinery," as White House counsel John Dean put it, to help the administration's friends, and "to screw our political enemies." [23] At its most sinister, such machinery could coordinate or even (as with the "Plumbers") direct illegal operations and domestic surveillance.

Less dramatically, a Domestic Council (and its staff) was created to serve as the counterpart to the National Security Council (and its staff); the NSC staff, which saw a tripling of its budget under key aide Henry Kissinger, was to be the main source of foreign policy advice and even operations. Nixon's major foreign policy endeavors ran through the Situation Room, not the State Department. The reorganization of the Bureau of the Budget into the Office of Management and Budget (OMB) emphasized Nixon's ambitions regarding how the departments and agencies were run. Along these lines Nixon charged OMB with reviewing agency regulations before they were issued.

But by 1972 Nixon's staffers felt the first term strategy had not been a success. "In the second term," they argued, "the President must gain control of the bureaucracy by staffing it with his people" – "Nixon loyalists" would be put in place to "re-take" the departments. [24]

To achieve that, the administration began an overt program of politicization complete with regular reports to Nixon chief of staff H.R. Haldeman on the progress made in "gaining control of the bureaucracy." When the credentials of one nominee were questioned by Haldeman, for example – "How tried and true a loyalist is he? " – personnel chief Fred Malek responded with a detailed description of the administration's plans for "further steps to politicize the individuals and gain their complete loyalty." This included significant training, including a seminar to teach Nixonians how to deal with recalcitrant career employees. [25] But given that the lower-level appointees of the first term, whom Nixon had allowed cabinet members to put in place, were "all but impossible to dislodge," Martin Anderson would later conclude that "Nixon lost his opportunity to govern before he started." [26]

Nixon's administrative strategy also included his aggressive interpretation of Article II's "executive power." What was new was the way the language of "rights" pervaded the administration's justifications for unilateralism. In some areas, it seemed, the separation of powers was absolute. As Nixon claimed in 1973, "the manner in which the president exercises his assigned executive powers is not subject to questioning by another branch of the government." [27] Attorney General Richard Kleindienst told the Senate in 1973 the president could direct *any* member of the executive branch, including those confirmed by the Senate, to refuse to give Congress information: "your power to get what the President knows," he said, "is in the President's hands." [28]

That claim dealt with process; but Nixon also made a play to define those "assigned executive powers" themselves. "In the president's hands," for instance, was apparently the location of the public purse. The administration argued that while Congress had the power to appropriate funds, the executive power covered their actual expenditure; as the OMB's Caspar Weinberger put it, "a law appropriating funds is permissive and not mandatory in nature." Thus, as Nixon himself claimed, "The Constitutional right of the President of the United States to impound funds…is absolutely clear." [29] The president's actions in this area had corresponding clarity: impoundments encompassed an astonishing 20% of discretionary spending by 1973. These were targeted at particular policies; in 1972, after Nixon's veto of a water pollution act was overridden, the president impounded more than half of the funds committed through the law. A federal court, overturning another impoundment, pointed out the implications for executive power: "if the power sought here were found valid, no barrier would remain to the executive ignoring any and all Congressional authorizations if he deemed them... to be contrary to the needs of the nation." [30]

In at least one signing statement, Nixon deemed just that. When Congress passed language in 1971 stating it was now United States policy to "terminate at the earliest practicable date" American involvement in Vietnam, Nixon declared it "without binding force or effect" since "it does not reflect my judgment about the way in which the war should be brought to a conclusion…. [It] will not change the policies I have pursued and that I shall continue to pursue toward this end." [31]

Yet even before Nixon's resignation Congress had begun to respond to these claims and actions with a long list of enactments seeking to extend legislative power over budgeting, war powers, and intelligence. Nixon's administrative strategy, then, was "the plot that failed," overwhelmed by his overreach and his administration's criminality.

Nathan concluded his discussion of Nixon's administrative efforts by noting that "it is possible that a president with a coherent program could organize his administration to navigate a course similar to Nixon's plan" but that Watergate's "aftertaste" would likely "discourage an American president from soon again attempting this kind of domestic strategy. Such a firm grabbing of the reins with an emphasis on administrative accomplishment may now be unacceptable." [32]

The Reagan Years: The Plot That Thickened

For the remainder of the 1970s, this proved true. But the Reagan administration entered office in 1981 with a strong feeling that the post-Watergate resurgence had gone too far. Reagan's White House counselor and attorney general, Edwin Meese bemoaned "the legislative opportunism" of the era, arguing it had created a "major threat to constitutional government." [33]

The administration responded accordingly. While Reagan may have been the "Great Communicator," it is too often forgotten that management was at the heart of the Reagan Revolution. Indeed, in a December 1980 transition memo to the incoming administration, longtime OMB stalwart and public administrator Dwight Ink warned, "The ability of the Reagan Administration to act will be no better than the capacity of the departments and agencies to manage." [34] And the Nixon model of the same – shy, they hoped, the detours into abuses of power – was present and correct, in the personae and plans of many of Reagan's new staffers, from George Shultz to Caspar Weinberger to Martin Anderson.

The first step was the appointment process, under the credo "Personnel is Policy." [35] Anderson, who had felt the Nixon politicization scheme was too little, too late, pushed for early and extensive planning on this front. [36] All Carter appointees were removed – Meese said "an empty office was better than a holdover" – including even ostensibly non-partisan slots. Appointees at both the cabinet and subcabinet level, along with members of the Senior Executive Service and judicial nominees, were centrally selected and vetted for ideological purity, then given what Anderson termed three rounds of "indoctrination," including one by conservative think tanks. [37] An internal memo stressed that departmental candidates must "have [a] clear understanding that being responsive to the White House is critical. Need someone loyal…. who can" serve as a "good communicator of RR goals." [38]

The Presidential Personnel Office forms required of those seeking non-career appointments asked candidates to provide information "pertinent to your philosophical commitment to the policies of this administration" along with the name of the campaign supervisor with whom they had worked during the Reagan/Bush campaign. [39] The same or stronger standards held for slots in EOP. After the creation of OMB, the agency had added a layer of political appointees, the PADs (program associate directors), between the substantive branches and the director's office. If such "politicization" of a staff long renowned for "neutral competence" was decried by most academics, presidents made no apologies, and PADs' roles remained critical to the White House as a means (as one staffer put it) "to ensure that th[e] temptation" of "softpedal[ing]" presidential priorities against legislative and departmental recalcitrance "is resisted." It was crucial for PADs to have "ideological commitment to the President's goal[s]," but negotiation skills were as important as "ideological fortitude"; better, the White House thought, to "have a savvy politician with only rudimentary knowledge of the relevant issue areas than an issues expert who is politically naïve." [40] Notably, budget director David Stockman was made part of the Reagan cabinet; his deputy, Ed Harper (another Nixon policy veteran), held the simultaneous title of assistant to the president, and attended White House senior staff meetings. [41]

This overlap of WHO and OMB was particularly important given that massive tax and domestic spending cuts drove Reagan's first year agenda. Impoundments, per se, were not on the table, but massive rescission proposals were. (OMB called this "Operation Flush," since it aimed to clear the budget "authority pipelines.") [42] On the "M" side, OMB's Lawrence Kudlow stressed in 1982 that "management initiatives are a serious part of the overall budget savings plan." [43] This included an array of strategies that included the tighter linkage of budgeting to management and the creation of various management councils to root out government waste. The Grace Commission became the best known of these, but there were also more permanent additions to the interagency firmament (such as the President's Council on Management Improvement) to flesh out the "Reform '88" initiative spearheaded by OMB. A Management Report was added to the president's annual budget presentation starting in fiscal 1986, and the administration pushed hard to create the government-wide position of Chief Financial Officer. [44]

The idea, as an OMB staffer noted, was to "get it institutionalized – or it will not survive in Washington, D.C." [45] One crucial advance along these lines was Reagan's formalization of a truncated initiative of the Nixon administrative presidency: the use of OMB to centralize the review of major regulations. Following Nixon, Presidents Ford and Carter had directed agencies to consider the inflationary impact and cost-benefit ratio of new regulations, but applied no sanctions; as a 1981 memo conceded, their efforts "did *not* make much of an inroad into the substance of regulations." [46] Reagan, by contrast, stated flatly in Executive Order 12291 that, by "the authority vested in me as President by the Constitution and laws of the United States" – though no laws or authorities were specified – ".... regulatory action shall not be undertaken unless the potential benefits to society for the regulation outweigh the potential costs to society." OMB, through the Office of Information and Regulatory Affairs (OIRA), had the power to recommend that regulations be withdrawn if they could not "be reformulated to meet its objections." As internal memos make clear, any objections of this kind were dictated at least in part by the West Wing: the "views ... of senior White House staff members are of course critical," OIRA head James C. Miller III assured one such staff member. [47]

The Administration sought diligently to publicize and enforce its new process to and upon the departments. The latter were not eager to comply: in 1983 the head of the Occupational Safety and Health Administration (OSHA) caused what OMB deputy director Joseph Wright told Ed Meese was a "run on E.O. 12291," when he declined to obtain final OMB clearance before sending a rule to the Federal Register. "A premeditated attempt to circumvent a Presidential Order should not be allowed to go unnoticed," Wright complained. "I would strongly suggest that you bring in [OSHA and Labor] and that we have a very serious discussion.... Last year, we brought in several Administrators from the Department of Transportation to have 'religious sessions' – I certainly think another one is required in this case." [48]

Another strategy for helping agencies to get presidential religion was the use of "signing statements." Nixon, as we have seen, did use statements designed to signal the administration's intent not to comply with legislative intent. But according to Phillip Cooper, "it was the Reagan administration that had taken what had been a relatively benign and largely ceremonial practice... and worked to make it a systematic and effective weapon to trump congressional action." [49] A 1986 memo by the Justice Department's Samuel Alito laid out the issues at hand. "Our primary objective," he wrote, "is to ensure that Presidential signing statements assume their rightful place in the interpretation of legislation." He noted the "potential increase of presidential power" this entailed and the likely resentment it would stir in Congress. He asked, but didn't answer, a key question: "what happens when there is a clear conflict between the congressional and presidential understanding? Whose intent controls?" [50]

But the administration's feelings on that point seemed clear nonetheless, grounded as they were in a broader theory of the "unitary executive" more coherent than Nixon's deeply-felt, but somewhat ad hoc, assertion of executive rights. The theory was developed (in Alito's phrase) as "the gospel according to OLC." [51] It was applied in cases such as the legislative veto. Brushing aside those pragmatists in the administration who wanted to work with Congress on the issue, Attorney General William French Smith told Reagan in 1981 that any such veto was "an unconstitutional encroachment by the Congress on the exercise of Presidential authority. It now represents a major danger to the independence and authority of the Executive branch." It didn't help that it also made it too easy for legislators to "thwart important proposals of your Administration." [52]

But the theory went further. Congress was not just Democratic, it was, well, Congress – interested mostly in district pork and in fine-tuning rather than eliminating the welfare state. Thus "the initial purpose of the unitary executive theory," Jeffrey Rosen has argued, "was to strike a blow at the heart of the regulatory state." [53] In this view the Congressional (and Court-aided) creation of putatively executive actors partially insulated from presidential reach was illegitimate.

As with Nixon, issues of information control and war powers were given special attention in this regard. Sometimes they were linked: for example, after Reagan had issued a national security directive governing the disclosure of information deemed sensitive, Congress passed a bill forbidding the administration from enforcing its punitive provisions. Reagan signed it – but stated that since it "impermissibly interfered with my ability to prevent unauthorized disclosures of our most sensitive diplomatic, military, and intelligence activities...., in accordance with my sworn obligation to preserve, protect, and defend the Constitution, [this section] will be considered of no force or effect. . ." [54]

While Reagan rarely invoked executive privilege by name, the Justice Department laid out legal justifications for restricting legislative access to "pre-decisional, deliberative" information. Reagan also sought rollbacks in the Freedom of Information Act, and he issued an executive order granting presidents executive privilege over the records due for release in their presidential libraries. The *Los Angeles Times* went so far as to complain that Reagan "set a policy and tone for secrecy in government that exceeds anything since Watergate. In fact, not even during the Nixon years were so many steps taken to establish secrecy as government policy." [55]

The Reagan attitude towards war powers and covert action flowed from similar assumptions about presidential power. The president shrugged off the War Powers Resolution's consultation and reporting requirements, [56] most notably perhaps in the invasion of Grenada in 1983 and retaliatory strikes in Libya in 1986 but not only then. In 1987-88, for example, the administration denied that troops were being introduced into hostilities in the Persian Gulf, despite a series of military incidents related to the Iran-Iraq war. [57] "Imminent danger" pay was approved for servicemen there; but this, the administration insisted, did not mean they were involved in the "imminent hostilities" that would trigger the WPR.

In one case the WPR *was* invoked, the only time its "clock" has ever been started. A full year after the president sent peacekeeping troops to Lebanon, Congress authorized their ultimately tragic mission Lebanon for eighteen months. The president accepted the legislative "support" but didn't agree he needed it. As he put it in a signing statement attached to the authorization, "I do not and cannot cede any of the authority vested in me under the Constitution as President and as Commander in Chief of the United States Armed Forces. Nor should my signing be viewed as any acknowledgment that the President's constitutional authority can be impermissibly infringed by statute." [58]

Statute did not affect U.S. policy in important cases of covert action, either. Most prominent was the Iran-*contra* affair, an operation centralized in the National Security Council staff and justified by the commander in chief power and the need for secrecy in pursuing the national interest. The president, independent counsel Lawrence Walsh would conclude, had not committed a crime. But he strongly scored "the President's disregard for civil laws enacted to limit presidential actions abroad" (the Boland Amendment, the Arms Export Control Act and congressional-notification requirements in covert-action laws) which "created a climate in which some of the Government officers assigned to implement his policies felt emboldened to circumvent such laws." [59]

GEORGE W. BUSH: ADVANCING THE PLOT

Given the political damage Iran-*contra* inflicted on Reagan, it can be argued that while the administrative plot had thickened, it had not fully gelled. Even so, the administration left important lessons in bureaucratic control to its heirs. In 2002 George W. Bush, echoing the Reagan years, emphasized his "obligation to make sure that the Presidency remains robust" and his "duty to protect the executive branch from legislative encroachment." [60] Bush's concern for his office was perhaps overblown: as we have seen, the tools of appointments, executive orders, regulatory review, signing statements, and even the language of executive unitary "rights," were all on the table well before 2001. But those tools were utilized skillfully, and unhesitantly, from the very start of the Bush term. [61]

James Pfiffner characterized the "Bush approach to executive management" as encompassing "secrecy, speed, and top-down control." [62] The Reagan approach to appointments, for example, was adopted and expanded. [63] Clay Johnson, head of the White House personnel office, interviewed and approved each candidate for appointment, giving Cabinet members a pre-approved short list of departmental senior staffers. In all cases loyalty was the paramount qualification. Michael Brown, later director of the Federal Emergency Management Agency (FEMA), became the poster child for the potential hazards of this approach after Hurricane Katrina; still, Bush, like his predecessors, viewed the appointment strategy as a necessary mechanism for asserting control over the wider executive branch. The president made it clear early on that he would not tolerate disobedient agency heads: when the head of the Army Corps of Engineers complained publicly about his allotted budget, for instance, he was summarily dismissed.

Throughout his term Bush promulgated the "President's Management Agenda" through OMB, rating agencies and programs on a variety of fronts, from personnel management to "e-government." By many accounts agency managers took quite the exercise more seriously than in past iterations – mainly because the administration made a renewed effort to tie management and program effectiveness to budgetary decisions. New personnel systems were created in the new Department of Homeland Security and within the Department of Defense, aiming to enhance executive control over pay, performance, and discipline for some 900,000 employees. The PMA also assessed the use of outside contracting, leading to the expansion of its use, even to military support positions. As with Nixon's earlier project, contracts were apparently at times tied to political responsiveness. [64]

Similar centralized discipline extended to the review of agency regulations by OMB. The agency was aggressively skeptical of the costs and benefits of agency action, bolstered when in his second term the president issued executive order 13422 adding internal "guidance documents" to the regulatory materials requiring review and mandating that a new political appointee sign off on anything included in an agency's annual rulemaking plan. [65] The emphasis on influencing statutory interpretation, and thus the practicalities of implementation, was particularly strong after Democrats regained congressional majorities in the 2006 elections. As John Graham (who headed OIRA during Bush's first term) noted, "creative lawyers can find lots of lawful ways for a determined president to advance an agenda." [66] As a backstop, presidential staffers energetically involved themselves in a wide range of other agency activities that threatened to prescribe policy divergent from presidential preferences. Bush's desire to impose his preferences on environmental policy attracted perhaps the most attention, but few areas escaped review. [67]

All this fell within the Bush administration's broader attitude towards executive power. The Bush version of the unitary executive, as laid out in memos by lawyers in the Justice and Defense Departments and the Office of the Vice President, made it clear that the executive would unilaterally draw the boundary lines between the branches. [68] Thus, to the notion that the executive power was the indivisible purview of the president was appended the assertion that the scope of that executive power was also defined by the president. This gave new resonance to the older claim that Congress could not infringe legislatively on the president's constitutional authority. In this view, not only could the president act when Congress had not acted in a given area, but even in the face of congressional opposition.

This philosophy suggested a new scope for controlling the bureaucracy. For example, after the September 11 terrorist attacks the president ordered the National Security Agency (NSA) to monitor certain international calls. On its face, this seemed to violate the requirements of the 1978 Foreign Intelligence Surveillance Act (FISA) that warrants for such surveillance be obtained when "U.S. persons" were involved. When the initiative was revealed in late 2005, the administration argued that the president had both inherent and statutory power to order such wiretaps. The Justice Department told Congress that "the NSA activities are supported by the President's well-recognized inherent constitutional authority of Commander in Chief .... The President has the chief responsibility under the Constitution to protect American from attack, and the Constitution gives the President the authority necessary to fulfill that solemn responsibility." While the administration argued that the Authorization for the Use of Military Force (AUMF) approved by Congress in September 2001 by-passed FISA's warrant requirement, this was secondary: to the extent that FISA infringed upon the Commander in Chief power, it was itself unconstitutional. [69]

Parallel claims were made in other areas. The administration claimed the authority to designate "enemy combatants," even U.S. citizens, and to place them outside the reach of the civilian court system. They were to be tried, if at all, by military tribunals, themselves established by a presidential order of November 2001. The procedures for those tribunals, and the treatment of detainees generally, were to be determined by the executive branch. A memo constructed by a working group of administration attorneys (dominated by the EOP) came to the same conclusion: "in order to respect the President's inherent constitutional authority to manage a military campaign, 18 U.S.C. § 2340A [the prohibition against torture] as well as any other potentially applicable statute must be construed as inapplicable to interrogations undertaken pursuant to his Commander-in-Chief authority." [70] When Congress passed an amendment reaffirming and clarifying that statutory ban, President Bush appended a signing statement to the statute; the administration would enforce the law, he informed Congress, "in a manner consistent with the constitutional authority of the President to oversee the unitary executive branch and as Commander in Chief." [71] Congressional offers to legalize the NSA surveillance program were rejected as unnecessary (though ultimately Congress would pass laws in 2007 and 2008 making the president's behavior legal.)

It should be noted that signing statements were a key part of the administration's process of beating the bounds of executive power, passing past precedent to become truly systematic. Bush issued more challenges to portions of legislation – 1,168 by one count -- than all his predecessors combined. Frequently these used the term "unitary executive" as a justification for restricting bureaucratic behavior (Reagan, by comparison, used that phrase itself only once). [72] Often such statements had to do with limiting the transfer of information outside the executive branch. Indeed, secrecy issues, as with Nixon and Reagan, were paramount with the Bush administration, which was far more successful than those predecessors in limiting outside access to executive branch decisions and deliberations. [73] "I'm the decider, and I decide what is best," the president said in 2006. [74] The statement became immediate shorthand for his administrative strategy.

BARACK AND BEYOND: THE FUTURE OF BUREAUCRATIC CONTROL

Richard Nixon, despite his overreach, laid out a set of administrative strategies that his successors could utilize and improve. They have sought to do just that. Indeed, while the lineage presented here suggests a partisan pattern, that pattern traces theory more than practice: for instance, President Clinton issued signing statements, invoked executive privilege, evaded the constraints of the War Powers Resolution, and creatively varied the types of directives used to control the bureaucracy. [75] The question is more one of "positionality" than personality. As Hamilton foresaw, antecedents lead to consequences – whether in the sequential policymaking between the branches, or the internal sequence of the presidential office itself.

Barack Obama's arrival in the White House in 2009 seemed to mark a major shift in the presidential attitude towards executive power, broadly defined. Aided by Democratic legislative majorities, Obama seemed content to seek major change by statutory means. His administration, he said, would be committed to "an unprecedented level of openness." [76] While not renouncing signing statements, he would use them sparingly, and "not use signing statements to nullify or undermine congressional instructions as enacted into law." [77] Far from saying the president was infallible, Obama's oratory seemed to suggest a willingness to listen to a range of views. Optimistic neo-Whigs contrasted, for example, Dick Cheney's justification of the Iran-contra affair – "an effort by the majority to criminalize what was really a policy difference in terms of how we dealt...with the situation in Nicaragua" -- with Obama's promise that "signing statements should not be used to suggest that the President will disregard statutory requirements on the basis of policy disagreements." [78]

Early on, Obama issued a series of executive orders lessening the presumption of government secrecy; pledging the closure of (though not closing) the Guantanamo Bay detention facility; reviewing "detention policy options" generally; and "ensuring legal interrogations." In the last order, most notably, Obama rejected the array of administration legal opinions underpinning the broadest reaches of the theory of the unitary executive described here. This was a major shift, buried in bureaucratic boilerplate: "officers, employees, and other agents of the United States Government... may not, in conducting interrogations, rely upon any interpretation of the law governing interrogation... issued by the Department of Justice between September 11, 2001, and January 20, 2009." [79]

Still, as former Clinton chief of staff Leon Panetta pointed out during the 2008 campaign, "I don't think any president walks into their job and starts thinking about how they can minimize their authority." [80] And the new administration's reversal of its predecessor's unilateral actions was conducted unilaterally. In the first two weeks of his term alone, President Obama issued ten formal orders and another ten memoranda to the executive agencies, on topics ranging from automobile emissions to Gazan refugees. He rejected the substance of past policy, that is, but not the manner of its formulation. Intriguingly, his choice for solicitor general (and, in May 2010, for the Supreme Court) was Elena Kagan, who as a Harvard Law professor had written approvingly of Bill Clinton's "assertion of personal ownership over regulatory product." [81] Obama's selection of Cass Sunstein (a high-powered academic proponent of cost-benefit analysis) to direct OIRA likewise suggested a strong emphasis by the administration on regulatory affairs.

And while the meat of the orders mattered, so, potentially, did the ellipses: in the executive order on interrogations noted above, for instance, they contain the proviso "unless the Attorney General with appropriate consultation provides further guidance." In early February 2009, the Obama Justice Department, to shrieks of protest from civil libertarians, endorsed the Bush administration strategy of invoking the "state secrets doctrine" in a court case involving the rendition program. The case, administration attorneys argued, should be dismissed, since even discussing it in court could jeopardize national security. [82] In May 2009, the president said that the detention regime "can't be based simply on what I or the executive branch decide alone"; but as 2010 began, it looked increasingly likely that Obama would issue an executive order deciding just that, continuing the regime of "preventive detention" without charge or trial: as one administration aide put it, "Legislation could kill Obama's plans." [83]

But legislation, too, might be finessed. The president's pledge not to use signing statements "to nullify or undermine congressional instructions as enacted into law" could not survive the issuance of an actual signing statement: evading such instructions is exactly their point. By July 2009, Obama had issued a dozen signing statements doing so, such as one noting that a provision of a supplemental spending bill dealing with the IMF and World Bank "would interfere with my constitutional authority to conduct foreign relations by directing the Executive to take certain positions in negotiations or discussions..."

The Obama administration, then, continued to utilize the administrative tools it inherited. Assuming this will stay constant, the future burden of research must shift to trace the *impact* of the efforts by presidents to control the bureaucracy. We know what presidents said; we don't know, at least not systematically, what agencies did in response. [84] That is: how well are presidential efforts to control implementation themselves implemented?

In fact, even if we make the heroic assumption that such efforts translate without bureaucratic, legislative, or judicial friction into outcomes, we should be careful to recognize other potential complications that may hinder an administrative strategy. Indeed, its very success could cause difficulties – both of coordination, as multiple actors in the bureaucracy (and "counterbureaucracy") are mobilized, and of quality (since responsiveness and competence may be negatively associated). [85] Appointees placed for patronage reasons into a more complex set of crosscutting White House institutional machinery may find themselves simply unable to work that machinery in a way that asserts the kind of control the president hoped to achieve in the first place.

The narrative here, then, is certainly incomplete. But I hope it has shown that a succession of presidents have thought bureaucratic issues important enough to spend their limited managerial resources on. They think it works – or at least that it matters. Presidents' emphasis on administrative direction helps explain how they have moved from "imperiled" (as Gerald Ford claimed) back towards imperial – and how they have learned to maneuver in such a way as to make the office increasingly unlikely to be imperiled again. The future of presidential power will be rooted in the administrative presidency.

REFERENCES

[1] Francis E. Rourke, "Whose Bureaucracy Is This, Anyway?: Congress, the President, and Public Administration," *PS: Political Science and Politics* 26 (December 1993), 687.

[2] Scalia, dissenting opinion in *Morrison v. Olson*, 487 U.S. 654 (1988), emphasis added.

[3] Quoted in Jane Mayer, "The Hidden Power: The Legal Mind behind the White House's War on Terror," *The New Yorker* (July 3, 2006); and see Jack Goldsmith, *The Terror Presidency* (New York: W.W. Norton, 2007), 124-25.

[4] Steven G. Calabresi and Christopher S. Yoo, *The Unitary Executive: Presidential Power from Washington to Bush* (New Haven, CT: Yale University Press, 2008).

[5] Thomas Hammond and Jack Knott, "Who Controls the Bureaucracy? Presidential Power, Congressional Dominance, Legal Constraints and Bureaucratic Autonomy in a Model of Multi-Institutional Policy Making," *Journal of Law, Economics, and Organization* 12:1 (1996): 119-66.

[6] *New York Trust Co. v. Eisner*, 256 US 345 (1921).

[7] Elena Kagan, "Presidential Administration," *Harvard Law Review* 114 (June 2001): 2245-2385.

[8] See Richard Neustadt's (p. 150) definition in (and of) *Presidential Power*: "governmental power… is influence of an effective sort on the behavior of men actually involved in making public policy and carrying it out." Earlier he notes (p. 4) that "not action as an outcome but his impact on the outcome is the measure of the man." *Presidential Power and the Modern Presidents* (New York: Free Press, 1990).

[9] Richard P. Nathan, *The Administrative Presidency* (New York: Macmillan, 1983).

[10] Richard P. Nathan, *The Plot That Failed: Nixon and the Administrative Presidency* (New York: Wiley, 1975).

[11] Andrew Rudalevige, *The New Imperial Presidency* (Ann Arbor: University of Michigan Press, 2005), 19-24.

[12] See http://press-pubs.uchicago.edu/founders/documents/a2_2_1s13.html [accessed October 13, 2009].

[13] Dissent to *Myers v. U.S.*, 272 U.S. 52 (1926), at 118.

[14] David Gray Adler and Michael Genovese, "Introduction," in Adler and Genovese, eds., *The Presidency and the Law: The Clinton Legacy* (Lawrence: University Press of Kansas, 2002), xxii.

[15] Rudalevige, *New Imperial Presidency*; Arthur M. Schlesinger, Jr., *The Imperial Presidency* (Boston: Houghton Mifflin, 1973); James Sundquist, *The Decline and Resurgence of Congress* (Washington: Brookings, 1982).

[16] Figures from Paul C. Light, as reported in Christopher Lee, "Big Government Gets Bigger," *Washington Post*, October 6, 2006, A21.

[17] Quoted in Mike Allen, "Bush to Change Economic Team," *Washington Post*, November 29, 2004, A1; see also Dana Milbank, "Bush Seeks to Rule the Bureaucracy: Appointments Aim at White House Control," *Washington Post*, November 22, 2004, A4. More generally see David E. Lewis, *The Politics of Presidential Appointments* (Princeton: Princeton University Press, 2008); Thomas J. Weko, *The Politicizing Presidency: The White House Personnel Office, 1948-1994* (Lawrence: University Press of Kansas, 1994).

[18] Nathan, *Administrative Presidency*, 82.

[19] See below or, more systematically, George A. Krause, "Organizational Complexity and Coordination Dilemmas in U.S. Executive Politics," *Presidential Studies Quarterly* 39 (March 2009): 74-88.

[20] Theodore B. Olson, et al., Brief for the Petitioners, *Cheney v. U.S. District Court for the District of Columbia*, U.S. Supreme Court case 03-475, April 2004, pp. 12-13. For a summary see Linda Greenhouse, "Administration Says 'Zone of Autonomy' Justifies Its Secrecy on Energy Task Force," *New York Times*, April 25, 2004.

[21] Rudalevige, *New Imperial Presidency*.

[22] Memo to the President, "The Second Administration Team: A Concept," 1972, Frederick Malek papers, Hoover Institution, Stanford, CA. Malek was Nixon's personnel czar and deputy director of the OMB.

[23] Rudalevige, *New Imperial Presidency*, 63-65.

[24] "Second Administration Team," p. 6.

[25] Haldeman notes on Jerry Jones to President, "Department of Commerce," memo of 30 January 1973; Malek to Haldeman, "Assistant Secretary for Administration/Tony Turner," memo of 2 February 1973. Both, along with the various progress reports, in Nixon Presidential Materials Project (NPMP), White House Special Files, H.R. Haldeman alpha files, Box 172, *Reorganization: Departments and Agencies I*.

[26] Martin Anderson, *Revolution: The Reagan Legacy*, expanded ed. (Stanford: Hoover Institution Press, 1990), 195; Frederic V. Malek, *Washington's Hidden Tragedy: The Failure to Make Government Work* (New York: Free Press, 1978).

[27] Nixon, "Statement on Executive Privilege," *Public Papers of the President* (March 12, 1973).

[28] Hearings before the Senate Subcommittee on Intergovernmental Relations, "Executive Privilege, Secrecy in Government, Freedom of Information," 93rd Congress, 1st session, April 10, 1973, Volume I, 20, 45, 51.

[29] Louis Fisher, *Congressional Abdication on War and Spending* (College Station: Texas AandM Press, 2000), 116; Schlesinger, *Imperial Presidency*, 239.

[30] *Local 2677 v. Phillips*, 358 F. Supp. 60 (1973).

[31] Nixon, "Statement on Signing the Military Appropriations Authorization Bill," *Public Papers of the President* (November 17, 1971). Two years later, in his veto of the War Powers Resolution (WPR), Nixon argued that its restrictions were "both unconstitutional and dangerous."

[32] Nathan, *Plot That Failed*, 93.

[33] Edwin Meese, III, *With Reagan: The Inside Story* (Washington: Regnery, 1992), 322.

[34] Dwight Ink, "Executive Branch Reorganization," 2 December 1980, National Archives (NARA), Record Group (RG) 51, Deputy Director's Subject Files: Ed Harper, 1981-82, Box 3, Reorganization.

[35] Weko, *The Politicizing Presidency*, 89.

[36] Anderson, *Revolution*, 193-205.

[37] Meese quoted in Dick Kirschten, "White House Strategy," *National Journal* (February 21, 1981); see also Robert Pear, "Ouster of All Inspectors General by Reagan Called Political Move," *New York Times*, February 3, 1981; Steven R. Weisman, "Reagan Moves Fast to Swear In Staff and Drop Holdovers," *New York Times*, January 22, 1981; Lewis, *The Politics of Presidential Appointments*; David A. Yalof, *Pursuit of Justices: Presidential Politics and the Selection of Supreme Court Nominees* (Chicago: University of Chicago Press, 1999), Ch. 6; Anderson, *Revolution*, 197.

[38] Dennis Thomas memo to Don Regan, "Secretary of HHS," 25 October 1985, Reagan Library (RRL), W. Dennis Thomas papers, Box 7, Regan Memorandum July-Dec 1985 (2 of 2).

[39] "PPO Non-Career Appointment Form," 18 November 1985, RRL, Presidential Personnel, Office of – Records, Box 18576, Alito Jr., Samuel A..

[40] Don Moran to Ed Harper, no title, 26 December 1981, NARA, RG 51, Deputy Director's Subject Files: Ed Harper, 1981-82, Box 3, Reorganization.

[41] See Anderson, *Revolution*, 246-248, who again discusses Nixon as an object lesson.

[42] Harper note on Don Moran to Stockman, "Summary of Agreements Reached at Budget Working Group Meeting with Secretary-Designate Bell," 27 January 1981, NARA, RG 51, Deputy Director's Subject Files: Ed Harper, 1981-82, Box 1, Budget Working Group Meetings.

[43] Lawrence Kudlow to Ed Harper, "Talking Points," 8 February 1982, NARA, RG 51, Deputy Director's Subject Files: Ed Harper, 1981-82, Box 1, Budget (general).

[44] Reagan went so far as to pre-emptively appoint OMB's Gerald Riso to this position in mid-1987. See "Status of Management Reviews – FY86 Budget," 12 November 1984, NARA, RG 51, OMB Director's Office File, 1981-88, Box 3, Management/Budget Presentations: March - December 1984; on the CFO, see folder entitled Chief Financial Officer, NARA, RG 51, Office of the Director: Deputy Director Joseph R. Wright, 1981-87, Box 1.

[45] Quote from "*Status of Management Reviews – FY86 Budget*," 12 November 1984, ibid.

[46] James C. Miller III to Ed Harper, memo of 27 January 1981, NARA, RG-51, Deputy Director's Subject Files: Ed Harper, 1981-82, Box 3, Regulatory Relief.

[47] Miller to Ed Harper, memo of 10 September 1981, NARA, RG-51, Deputy Director's Subject Files: Ed Harper, 1981-82, Box 3, Regulatory Relief.

[48] Joseph R. Wright, Jr, to Edwin Meese III, "Run on E.O. 12291," 3 October 1983, RRL, White House Office of Records Management Subject Files, FG 006-11 (OMB).

[49] Phillip J. Cooper, *By Order of the President: The Use and Abuse of Executive Direct Action* (Lawrence: University Press of Kansas, 2002), 201.

[50] Samuel A. Alito, Jr, to Litigation Strategy Working Group, "Using Presidential Signing Statement to Make Fuller Use of the President's Constitutionally Assigned Role in the

Process of Enacting Law," NARA, RG 60, Files of Stephen Galebach, Box 6, SG/Litigation Strategy Working Group.

[51] That is, Reagan's Office of Legal Counsel in DOJ. Jess Bravin, "Judge Alito's View of the Presidency: Expansive Powers," *Wall Street Journal* (January 5, 2006): A1.

[52] Smith to the President, "Congressional Vetoes," 5 March 1981, RRL, Papers of Michael Uhlmann, Box 3, Legislative Veto (3 of 7); on the other side see Stockman comments on Ed Harper to Stockman, "Legislative Veto," 21 February 1981, RRL, Papers of Martin Anderson, Box 4, Staffing Memorandums, February 1981 (1).

[53] Jeffrey Rosen, "Power of One," *New Republic* (July 24, 2006).

[54] Cooper, *Order of the President*, 204-05

[55] Quoted in Mark Rozell, *Executive Privilege: Presidential Power, Secrecy, and Accountability*, 2nd rev. ed. (Lawrence: University Press of Kansas, 2002), 98.

[56] Richard F. Grimmett, *The War Powers Resolution: After Thirty Years*. CRS Report RL32267 (Washington: Congressional Research Service, March 2004).

[57] Most notably, three dozen U.S. sailors were killed by an Iraqi missile on the *USS Stark* in May 1987 and a civilian Iranian airliner was mistakenly downed by the *USS Vincennes* in July 1988.

[58] Reagan, "Statement Upon Signing Multinational Force in Lebanon Resolution," *Public Papers of the President* (October 12, 1983).

[59] Lawrence Walsh, *Final Report of the Independent Counsel for Iran-Contra Matters* (Washington, D.C.: Government Printing Office, 1993).

[60] "President Bush Holds Press Conference," Office of the White House Press Secretary (March 13, 2002).

[61] James P. Pfiffner, "The First MBA President: The Public Administration Legacy of George W. Bush," *Public Administration Review* (January/February 2007); Andrew Rudalevige, "'The Decider': Issue Management in the Bush White House," in Colin Campbell, Bert A. Rockman, and Andrew Rudalevige, eds., *The George W. Bush Legacy* (Washington, DC: CQ Press, 2008).

[62] Pfiffner, "M.B.A. President," 31.

[63] Martha Joynt Kumar and Terry Sullivan, *The White House World: Transitions, Organization, and Office Operations* (College Station: Texas A&M Press, 2003); Charlie Savage, *Takeover*, paperback ed. (Boston: Back Bay Books, 2008); Warren P. Strobel, "Career Weapons Experts Booted by Bush Team," *Philadelphia Inquirer*, February 8, 2006, A2; Mark Thompson, Karen Tumulty, and Mike Allen, "How Many More Mike Browns Are Out There?" *Time* (September 25, 2005).

[64] Note for instance HUD Secretary Alphonso Jackson's boast that he had denied one contractor's bid after learning of his political views. Christine Perez, "HUD Secretary's Blunt Warning," *Dallas Business Journal* (May 5, 2006).

[65] Rudalevige, "The Decider," 139-45; Curtis Copeland, "Executive Order 13422: An Expansion of Presidential Influence in the Rulemaking Process," *Presidential Studies Quarterly* 37 (September 2007): 531-44.

[66] Quoted in Rebecca Adams, "Lame Duck or Leapfrog?" *CQ Weekly* (February 12, 2007), 450.

[67] Barton Gellman, *Angler: The Cheney Vice Presidency* (New York: Penguin, 2008), especially Ch. 8; James Glanz, "At the Center of the Storm Over Bush and Science," *New York Times*, March 30, 2004; Andrew Revkin, "A Young Bush Appointee Resigns

His Post at NASA," *New York Times*, February 8, 2006; Christopher Lee, "Scientists Report Political Interference," *Washington Post*, April 24, 2008; Michael Hawthorne, "EPA Official Ousted While Fighting Dow," *Chicago Tribune*, May 2, 2008; Felicity Barringer, "White House Refused to Open Pollutants E-mail," *New York Times*, June 25, 2008.

[68] See James P. Pfiffner, *Power Play: The Bush Presidency and the Constitution* (Washington, DC: Brookings, 2008); John Yoo, *War by Other Means* (New York: Atlantic, 2005); Mayer, "The Hidden Power"; Gellman, *Angler*.

[69] U.S. Department of Justice, *Legal Authorities Supporting the Activities of the National Security Agency Described by the President (*January 19, 2006).

[70] Working Group Report on Detainee Interrogations in the Global War on Terrorism: Assessment of Legal, Historical, Policy, and Operational Considerations, U.S. Department of Defense, April 4, 2003, p. 21 and Section III generally. See Jane Mayer, *The Dark Side* (New York: Doubleday, 2008); Karen Greenberg and Joshua Dratel, eds., *The Torture Memos* (New York: Cambridge University Press, 2005), provide a useful compilation of similar memos.

[71] Bush, "President's Statement on Signing of H.R. 2863," Office of the White House Press Secretary (December 30, 2005).

[72] This count is from Prof. Christopher Kelley: see http://www.users.muohio.edu/kelleycs/ [accessed October 12, 2009]. See also Phillip Cooper, "George W. Bush, Edgar Allen Poe, and the Use and Abuse of Presidential Signing Statements," *Presidential Studies Quarterly* 35 (September 2005): 512-32; Rosen, "Power of One."

[73] Rudalevige, *New Imperial Presidency*, 189-92, 237-40.

[74] Bush, "President Bush Nominates Rob Portman as OMB Director…," Office of the White House Press Secretary (April 18, 2006).

[75] Kagan in "Presidential Administration" argues that this "expanded dramatically during the Clinton years, making the regulatory activity of the executive branch agencies more and more an extension of the President's own policy and political agenda" (p. 2248).

[76] Obama, "Transparency and Open Government," Office of the White House Press Secretary (January 21, 2009).

[77] Charlie Savage, "Barack Obama's Q and A," *Boston Globe*, December 20, 2007; and see Obama, "Presidential Signing Statements," Office of the White House Press Secretary (March 9, 2009).

[78] Kenneth T. Walsh, "The Cheney Factor," *U.S. News and World Report* (January 23, 2006): 48; Obama, "Presidential Signing Statements."

[79] Executive Order 13491, Section 3(c).

[80] Quoted in David Nather, "New Handshake, Same Grip," *CQ Weekly* (December 17, 2007), 3702.

[81] Kagan, "Presidential Administration," 2250.

[82] John Schwartz, "Obama Backs Off a Reversal on Secrets," *New York Times*, February 9, 2009, A12.

[83] Obama, "Remarks by the President on National Security," Office of the White House Press Secretary (May 21, 2009); Dafna Linzer and Peter Finn, "White House Weighs Order on Detention," *Washington Post*, June 27, 2009; Peter Baker, "Obama to Use Current Law to Support Detentions," *New York Times*, September 23, 2009.

[84] For one attempt to measure this impact, see Government Accountability Office, *Presidential Signing Statements: Agency Implementation of Selected Provisions of Law*, GAO-08-553T (March 11, 2008).

[85] See Krause, "Organizational Complexity"; David E. Lewis, "Revisiting the Administrative Presidency: Policy, Patronage, and Agency Competence," *Presidential Studies Quarterly* 39 (March 2009): 60-73.

PART III:

THE FUTURE OF PRESIDENTIAL POWER

In: President or King?
Editor: Meena Bose, pp. 143-155 ISBN: 978-1-61324-655-9

HARM TO THE NATION FROM EXCESSIVE EXECUTIVE BRANCH SECRECY

Frederick A. O. Schwarz, Jr.

ABSTRACT

For decades, presidential power has been on the rise. This article asserts that excessive executive branch secrecy has been a central root cause. Excessive secrecy has both contributed to the growth of presidential power and has added to its potential for harm.

The article touches upon harms from overclassification and from claims of executive privilege and state secrets. It also presents four "what if" questions from the Bush (II), Kennedy, Eisenhower, and Truman Administrations about how American history might have been changed (for the better) if crucial secrets had been revealed.

But the heart of the paper is its analysis of how the shaping of secret decisions by presidents listening only to a small coterie of like-minded advisors increases the likelihood of unwise, or even abusive, decisions. Examples discussed are decisions to use torture (Bush II); expand the domestic jurisdiction of the FBI (FDR); have the CIA engage in covert action (Truman); and Iran/Contra (Reagan).

INTRODUCTION

For decades, for many reasons, presidential power has been on the rise.

A central root cause has been excessive secrecy, which both contributes to the growth of presidential power, and adds to its potential for harm.

Secrecy is seductive. Excessive secrecy stifles debate. It increases the chance of unwise policy decisions. It neuters checks and balances. It smothers the popular judgment that gives life to democracy.

Broadly speaking, there are two aspects of excessive executive branch secrecy. The first is close-to-the-vest decision-making by presidents, aided by small coteries of like-minded executive branch officials, without meaningful debate or discussion. The second is the secrecy stamp that blinds outsiders to documents, coupled with claims of privilege — for example, executive privilege and "state secrets" — that stitch up the lips of witnesses, and fend off checks by Congress or the courts.

While both aspects of excessive secrecy are important, and both often cause harm, the vast mountain ranges of classified documents get more attention. But excessive secrecy in shaping government policy merits greater — or at least equal — attention. Indeed, it probably causes more harm. In this paper, I explore ways in which decisions shaped and implemented in secret have led to harmful policy choices and abuses of executive power.

Some Perspectives on the Growth of Presidential Power

Throughout American history, crises have always made it tempting to ignore the wise restraints that keep us free. From the Founding to the 1940s, these actions largely took place in public. Thus, the Alien and Sedition Acts of 1798, the Palmer Raids in 1919, and the herding of Japanese-Americans into concentration camps early in World War II, however wrong, were all public acts. So too was Lincoln's unilateral suspension of habeas corpus.

But starting in the late 1940s with the Cold War, and more recently in reaction to the murders of 9/11, more and more questionable or improper executive actions have been shaped in secret without meaningful debate. Their implementation as well has all too often been hidden from the public, and even from Congress. The number of documents that have been stamped secret has also grown exponentially, particularly in the last eight years.

The growth of executive secrecy is not a partisan phenomenon. Presidents from both parties have used their powers to foster excessive secrecy, thereby undermining the Constitution's checks and balances.

The work of the Church Committee illustrates this point. Established in the wake of Watergate, the Committee was expected by some merely to elaborate upon the excesses of Richard Nixon. Nixon had just resigned in disgrace, with the coup de grâce coming from the Supreme Court lifting the lid upon his secret tapes of talks with top advisors in the White House. [1] These talks included Nixon's instructions to use the CIA, and a "national security" claim, to stymie the FBI's Watergate investigation. But, in my opinion, one of the signal accomplishments of the Church Committee was to show that all presidents from Franklin Delano Roosevelt through Richard Milhous Nixon had abused their secret powers. A key tool was that they, and their security agencies, had kept much of the truth secret from the American public, usually from Congress, and often from rival government agencies.

All of these presidents, and the intelligence officials who carried forward their plans or desires, generally thought they were serving the nation's needs. The same is true, I believe, for the Bush/Cheney Administration. During the Cold War, and in response to 9/11 and other terror attacks, America faced real dangers. But while danger often drove decisions, and presidents and intelligence officials often did much good, danger does not automatically make decisions wise. And shaping decisions by a small coterie of like-minded officials increases the chance of unwise decisions by reducing thoughtful consideration. Moreover, as Justice Louis Brandeis warned, in a somewhat narrower context, often the "greatest dangers to liberty lurk in insidious encroachment by men of zeal, well meaning, but without understanding." [2]

WHY DO WE CARE?

Everybody who knows modern American government knows there is far too much secrecy. Lee Hamilton, as Vice Chair of the 9/11 Commission, for example, estimated that 70 percent of the classified information he saw was "needlessly classified." Some estimates are lower; some are higher; but all agree there is vast over-classification. [3]

My own observation in the mid 1970s as Chief Counsel for the Senate's Church Committee was more qualitative than quantitative. While there were obviously legitimate secrets that must be respected and protected, [4] it seemed to me that far too much was kept secret not to *protect America,* but to keep embarrassing and improper information *from Americans.* Of course, that conclusion might be expected in the context of an investigation mandated by the Senate to focus on "the extent, if any, of illegal, improper or unethical activities," an investigation which, in fact, uncovered vast amounts of such activities. [5]

But while valid then, and valid now, my observation three decades ago was too narrow. For the seduction of secrecy sinks much deeper than hiding impropriety or embarrassment. Secrecy is a tool of power. Human nature pushes powerful people toward secrecy. It limits challenges. And pesky questions. It seems easier. And faster. It fosters illusions of grandeur.

A LITTLE HISTORY

This has been forever so. At the dawn of history, leaders controlled the spigots of information from the gods to the people. [6] Later, Popes forbade translation of the Bible into vernacular languages. They feared that versions of the Bible written in the peoples' language, and not in Latin — which neither Moses nor Jesus had spoken — might lead to challenges to Church authority.

Later, secrecy supported the sway of monarchs, who announced "L'état, c'est moi," [Louis XIV of France], and who claimed the prerogative to ignore laws of Parliament, [the Stuart Kings of England]. Thus, England's King James I ordered the Speaker of the House of Commons "to acquaint that house with our pleasure that none therein shall presume to meddle with anything concerning our government or mysteries of State." [7] In pre-revolutionary France, the "absolute authority of the King was bolstered by a practice of strict secrecy in public affairs." The "law of silence" prohibited public discussion of matters of state. Supportive French theorists warned that, with publicity, the King's plans "'would be as effective as an exploded mine'." [8]

The Founders of this nation, however, rejected monarchical notions that power was best exercised in secret.

In the Declaration of Independence, Jefferson began by saying that "a decent respect to the opinions of mankind requires that they [the united [sic] States] should declare the causes which impel them to the separation." Jefferson was using openness to help prove the case for independence was just. But, nonetheless, it stands as a recognition that openness in explaining decisions is a bedrock principle.

The Founders had a sophisticated understanding of human nature. They knew that power that is unchecked and unchallenged is less likely to be wisely exercised. Decisions made in secret without popular information are more likely to be bad decisions. As James Madison put it:

> "[A] popular government, without popular information, or the means of acquiring it, is but a prologue to a Farce or a Tragedy; or, perhaps both. Knowledge will forever govern ignorance. And a people who mean to be their own governors, must arm themselves with the power which knowledge gives." [9]

In the Federalist Papers, supporting ratification of the Constitution, Madison made his most powerful arguments about human nature and its implications for government and society. Thus, as Madison explained in the 51st Federalist, because people are not "angels," government must, among other things, "control itself." But, if secrecy blinds Congress, and the people, to the truth, "control" is impossible.

In the 10th Federalist, Madison made a revolutionary argument. Before our Constitution, conventional wisdom had been that republics could thrive only when the polity was small. (As an extreme example, Aristotle had argued that citizens could not manage government unless all citizens knew one another. [10]) Madison turned all this upside down, arguing that the United States' great size would actually mean more diverse voices would debate public policy issues. And this would reduce the risk of a single "faction" adopting oppressive or unwise measures. A corollary to this principle is that when important policy decisions are shaped in secret by presidents, listening only to a narrow coterie of like-minded aides, the risk of unwise, or even oppressive, decisions is magnified.

Madison was also, however, a leading advocate of secrecy at the Convention that wrote our Constitution. And opponents of excessive secrecy must wrestle with that example. Meeting for four months in Philadelphia during the spring and summer of 1787, the delegates at the outset passed a "Secrecy Rule" not to let a whisper of their deliberations leak out. [11] As Madison explained to Thomas Jefferson, who was away serving as Ambassador in Paris, the Secrecy Rule was "thought expedient" to "secure unbiased discussion within doors and to prevent misconceptions and misconstructions without." [12] Jefferson's reaction, in a letter to John Adams, was to express sorrow at the "abominable" "tying up of tongues." This, he wrote, could be explained only by "the innocence of their intentions, and ignorance of the value of public discussions." [13] Some Convention members criticized the Secrecy Rule. But most either agreed or kept quiet.

At the Convention, George Washington, Convention Chair, and the young nation's most revered, respected — and feared — leader, scared the members about leaks. After one (unknown) delegate left on the floor a copy of propositions before the Convention, Washington reprimanded the delegate for his carelessness:

> "'I must entreat gentlemen to be more careful, lest our transactions get into the newspapers, and disturb the public repose by premature speculations. I know not whose paper it is, but there it is (throwing it down on the table), let him who owns it take it.' At the same time, he bowed, picked up his hat, and quitted the room with a dignity so severe that every person seemed alarmed .... It is something remarkable that no person ever owned the paper'." [14]

Proponents of secrecy rely on the Secrecy Rule at the hallowed Constitutional Convention. But even though the Constitution and our Founding Fathers generally hold a sacred place in America, the tale of the 1787 Constitutional Convention does not make a broad case for secrecy. For one thing, many of the harmful handmaidens of secret decision-making were absent:

- The participants in the Convention were not a narrow coterie of like-minded thinkers. They had different interests. There were real debates. There were shifting coalitions.
- The decisions of the Convention were publicly released as soon as the document had been agreed upon.
- Before the proposed new Constitution could go into effect it was publicly, and vigorously, debated in ratification campaigns and conventions in the states.

Moreover, all subsequent constitutional amendments have been formulated and extensively debated in public. These included the Civil War Amendments which, as Abraham Lincoln prophesized in the Gettysburg Address, gave rise to "a new birth of freedom." And the Amendment granting the right of women to vote. The fact that these momentous developments could occur in broad sunlight casts doubt upon any assumption that public scrutiny of such deliberations stymies progress.

In any event, the secrecy surrounding the Constitutional Convention at most supports the argument that there are some circumstances where meetings considering public policy issues ought not be held in the open. [15] This article, however, is focused on the case against keeping major public policy decisions secret after they have been made, and on the case against secret decision-making by narrow coteries of like-minded officials.

Three Examples of Harm through Secretive Decision-Making by Small Coteries of Like-Minded Officials

In widening the scope of the power of both the FBI in the 1930s and the CIA in the 1940s, presidents made a conscious decision to hide these expansions from the American public, and even from Congress. Thus, leading up to World War II, Franklin Roosevelt authorized the FBI to go beyond investigating "conduct forbidden by the laws of the United States" by casually throwing in the amorphous term "subversion." In ordering the Bureau to expand its domestic security role, Roosevelt agreed with Bureau Director J. Edgar Hoover that it was "imperative" to proceed "with the utmost degree of secrecy. . . to avoid criticism or objections." Therefore, the expansion was not revealed — even to Congress. [16]

As it turned out, over the following decades, the vague term "subversion" opened the door to many secret FBI misdeeds. Because the expansion was blessed in secret, neither Congress nor the public had a chance to debate the issues. Nor was Congress alerted to the importance of watching how such an open-ended grant of authority to the Bureau was in fact exercised. It awaited the Church Committee almost forty years later to reveal how much had gone wrong. [17]

The story is similar for the CIA. In creating the CIA, the 1947 National Security Act emphasized coordination and evaluation of intelligence. It did not even mention covert action. However, a year later, the National Security Council secretly authorized the CIA to engage in covert action. Neither Congress, nor the public, had any chance to debate this transformative change, or to consider what covert tactics might be consistent with the nation's character. Once again, much was done that seemed a success, but turned out to cause lasting harm to America. One example is the 1953 CIA-backed overthrow of Mohammad Mossadegh, the Prime Minister of Iran's democratic (though economically radical) government.

Jumping ahead to the Bush/Cheney Administration's secret decision to authorize torture, we now know a lot about the flawed way in which that decision was reached. An opinion by John Yoo, a deputy in the Justice Department's Office of Legal Counsel, was kept secret within the Justice Department, bypassing its normal review process. It was kept secret from Congress and the public even though it purported to say what the law was. [18] When the opinion was revealed later, it was a professional embarrassment. [19]

Moreover, the White House decided to open the door to torture without consulting key government officials in the Department of State and the military. Those shut out could have made the case that adopting torture would weaken America with its allies, strengthen its enemies, and risk harm to our soldiers or CIA agents when they were captured. Those who were shut out could have reminded the "deciders" that, starting with George Washington, the United States had led the way on restricting coercion of prisoners of war. [20]

Those who were shut out could have protested our use of waterboarding by pointing out that after World War II, the United States had prosecuted Japanese soldiers as war criminals for using waterboarding on American prisoners. And those who were shut out could have shown that many other techniques authorized by the Bush/Cheney Administration were copied from techniques used *against* American prisoners in the Korean War.

Most importantly, the secrecy surrounding the descent to torture shut out any debate about American values within the White House, the Congress, and the country.

Four "What If" Questions

Might American history might have changed (for the better) if certain crucial secrets had been revealed? A quick look at a secret from four administrations — those of Bush II, Kennedy, Eisenhower and Truman — provides food for thought. In each case, there are additional complexities to the story. And plausible arguments why secrecy was appropriate could be made. But the case in favor of openness simply does not get made.

In August 2001, President George W. Bush was vacationing at his Crawford, Texas, ranch. Nevertheless, the CIA regularly gave him the President's Daily Brief (or PDB) containing information the CIA regarded as particularly important. On August 6, the CIA's PDB was headlined: "Bin Laden Determined to Strike at U.S." Thirty-six days later, on September 11, Bin Laden did strike at the U.S., slaughtering almost 3,000 innocents, by crashing two airplanes into the World Trade Center in New York City, a third into the Pentagon in Virginia, and a fourth plane heading for the Capital, but crashing into a Pennsylvania field because of the bravery of its passengers.

The PDB was stamped "Top Secret" "For the President Only." It did not see the light of day until about three years later, when, over the strident protests of the Administration, it was obtained and publicly released by the 9/11 Commission.

Might the murders of 9/11 have been averted if the Bin Laden PDB had been released in August, 2001?

In October 1962, President John F. Kennedy and his closest advisors wrestled with the Cuban Missile Crisis, a crisis that brought the world its closest to nuclear Armageddon. The Soviet Union had secretly sneaked missiles into Cuba, ninety miles off the coast of Florida. After thirteen tense days, Nikita Khrushchev, Chairman of the Supreme Soviet, backed down. The missiles were removed from Cuba.

President Kennedy was a hero for America — and for the planet. He was lionized for his toughness, as well as for his subtlety in ignoring a threatening, bellicose letter from Chairman Khrushchev and instead replying to an earlier letter that seemed to seek a solution. But it was toughness that produced the most enduring metaphor of the crisis: Secretary of State Dean Rusk summed up by boasting: "we were eyeball to eyeball, and the other fellow just blinked."

The only problem with glorification of JFK's toughness is that it left out a secret deal we made with the Soviets. The President, through a secret visit by his brother, Robert, to the Soviet Ambassador in Washington, had made clear that if the Soviets withdrew their nuclear missiles from Cuba, we would shortly thereafter withdraw *our* nuclear missiles sitting in Turkey just across the Soviet border. But the Soviets had to agree to keep this understanding secret. And the Administration concealed it from the American public. Meanwhile, publicity emphasized the President's toughness.

Would President Lyndon Johnson have felt freer to make a deal in Vietnam if the memory of America's most recent harrowing crisis, as handled by his martyred predecessor, had been that both sides gave, rather than simply that the other side blinked?

In 1954, with our nation in the grip of a Cold War with the Soviet Union, a high-level special Commission advised President Dwight Eisenhower in a "Top Secret" report that, among other things, the Soviets were making "spectacular progress" economically — so much so that they would surpass the United States in the foreseeable future. This contributed to massive Cold War spending and questionable covert actions.

Had the report been made public, its economic analysis would have been exposed to critiques by knowledgeable experts on, and observant visitors to, the Soviet Union. Would this have lessened our spending or altered our tactics?

Early in World War II, President Franklin Roosevelt accepted the advice of Albert Einstein and other scientists that the vast power of atomic energy could be harnessed in a bomb of unprecedented power. And that Nazi Germany also had scientists capable of harnessing the awesome power of atoms. Recognizing the need to develop the bomb, and to stay ahead of Nazi Germany, Roosevelt initiated the super-secret Manhattan Project.

Roosevelt died in April 1945. Vice President Harry Truman became President. Truman had previously known next to nothing about the super-secret bomb.

On May 7, 1945, shortly after Truman was sworn in, Germany surrendered. In July, a secret test of the atomic bomb in the remote Nevada desert proved that our bomb worked and had stupendous power. The German surrender was no reason to relax the secrecy of bomb-making technology. But with the only threat of use of an atomic bomb against America gone, should Truman, after knowing that our bomb worked, and before using the bomb against the Japanese in early August 1945, have revealed the bomb's existence, and its massive, frightening power? Might this have led to the end of the war without the overwhelming loss of civilian life in Hiroshima and Nagasaki? And would doing this have strengthened America's moral position even if use of the bomb had nonetheless proved necessary?

Suffice it to say here that the answers are not simple. There are, in each case, plausible arguments why the secrets should have been kept secret. But the key problem is that the case in favor of openness never gets made. The culture of secrecy is so powerful that it suffocates debate, increases the risk of error, and saps our democracy.

SOME OF THE HARMS OF SECRECY IN SHAPING DECISIONS

This section emphasizes harm in shaping decisions by small groups of Executive Branch officials. It then moves to some of the more general harms caused by excessive secrecy.

Within the White House, presidents are often tempted to listen only to small numbers of like-minded advisors. As pointed out above, the Bush/Cheney Administration's decision to opt for "enhanced interrogation" tactics — which, without euphemism, were torture — was reached without a chance for high-ranking expert voices from the military and the State Department to be heard. Four decades earlier, James C. Thomson, Jr., who worked in the White House and the State Department from 1961 to 1966 asked "How Could Vietnam Happen?" A "central question at the heart of the policy process" was "where were the experts, the doubters, and the dissenters?" Thomson's answer included:

> [A] recurrent and increasingly important factor in the decision-making process was *the banishment of real expertise*. Here the underlying cause was the 'closed politics' of policy-making as issues become hot: the more sensitive the issue, and the higher it rises in the bureaucracy, the more completely the experts are excluded while the harassed senior generalists take over (that is, the Secretaries, Undersecretaries, and Presidential Assistants). The frantic skimming of briefing papers in the back seats of limousines is no substitute for the presence of specialists; furthermore, in times of crisis such papers are deemed 'too sensitive' even for review by the specialists." [21]

The pages of American history are filled with other examples of where decisions shaped in secret, without debate, have harmed the nation, as well as damaging the presidents who made them. Two more examples:

- Frustrated by the Supreme Court and flush with his huge electoral success, FDR came up with his "court-packing" plan without talking to Congress or even to his own most savvy White House advisors. The plan was overwhelmingly rejected by members of Congress of both parties, and undermined the Administration's momentum, though it may have influenced the Court.
- Ronald Reagan's Administration put the final touches on Iran/Contra in meetings that excluded the Secretaries of State and Defense. Iran/Contra caused a constitutional crisis, embarrassed Reagan, and hurt his popularity. It required him to cast out his White House team.

Outside the White House, but still within the executive branch, the culture of secrecy often harmfully inhibits information flows between agencies or even within agencies. One example is that leading up to the failed Bay of Pigs invasion of Cuba in 1961, the CIA's covert action wing did not tell the Cuba experts in the CIA's Intelligence Division about the plans. Had they done so, it is likely the Intelligence Division's experts would have said the hopes of an uprising within Cuba were fanciful. [22]

A more recent example, emphasized by the 9/11 Report, is that the CIA, the FBI and the State Department did not effectively share information about two known terrorists who later came to the United States and participated in the 9/11 hijacking. Had they done so, they should have been put under surveillance or apprehended. This could have disrupted Bin Laden's plan.

Of course, the traditional jealousies and rivalries between the CIA's covert action and intelligence wings, and between the FBI and the CIA, are important factors in these events. As Senator Moynihan elaborated in his book *Secrecy*, "owning" information is power. [23] But, for that very reason, these stories are best seen as part of the powerful culture (or cult) of secrecy, a culture that constantly leads to decisions to keep information too close to the vest.

More General Harms from Excessive Secrecy

That culture of secrecy underlies decisions by the executive branch to withhold information from Congress and from the people. To apply the title of this special issue, that tendency has been a major root cause of our moving the presidency farther and farther away from the "original" ideas of our Constitution, and more and more toward the monarchical trappings that we fought the Revolution to shed.

While a detailed exploration of the issue is beyond the scope of this paper, it should be briefly noted that the other putatively "co-equal" branches of government have not been free from fault in the rise of executive secrecy and power. Congress has let its power "slip between its fingers." In the last few decades, it has lost sight of the role that James Madison envisaged of defending its own institutional prerogatives. Instead, it has lapsed into divisive partisanship. This, plus fear cleverly fomented by the White House, has led, among other things, to a far too ready acceptance of secrecy claims. The courts as well have generally shied away from their constitutional obligation to independently evaluate the executive branch's secrecy claims.

At bottom, our culture of secrecy, and the undue deference to the executive that both enables and flows from that culture, have weakened our democracy. As Nicholas Katzenbach, former Attorney General and Deputy Secretary of State, noted more than three decades ago:

> "Those responsible for the creation and execution of our foreign policy must be responsive to public attitudes and cannot seek to repress dissent and disagreement, conceal the truth from the public, or violate the letter and the spirit of the Constitution. There is no 'country' whose interests they serve apart from the people of the United States. There are no 'interests' of that country apart from the interests of its citizens. However difficult and complex our foreign policy may be, there is no license to free it from the mandates of the Constitution or the constraints of public views, interests and wants, any more than any other difficult and complex problem can be freed from the same constraints." [24]

Of course, citizens have the final checking power at the ballot box. But, to play their proper role, citizens must know what is being done by their government. Excessive secrecy by the executive branch blinds the public. Citizens themselves must "arm themselves with the power that knowledge gives." Civic literacy is a must. [25] The Constitution is necessary, but not sufficient. For "[l]iberty lies in the hearts of men and women; when it dies there, no constitution, no law, no court can save it." [26]

A Few Words about Lincoln

The title of this special issue refers to Lincoln. And 2009 was the two hundredth anniversary of his birth. What can we briefly say about Lincoln that bears upon the subject? First, on one aspect of secrecy that this paper emphasizes — decision-making by presidents who listened only to like-minded advisors and who turned a deaf ear to debate and discussion — Lincoln was exemplary in hearing all positions, as Doris Kearns Goodwin's book *Team of Rivals* illustrates. (The same can be said about President Obama.)

Second, Lincoln, at the start of the Civil War, did suspend habeas corpus, and then ignored a judicial order that, under the Constitution, only Congress has that power. But Congress was in recess and the emergency was dire. [27] Most importantly, Lincoln did not act in secret, hiding his actions from Congress and the public. Moreover, as soon as Congress was back in session, Lincoln recognized Congress' power by seeking ratification for his actions. He obtained it.

References

[1] For a critique of the lesser known part of the Court's decision that held that there should be a lasting presumption of secrecy for communications between presidents and presidential advisors, see Eric Lane, Frederick A. O. Schwarz, Jr., and Emily Berman, "Too Big A Canon in the President's Arsenal: Another Look at *United States v. Nixon*, 17 *Geo. Mason L. Rev.* (Spring 2010).

[2] See *Olmstead v. United States*, 277 U.S. 438, 479 (1928) (Brandeis, J. dissenting).

[3] For a collection of estimates of the extent of overclassification, see Testimony of Thomas Blanton, Executive Director, National Security Archive, at Hearing of the Subcommittee of the House Committee on Governmental Reform, on National Security, Emerging Threats and International Relations, May 2, 2005, at p. 110.
As Mr. Blanton's examples show, the concern for overclassification comes from members of both parties. See also, e.g., Trent Lott and Ron Wyden, "Hiding the Truth in a Cloud of Black Ink," Op. Ed, *The New York Times*, August 26, 2004, p. A27.

[4] See, e.g., Frederick A.O. Schwarz, Jr., "Intelligence Oversight: The Church Committee," in Loch Johnson, ed., *Intelligence and Accountability* (Praeger Security Intl., 2007); and "The Church Committee: Thirty Years Ago and Today," in Russell A. Miller, ed., *U.S. National Security Intelligence and Democracy*, (Routledge, 2008).

[5] S. Res. 21, 1st Resolved Clause. For summaries of the Church Committee's disclosures, see Frederick A.O. Schwarz, Jr., and Aziz Huq, *Unchecked and Unbalanced: Presidential Power in a Time of Terror* (The New Press, 2007; paperback, 2008), Chap. 2, pp. 21-49, "Revelations of the Church Committee"; and Loch K. Johnson, *A Season of Inquiry: The Senate Intelligence Investigation* (University Press of Kentucky, 1985).

[6] Robert Wright, *The Evolution of God* (Little, Brown, 2009) uses the term "divine spigot" in describing the role of Polynesian chiefs who were the "conduits through which mana [i.e., "a magical or divine power"] entered society and then trickled down the social scale to lesser folks." (Wright at p. 52, citing Raymond Frith, "The Analysis of Mana: An Empirical Approach," *Journal of the Polynesian Society*, 49: p. 491 (1940). Similarly, "Mayan kings were 'conduits through which supernatural powers were channeled into the human realm.'" And "the Egyptian [pharaoh] was 'the sole intermediary who could serve the gods and hence maintain the flow of energy into the world.'" (Wright, p. 75, citing Lynn V. Foster, *Handbook to Life in the Ancient Maya World*, Facts on File, p. 178; and Bruce G. Trigger, *Early Civilizations*, (The American University in Cairo Press, 1993), p. 102.

[7] See Ernst H. Kantorowicz, "Mysteries of State: An Absolutist Concept and Its Late Medieval Origins," *The Harvard Theological Review*, Vol. 48, No. 1 (Jan. 1955) (Published by Cambridge University Press), p. 68.

[8] See materials referenced in Alasdair Roberts, *Blacked Out: Government Secrecy in the Information Age* (Cambridge University Press, 2006), pp. 9-10.

[9] James Madison to W. T. Barry, Aug. 4, 1822, reprinted 1 *The Founders' Constitution* (Philip B. Kurland and Ralph Lerner, eds., 1987), p. 690. This quote is widely cited in many books and articles that decry excessive secrecy. But, to be fair, its purpose was not to condemn excessive secrecy, but to support enactment of a proposed Kentucky law expanding public education. Moreover, it was written in 1822, after Madison had finished his government service. (See Paul H. Gates, Jr. and Bill C. Chamberlin, "Madison Misinterpreted: Historical Presentation Skews Scholarship," 13 *Am. Journalism* 43 (1996), p. 39.)

[10] See, Aristotle, *Politics*, Benjamin Jowett transl., bk. VII, chap. 4 (Oxford, Vol. I, p. 215).

[11] For the "Secrecy Rule," see Charles Warren, *The Making of the Constitution* (Little, Brown, 1928), p. 135.

[12] Madison to Jefferson, June 6, 1787. See also Madison to James Monroe, June 10, 1787, referring to the Rule as being "prudent," which will "effectively secure the requisite freedom of discussion," and "save both the Convention and the community from a thousand erroneous and perhaps mischievous reports." Other comments about the Rule are collected in Warren, pp 134-139.

[13] Warren, p. 137.

[14] Warren, p. 139, citing an anecdote related by Major William Pierce, a delegate from Georgia.

[15] Two examples where most would say a decision-making meeting on a public matter ought not to be open are jury deliberations, and Supreme Court or other judges deliberating on how to decide. Both examples share with the Constitutional Convention an absence of some of the harmful handmaidens of secret-decision making. Thus, for both juries and judges, the arguments had previously been fully laid out in public. Moreover, in both cases, the decision is subsequently made public; and with judges their decisions are also publicly explained.

Attempting to work out principles and workable criteria to separate "bad" government secrets from "good" ones will be a part of The New Press book on government secrecy that I am writing with my colleague Elizabeth Goitein.

[16] See *Unchecked and Unbalanced,* supra, n. 5, at pp 14-17 ("Flawed Mandates, The FBI"), and see its n. 12 at p. 212, citing Church Committee Reports and memos from J. Edgar Hoover, sent to President Roosevelt by Attorney General Homer Cummings, and Cummings to Roosevelt, October 20, 1938.

[17] After the Church Committee finished its hearings and reports, I gave a speech about its work that included "General Lessons," the fifth of which was:
"Abuse thrives on secrecy. Public disclosure of matters such as the names of intelligence agents or the technological details of collection methods is, our Committee unanimously believed, inappropriate. But in the field of intelligence, secrecy was extended much further. It served to inhibit review of the basic programs and practices themselves. I believe that if the excesses had been known, the good sense of the American people would have stopped them. I am sure all those officials would not have sanctioned the programs had they known they would be exposed." (See "Intelligence Activities and the Rights of Americans," *The Record of the Association of the Bar of the City of New York*, January/February 1977, pp 43-52, at pp 50-51.)

[18] See Nicholas deB Katzenbach and Frederick A. O. Schwarz, Jr., "Release Justice's Secrets," op. ed. *The New York Times*, Nov. 20, 2007, p. A23.

[19] See, e.g., *Unchecked and Unbalanced*, n. 5 supra, at Chapters 7 and 8, passim.

[20] At the dawn of the United States, George Washington explicitly rejected using tactics of the enemy on prisoners we had captured: "Treat them with humanity, and Let them have no reason to Complain of our Copying the brutal example of the British army in their Treatment of our unfortunate brethren." Washington to Samuel Blachley Webb, New Jersey, Jan. 8, 1777, reprinted in 8 *The Papers of George Washington: Revolutionary War Series* 16 (W.W. Abbot ed., 1985). Similarly, the code (drafted by Columbia University scholar Francis Lieber) that President Lincoln approved in the Civil War forbade Union soldiers using "torture to extort confessions." Instructions for the Government of Armies of the United States in the Field, Art. 16, Apr. 24, 1863, General Orders No. 100, *available at* http://www.yale.edu/lawweb/avalon/lieber.htm. Finally, the United States was deeply involved in drafting the Geneva Conventions after World War II. (See Raymond T. Yingling and Robert W. Ginnane "The Geneva Convention of 1949," *American Journal of International Law*, Vol. 45 (1951), 407.)

[21] James C. Thomson, Jr., "How Could Vietnam Happen? — An Autopsy," *The Atlantic Monthly*, April 1968 (emphasis in original).

[22] John McCone, who took over as CIA Director after the Bay of Pigs, issued an order that thereafter relevant Intelligence Division personnel had to be informed of covert action plans. How well this worked needs to be explored. However, one indication that information sharing was hardly guaranteed is the fact that McCone himself was not informed by the CIA's covert operators about the CIA's role in ongoing plots to assassinate Cuba's Fidel Castro. (See, Church Committee, *Alleged Assassination Plots Involving Foreign Leaders*, pp. 99-108.)

[23] See Daniel Patrick Moynihan, *Secrecy: The American Experience* (Yale University Press, 1998), passim. Although Moynihan refers to "Secrecy as Regulation," p. 59, the thrust of his book is really about power, and at places he uses, or quotes others as using, the more apt power word (e.g., p. 186).

[24] Nicholas deB Katzenbach, "Foreign Policy, Public Opinion and Secrecy," *Foreign Affairs*, Vol. 52, No. 1, October 1973, p. 3.

[25] See Eric Lane and Michael Oreskes, *The Genius of America: How the Constitution Saved Our Country and Why It Can Again* (Bloomsbury, 2007), Conclusion: "We," pp. 191-221.

[26] Learned Hand, "*The Spirit of Liberty*," 1941.

[27] An angry Baltimore mob had attacked Union troops who were marching through the City. Sixteen soldiers were killed. Baltimore's Mayor ordered the destruction of railroad bridges connecting the city to the north, seeking to prevent the movement of more Union troops heading south to protect Washington from the Confederate army in Virginia.

In: President or King?
Editor: Meena Bose, pp. 157-167
ISBN: 978-1-61324-655-9

CIVIC IGNORANCE AND THE RISE OF THE PRESIDENT-KING [1]

Eric Lane

ABSTRACT

Everybody wants to be a king, to be free to do what they want. Presidents particularly want to be kings. After successfully negotiating the gauntlet of the modern presidential campaign, they arrive at the White House profoundly determined to realize their visions for the country. The framers would have expected no less. They understood all about this "monarchial" view of human nature. They designed a government to restrain it. At the White House this design of American government becomes, at least from a presidential perspective, a presidential problem. To succeed Presidents must act "unkingly." Usually they conform in one way or another to this rule, but sometimes they don't. They act in a kingly fashion. They ignore constitutional restraints and the law.

The Bush administration provides the most recent and the most expansive example. A compliant legislature and public has made this possible. Such compliance is a product of both anxiety and civic ignorance. Anxiety has been a product of 9/11 and the on-going war on terrorism. Civic ignorance has been the consequence of a school system that no longer sees its mission as teaching students, as William Galston wrote, to be willing and able "to engage in public discourse and evaluate the performance of those in office." A citizenry lacking this capacity opens the door to expanding monarchial behavior, undermining American democracy.

The challenge of accommodating a vigorous executive power within the framework of the rule of law remains formidable even eight centuries later. Consequently, whether it is seen as imperial or simply magisterial – or as "close to the people" as ambition and the media can make it – the American Presidency will never be easy to locate within our constitutional framework. . . . [T]he President like the English kings before him is a person as well as an institution; and unlike other institutions, the Presidency is led by an individual elected by the entire Nation to secure its survival, to represent it to the world, and to voice its aspiration to all the people. Thus it is only by an extraordinary triumph of constitutional imagination that the commander-in-chief is conceived as commanded by law.

Laurence Tribe [2]

Few people want to be president, but everyone wants to be a king. Writes Homer: "I . . . maintain . . . that it is no bad thing to be a king - to see one's house enriched and one's authority enhanced." [3] Or as the screen writer Mel Brooks wrote in *History of the World Part I*: "It's good to be the king." [4] We all understand this. The common proverb about being a master in one's own castle captures the sentiment. In that space, whether bedroom size or boardroom size or nation size, "you are the boss and no one can tell you what to do." [5] Being a king is about the unfettered power to do what you want, about getting your way.

This monarchial element of human nature is particularly applicable to modern presidents. Presidents want to be kings. They want to effect the "energy" Hamilton attributed to the office, [6] to be the "big" men that President Woodrow Wilson declared they all could be. [7] After successfully negotiating the gauntlet of the modern presidential campaign they arrive at the White House profoundly determined to realize their visions for the country, to fulfill their campaign promises, and to make their historical mark. Behind whatever façade they may effect, they are driven to get their way.

The framers would have expected no less. They understood all about this "monarchial" view of human nature. Over the eleven years that separated independence from the constitutional convention, they observed a new nation almost destroy itself from multiple factions clashing over multiple interests, each trying to get its way. The earlier utopian hope that Americans could be publically virtuous—capable of repressing their own self-interest for the greater good—had been dashed by factionalism, leaving a nation described by John Quincy Adams as "groaning under the intolerable burden of . . . accumulated evils." [8] Or as the historian Gordon Wood has written: the framers saw in America "mistrust, the breakdown of authority, the increase of debt, the depravity of manners, and the decline of virtue." [9]

The problem was Americans themselves. As Madison observed, the more fatal cause of the nation's crisis "lies among the people themselves." [10] Only months before the convention George Washington wrote to John Jay: "We have probably had too good an opinion of human nature in forming our confederation. . . . We must take human nature as we find it. Perfection falls not to the share of mortals." [11] As "mortals," we passionately pursue our own self-interests, thinking what is right for us is right for everyone else. Americans, like all others, "think of themselves in possession of all truth, and that whatever others differ from them it is so far error," Benjamin Franklin observed. [12] And they will act on this. Noted Alexander Hamilton more bluntly about the monarchial nature of Americans: "Men love power. . . . Give all the power to the many, they will oppress the few. Give all power to the few, they will oppress the many." [13]

To counter this aspect of human nature the framers established a system of government designed to make a virtue of the vice of self-interest. The basic details are the contents of what once was Civics 101 (more on this later). Freedom was to be preserved first through representation to assure the nation's multiple interests (as the framers then defined them and later amendments expanded them) could be heard, and then by the separation of political power, "the best defense of liberty," [14] to make sure no particular interest could dominate another and that Americans would suffer neither executive or legislative (majority) tyranny. Of this latter form of tyranny wrote Madison: "[t]here is no maxim in my opinion which is more liable to be misapplied, and which therefore more needs elucidation than the current one that the interest of the majority is the political standard of right and wrong." [15] In short, a reliance on public virtue was to be replaced by a "policy of supplying, by opposite and rival interest, the defect of better motive." [16] Or more bluntly put, "[a]mbition must be made to counteract ambition." [17] Success would require compromise and consensus.

This view was not restricted to domestic law making power, but also informed how the constitution assigned responsibilities for the historically royal powers for the conduct of foreign policy and war. Observes Professor David Adler in this book: "The Constitution assigns to Congress senior status in a partnership with the president for the purpose of conducting foreign policy [including war]." [18] Again the arrangement flowed from the framers' view of human nature. Wrote Alexander Hamilton, among the most monarchial of the framers, [19] in Federalist No. 75: "The history of human conduct does not warrant that exalted opinion of human virtue" which allow the granting of power over foreign affairs "to the sole disposal of a magistrate created and circumstanced as would be a president of the United States." And similarly about the war powers Madison wrote: "The constitution supposes, what the History of all governments demonstrates, that the Executive is the branch of power most interested in war, and most prone to it. It has accordingly with studied care, vested the question of war in the Legislature." [20]

At the White House this complex, power sharing design of American government becomes, at least from a presidential perspective, a presidential problem. "Congress' separate power is an obstacle to modern policy making," wrote then-Nixonian philosopher Kevin Phillips, [21] a view later expanded upon by President Jimmy Carter's Counsel Lloyd Cutler, who called for replacing Congress with a parliamentary form of government. [22]

The problem is simple. The president cannot change the law himself. The president's inevitable monarchial temperament encounters a system designed, as Louis Brandeis wrote, "not to promote efficiency, but to preclude the exercise of arbitrary power." [23] Presidents must convince Congress that there is a problem worth addressing and that he has the appropriate solution. Recall, in the extreme, President Clinton's failure to convince a Democratic Congress that they needed to turn their attention to health care and that he had the solution to the problem. Or President George W. Bush's failure to convince a Republican Congress to support his major domestic initiative, the privatization of social security.

To negotiate such obstacles, presidents must act less kingly. They must entertain objections to their vision and compromise for success. For some this is not an uncomfortable role. President Lyndon Johnson, for example, was a master of the process and, by all accounts, relished its incredible demands. But not every president is game for such work. Some simply find, for various reasons, these efforts "unkingly." Wrote Arthur Schlesinger about President Nixon: he "aimed at reducing the power of Congress at every point along the line and moving toward rule by presidential decrees." [24] An example was the presidentially approved secret Huston Plan to spy on American citizens in the anti war movement or on the political left, justified, after exposure, by the assertion: "Well, when the president does it that means that it is not illegal." [25]

But probably no administration has embraced kingly conduct with more vigor and aim than that of the President George W. Bush. The grave security concerns created by 9/11 provided an opportunity for the Bush administration to effect its monarchial view. The goal was to restore to the presidency the powers perceived to have been stripped from it since, and as a result of, the ignominious fall of President Richard Nixon. "In 34 years, I have repeatedly seen an erosion of the powers and the ability of the president of the United States to do his job," declared Bush's Vice President Dick Cheney on ABC in January 2002. [26] "I feel an obligation . . . to pass on our offices in better shape than we found them to our successors."

[27] And what needed to be restored, Cheney noted in 2005, could be found in an "obscure text," the minority report that accompanied the Iran Contra Report of 1987. [28] In that report the Vice President wrote: "the Chief Executive will on occasion feel duty bound to assert monarchical notions of prerogatives that will permit him to exceed the law." [29] And that argument of a then young Wyoming minority congressman became the openly expressed rational for the Bush Administration rejection of laws prohibiting torture or the wiretapping of American citizens. According to Frederick A. O. Schwarz and Aziz Huq: "No sitting president before President Bush asserted or used power under the Constitution to set aside laws wholesale. Such power means a president can ignore statutes passed by the Congress whenever he claims that 'national security or military necessity' is at issue." [30]

Beyond simply exercising the monarchial prerogative to ignore the law, the Bush administration did everything it could to ignore or circumvent Congress. Many of its actions, observes Louis Fisher in his essay, "evaded normal checks and balances for years because they were done in secret." [31] Wrote former Republican Senator Lincoln Chafee: "The White House was out to neuter Congress . . . [to] set the stage for one-branch rule in America and all the consequences we live with today." [32] And the prime strategy adopted for this purpose was the extensive use of another monarchial prerogative, secrecy. Asked the Senator from Virginia and the philosopher of Jeffersonianism, John Taylor of Caroline in 1814, about the "monarchical custom" of "executive secrecy," how "can legislatures be wise or independent, who legislate in the dark upon the recommendation of one man?" [33] Then and now, the answer is they cannot. A 2007 report on governmental secrecy found:

> In the past six years, the basic principle of openness as the underpinning of democracy has been seriously undermined and distrust of government is on the rise.
>
> The Administration has taken an extreme view of the power of the presidency. In its view, its powers to operate are largely unchecked by the Congress, courts, states, or the public. The number of secrets generated has substantially increased, while release of information has declined. [34]

Through the control and management of information, the Bush Administration steered Congress and the public toward the policies the administration favored. The most striking and serious example of this was the Iraq war. [35]

It is pretty clear that, at least after September 11, President Bush wanted to go to war with Iraq to effect regime change. The administration judged such a war could not be undertaken without congressional and public support. So they had to convince both that the war made sense. To this end they conducted a marketing campaign "to convince the American people that Iraq was in possession of weapons of mass destruction and had contacts with the al Qaeda terrorist organization." [36] Approaching a war like a marketing campaign, writes Gary Jacobson, "[breeds] a cavalier approach to truth: dishonesty not by lying, but by a deceptive selection of truthful but misleading statements." [37] And this was certainly true in this case. As part of this campaign, as I have written elsewhere:

> [A]dministration officials concealed both the paucity of evidence in support of their claims and any evidence that contradicted them. They touted questionable information regarding the existence of weapons of mass destruction, they claimed a connection to the 9/11 attacks where none existed, and they minimized concerns over problems that might arise in the post-invasion phase. Through distortions and half-truths, the administration was able to

portray the specter of an Iraq that posed a direct threat to America through its weapons of mass destruction and it support of the 9/11 terrorists. [38]

Would Congress and the American public have supported the war if the administration had been more forthcoming about the factual basis for its support? I think not, but regardless of one's view of the war's virtue, it is hard, I think, to justify the administration's decision under a constitution that requires war to be declared and paid for by Congress in order to assure that such a profound decision be the subject of real public debate. Unless you want to be a king.

The path from president to king should not be unfamiliar to Americans. Throughout our history we have off and on flirted with monarchial rule. Wrote Washington to John Jay in August of 1786, as the new country seemed to be imploding: "What astonishing changes a few years are capable of producing! I am told that even respectable characters speak of a monarchical form of government without horror. From thinking proceeds speaking, thence to acting is often but a single step. But how irrevocable and tremendous!" [39] And during this same period of time it has been reported that Nathaniel Gorham, a member and then president of the Continental Congress and delegate to the Constitutional Convention, wrote to Prince Henry of Prussia inquiring if he would be interested in assuming "regal powers" over America. [40] The Prince declined. And the historian Max Farrand reports that during the constitutional convention some of the delegates "may have been circulating rumors of establishing a monarch in order to try out public opinion." [41] In the early 1930s as the depression deepened, the journalist Henry Hazlitt suggested replacing Congress with a twelve-man directorate [42]. Republican Senator David Reed of Pennsylvania suggested that "a Mussolini" may be needed [43]. Barron's Magazine called for a "genial and lighthearted dictator." [44] And the renowned journalist Walter Lippmann advised Franklin Delano Roosevelt: "The situation is critical Franklin. You may have no alternative but to assume dictatorial powers." [45]

Anxiety over social and political upheaval has been the common threads of these separate events. In his profoundly disturbing book *Escape from Freedom*, the psychologist Erich Fromm explores how anxiety and its consequential feeling of helplessness produce a powerful attraction to authoritarian figures that promise some form of salvation, secular or religious. [46] And the political scientist William Scheuerman has recently translated this urge into the president–king context:

> As in the distant past, social and political anxiety apparently leads many to develop a deep emotional identification with the most concrete and seemingly unmediated representative of the political community, namely the single person of the presidency, whose every staged word and action can now be communicated into the recesses of the private abode of even the most apathetic member of the political community to a degree to which his royal predecessors could only have fantasized. In the contemporary U.S. version of this popular ideology, the president alone represents the popular will, whereas our numerous elected representatives in Congress—whose organizational complexity, it seems, is inconsistent with the emotionally charged sense of identity with a concrete personal symbol apparently called for by our anxiety-ridden times—stands for nothing more than particularized ''special interests." [47]

Once again, as in 1787, the cause of the problem, as Madison reported then, "lies among the people themselves." [48] Despite polls that find that eighty-four percent of Americans believe that for America's government to work citizens needed to be informed and active, and that three-quarters of those polled claimed that the Constitution mattered in their daily lives, [49] the reality brutally undermines the rhetoric. Americans know almost nothing about their government: about its structures, processes, or the principles or values that over time have formed our constitutional conscience. And it is this knowledge that pushes back against a president who wants to become a king and against our natural tendency to measure our government's legitimacy through outputs that are favorable to ourselves. On this point a public opinion survey once asked Americans to "[s]uppose the President and Congress have to violate a constitutional principle to pass an important law the people wanted. Would you support them in this action?" [50] Only 49% of the public said flatly, no. [51] The other half were a mix of yes (22%) and undecided or neither (29%). [52] And it is hard to imagine that most Americans appreciate the extraordinary display of public deliberation that surround the healthcare legislation, measuring the process only by projected outcomes and by their perspective on whether the President is being strong enough.

American's ignorance about their government is often and well documented. For example a National Constitution Center (NCC) survey found that 41% of respondents were not aware that there were three branches of government, and 62% couldn't name them; 33% could not even name one. Over half of all those answering the NCC survey did not know the length of a term for a member of the Senate or House of Representatives. And another NCC study found that while 71% of teens knew that "www" starts an online web address, only 35% knew that "We the People" are the opening words of the Constitution. A study by the Intercollegiate Studies Institute found that "the average college senior knows astoundingly little about America's history, government, international relations and market economy, earning an 'F' on the American civic literacy exam with a score of 54.2 percent." [53] And most Americans would have a very tough time passing the recently adopted test for citizenship, heralded by the government as a real measure of "what makes an American citizen," [54] which asks such questions as: "What is the supreme law of the land?" "What does the Constitution do?" "The idea of self-government is in the first three words of the Constitution. What are these words?" and "What is the rule of law?" [55]

And these questions just touch the edge of civic literacy. Imagine the results if we asked Americans the much more important questions of what vision of human nature informed the Constitution and how does the Constitution reflect its answer?

Civic ignorance threatens the American Republic. Without civic knowledge we cannot understand why it is important to balance our output measure of government legitimacy with an input measure. We cannot understand that American government is far more about process than products. Only with civic knowledge can we fulfill the constitutional obligation Madison imposed on all of us. "[Y]ou must," he wrote in *Federalist 51*, "oblige [the government] to control itself." [56] This is the same message that two recently retired Supreme Court Justices, O'Connor and Souter, have delivered around the nation in recent months. Declares Souter: the republic "can be lost, it is being lost, it is lost, if it is not understood." [57] It is through civic literacy, William Galston writes, that we gain both the willingness and ability to engage in public discourse and evaluate the performance of those in office. [58] And proof of this proposition is offered in Henry Milner's *How Informed Citizens Make Democracy Work.* [59] Two scholars, Michael Delli Carpini and Scott Keeter, also detail this same point in their

1996 study *What Americans Know About Politics and Why It Matters*. They find that civic literacy provides meaningful understanding and support for a number of core constitutional values, including compromise and tolerance, and promotes meaningful political participation. [60] They also argue that "a better-informed citizenry places important limitations on the ability of public officials, interest groups, and other elites to manipulate public opinion and act in ways contrary to the public interest." [61]

Thomas Mann and Norman Orenstein provide an example of the negative consequence of this civic ignorance. Discussing the six year relationship between President Bush and the Republican controlled Congress, they write: "Members of the majority party, including the leaders of Congress, see themselves as field lieutenants in the president's army far more than they do as members of a separate and independent branch of government." [62] And in this mode they failed to fulfill their constitutional obligation, particularly as it relates to congressional responsibility for declaring war. As seen by two foreign policy experts, Stefan Halper and Jonathan Clark, the run-up to the Iraq was a quintessential breakdown of the roles of Congress and the media. "Those institutions that could have challenged the scare scenarios governing the nation's perception of the terror challenge and Saddam Hussein failed to do so." [63]

But perhaps the more powerful expression of the nexus between kings and civic ignorance is that set forth, not by a scholar or journalist, but by a President, Dwight Eisenhower. In 1959, he received a letter from the dying World War II veteran Robert Biggs challenging his leadership qualities because of what Biggs thought an inadequate public response to public feelings of insecurity that "manifest themselves in the guise of a recession . . ." [64] For Eisenhower the letter provided an opportunity to discuss what he saw as a powerful connection between Americans' demands for presidential certainty and authority and civic knowledge. Using the ideas of Eric Hoffer as a reference point, Eisenhower wrote "dictatorial systems make one contribution to their person which leads them to tend to support such systems—freedom from the necessity of informing themselves and making up their own minds concerning these tremendous complex and difficult questions." [65] To which he then added that though such education "is a taxing one to a free people," it is a critical one, not only because of new ideas and "tremendous vigor, vitality and progress" that will ensue, but because of its critical value to self government. [66]

Through being better informed, they can best gain greater assurance regarding our nation's situation and participate in establishing policies and programs which they think to be sound and right. The quest for certainty is at best, however, a long and arduous one. While complete success will always elude us, still it is a quest which is vital to self-government and to our way of life as free men. [67]

As Eisenhower pointed out, it is hard work to be civically literate, made harder by our complacency. Despite Benjamin Franklin's often repeated response to a woman's question concerning the nature of the new government—"a republic, madame, if you can keep it" [68]—most Americans have absolutely no concern about its endurance. "Of course the Republic will survive, how can it be otherwise? We have always been free, and we will always be free," I have heard more than a few people—educated, politically conscious people—say. I recently tested this issue with a class of mine. Almost all of these students thought we were experiencing a decline in civil liberties and growing challenges to our constitutional system. But few thought it was possible that today's democracy would be dramatically different fifty years hence. While they all thought that presidential power would continue to grow, none saw a democratic crisis ahead. Such complacency forecloses serious reform.

Civic illiteracy is the fault of our schools and our expectation for them. Declared James Madison: "Learned institutions ought to be favorite objects with every free people. They throw that light over the public which is the best security against crafty and dangerous encroachments on the public liberty." [69] And in fact public schools were founded for that very purpose. But since the industrial revolution, and now, they are committed almost exclusively to the industrial education of our children. The focus is on jobs, and, of course, that is an important focus, but the exclusivity of that focus leaves little time for thinking about citizenship. As retired Supreme Court Justice Sandra Day O'Connor recently noted, the current emphasis on science and math "has effectively squeezed out civics education because there is no testing for that anymore and no funding for that." [70] Not once, that I have found, has President Obama or his Secretary of Education in heralding their new educational efforts touted civic literacy as a goal of public education. A competitive America seems their only goal, as if Americans are civically literate or can home school themselves to become so. As I have written elsewhere:

> Public schools have an obligation to teach children about our history and civic institutions including the Constitution. This obligation trumps even math and science education: After all, what is the value of either math or science, if we don't have our democracy? Or as Amy Gutmann, the President of the University of Pennsylvania, asserted, "'political preparation'—the cultivation of virtues, knowledge, and skills necessary for political participation—has moral primacy over other purposes of public education in a democratic society. [71]

President or king? It's up to us.

REFERENCES

[1] A draft of this paper was presented at the Hofstra University Peter S. Kalikow Center for the Study of the American Presidency in November of 2009. I would like to thank Professor Meena Bose, Peter S. Kalikow Chair in Presidential Studies, for organizing this conference and insisting on my participation. I would also like to thank the Hofstra Law School for its support of these efforts.

[2] Laurence H. Tribe, *American Constitutional Law* (Mineola, N.Y.: Foundation Press, 2000), 631.

[3] Homer, *The Odyssey* (New York: Penguin Classics, E. V. Rieu trans., 2003), 13.

[4] *History of the World Part I* (Twentieth Century Fox 1981).

[5] Gregory Y. Titelman, *Random House Dictionary of Popular Proverbs and Sayings* (New York: Random House, 2000).

[6] *The Federalist No. 70* (Alexander Hamilton).

[7] Woodrow Wilson, *Constitutional Government in the United States* (New York: Columbia University Press, 1908), 70.

[8] Robert A. East, *John Quincy Adams: The Critical Years: 1785-1794* (New York: Bookman Associates, 1962), 85.

[9] Gordon S. Wood, *The Confederation and the Constitution: The Critical Issues* (Washington: University Press of America, 1979), 87.
[10] James Madison and Jack N. Rakove, *Writings* (New York: Library of America, 1999), 76.
[11] Letter from George Washington to John Jay (Aug.15, 1786).
[12] Carol Berkin, *A Brilliant Solution: Inventing the American Constitution* (Orlando: Harcourt, 2002), 163.
[13] James Madison, *Notes of Debates in the Federal Convention of 1787* (New York; London: Norton, 1987), 131-35.
[14] Gordon S. Wood, The *Creation of the American Republic 1776-1787* (Chapel Hill, University of North Carolina Press, 1969), 598.
[15] Ralph Ketcham, *James Madison: A Biography* (New York: Macmillan, 1971), 181.
[16] The Federalist No. 51 (James Madison).
[17] Id. See also Wood, supra note 8, at 608.
[18] David Gray Alder, "Presidential Ascendancy in Foreign Affairs and the Subversion of the Constitution," *White House Studies* 10, no. 1 (2010).
[19] See generally William E. Scheuerman, "American Kingship?: Monarchical Origins of Modern Presidentialism," *Polity* 1 (2005).
[20] Letter from James Madison to Thomas Jefferson (April 2, 1798), in *Letters and Other Writings of James Madison: 1794-1815*, vol. 2 (Philadelphia: J.B. Lippencott and Co., 1865), 131.
[21] Kevin Phillips, "Our Obsolete System," *Newsweek* (Apr. 23, 1973), 13.
[22] Lloyd N. Cutler, "To Form a Government," *Foreign Affairs* (1980), 132.
[23] *Meyers v. United States*, 272 U. S. 52, 293 (1926).
[24] Arthur Schlesinger, Jr., *The Imperial Presidency* (Boston: Houghlin Mifflin, 1973), 246.
[25] Interview by David Frost with Richard M. Nixon (television broadcast May 19, 1977).
[26] Charlie Savage, "Hail to the Chief: Dick Cheney's Mission to Expand—or 'Restore'—the Powers of the Presidency," *Boston Globe* (Nov. 26, 2006), C1.
[27] Id.
[28] Charlie Savage, "Cheney Aid is Screening Legislation; Advisor Seeks to Protect Bush Power," *Boston Globe* (May 28, 2006), A1.
[29] Senate Select Comm., Report of the Congressional Committees Investigating the Iran-Contra Affair, S. Rep. No. 100-216, at 465 (1987).
[30] Frederick A. O. Schwarz, Jr. and Aziz Huq, *Unchecked and Unbalanced: Presidential Power in a Time of Terror* (New York: New Press: Brennan Center for Justice at NYU School of Law, 2007), 153.
[31] Louis Fisher, "Presidents Operating Under the Law," *White House Studies* 10, no. 1 (2010). Article reprinted in this volume.
[32] Lincoln Chafee, *Against the Tide: How a Compliant Congress Empowered a Reckless President* (New York: St. Martin's Press, 2008), 54.
[33] Schlesinger, supra note 23, at 450, quoting John Taylor, *An Inquiry into the Principles and Policy of the Government of the United States* (New Haven: Yale Univ. Press, 1950), 194.
[34] David Banisar, *Government Secrecy: Decisions Without Democracy* (Washington, D.C.: People for the American Way, 2007), 13.

[35] See generally Eric Lane, Frederick A.O. Schwarz, and Emily Berman, "Too Big a Canon in the President's Arsenal: Another Look at United States v. Nixon," *George Mason Law Review* (forthcoming April 2010).

[36] Banisar, supra note 33, at 36.

[37] Gary C. Jacobson, *A Divider, Not a Uniter: George W. Bush and the American People* (New York: Pearson Longman, 2007), 75.

[38] Lane, Schwarz, and Berman, supra note 34, at 36-37 (footnotes omitted).

[39] Letter from George Washington to John Jay (Aug.15, 1786).

[40] David P. Szatmary, *Shays' Rebellion: The Making of an Agrarian Insurrection* (Amherst: University of Massacusetts Press, 1984), 82.

[41] Max Farrand, *The Framing of the Constitution of the United States* (New Haven: Yale University Press, 1913), 175.

[42] William E. Leuchtenburg, *Franklin D. Roosevelt and the New Deal: 1932-1940* (New York: Harper and Row,1963), 30.

[43] Cass R. Sunstein, *The Second Bill of Rights: FDR's Unfinished Revolution and Why We Need It More Than Ever* (New York: Basic Books, 2004), 40.

[44] Leuchtenburg, supra note 41, at 30.

[45] David M. Kennedy, *Freedom from Fear: The American People in Depression and War, 1929-1945* (New York: Oxford University Press, 1999), 111.

[46] See generally Erich Fromm, *Escape from Freedom* (New York: Henry Holt and Co., 1994).

[47] Scheuerman, supra note 18, at 47.

[48] *Letters and Other Writings of James Madison*, Published by Order of Congress, vol. 1 (New York: R. Worthington, 1884), 325.

[49] Eric Lane, "America 101: How We Let Civic Education Slide—And Why We Need a Crash Course in the Constitution Today," *DemocracyJournal.org* 10 (2008), 54.

[50] Herbert McKlosky and Alida Brill, *Dimensions of Tolerance: What Americans Believe About Civil Liberties* (New York: Russell Sage Foundation, 1983), 148, Table 4.1.

[51] Id.

[52] Id.

[53] Intercollegiate Studies Institute, Failing Our Students, Failing America: Holding Colleges Accountable for Teaching America's History and Institutions, http://www.americancivicliteracy.org/2007/summary_summary.html (last visited Oct. 31, 2009).

[54] Julia Preston, "Tough Questions for a New Test: What Does 'American' Mean?," *New York Times* (Sept. 28, 2007), A26 (quoting Emilio Gonzalez, Director of Citizenship and Immigration Services).

[55] U.S. Citizenship and Immigration Services, Civics (History and Government) Items for the Redesigned Naturalization Test, http://www.uscis.gov/files/nativedocuments/100q.pdf (last visited Oct. 31, 2009).

[56] *Federalist No. 51* (James Madison).

[57] Debra Cassens Weiss, "Souter Decries Lack of Civics Knowledge, Plans to Do Something About It," *ABAJournal.com* (May 21, 2009), http://www.abajournal.com/news/souter_decries_lack_of_civics_knowledge_plans_to_do_something_about_it/.

[58] William A. Galston, *Liberal Purposes: Goods, Virtues, and Diversity in the Liberal State* (New York: Cambridge University Press, 1991), 221-24.

[59] See generally Henry Milner, *Civic Literacy: How Informed Citizens Make Democracy Work* (Hanover: University Press of New England, 2002).
[60] See generally Michael X. Delli Carpini and Scott Keeter, *What Americans Know About Politics and Why It Matters* (New Haven: Yale University Press, 1996).
[61] Id., 220.
[62] Thomas E. Mann and Norman J. Ornstein, *The Broken Branch: How Congress is Failing America and How to Get It Back on Track* (New York: Oxford University Press, 2006), 155.
[63] Stefan Halper and Jonathan Clarke, *The Silence of The Rational Center* (New York: Basic Books, 2007), 70.
[64] Dwight David Eisenhower et al., *The Papers of Dwight David Eisenhower: Keeping the Peace* (Baltimore: Johns Hopkins Press, 2001), 1342, n. 2.
[65] Id. at 1341.
[66] Id.
[67] Id. at 1341-42.
[68] William Lockhart Morrow, *A Republic, If You Can Keep It: Constitutional Politics and Public Policy* (Upper Saddle River, N.J.: Prentice Hall, 2000), 2.
[69] *The Writings of James Madison: 1819-1836* (New York: G.P. Putnam's Sons, 1910), 105.
[70] Seth Schiesel, "Former Justice Promotes Web-Based Civics Lessons," *New York Times* (June 9, 2008), C7.
[71] Lane, *supra* note 48, at 60-61.

CONCLUSION

In: President or King?
Editor: Meena Bose, pp. 171-177
ISBN: 978-1-61324-655-9

CONCLUSION: WHY THE FUTURE OF PRESIDENTIAL POWER WILL RESEMBLE THE PAST

Julian Ku

Each of the papers in this book offers a critical view of the modern presidency. The criticisms flow in a number of directions: excessive secrecy, unilateralism in foreign policy to the detriment of Congress, and even unlawful claims about the President's constitutional powers. In all cases, our contributors take aim at the centralizing "unitary" tendencies of the modern presidency and most cite the George W. Bush administration as an example of this troubling tendency.

Although they focus on the modern presidency, all of the contributions might also be described as responses to the presidency envisioned at the establishment of the Constitution. In his manifesto on executive power in Federalist 70, Hamilton argued in favor, above all, for a single executive to maintain "unity" in the executive branch

> Those politicians and statesmen who have been the most celebrated for the soundness of their principles and for the justice of their views, have declared in favor of a single Executive and a numerous legislature. They have with great propriety, considered energy as the most necessary qualification of the former, and have regarded this as most applicable to power in a single hand, while they have, with equal propriety, considered the latter as best adapted to deliberation and wisdom, and best calculated to conciliate the confidence of the people and to secure their privileges and interests.

He then goes on to say,

> That unity is conducive to energy will not be disputed. Decision, activity, *secrecy*, and despatch will generally characterize the proceedings of *one man* in a much more eminent degree than the proceedings of any greater number; and in proportion as the number is increased, these qualities will be diminished. [1]

In other words, our contributors raise important criticisms, but the issues they raise are neither novel nor unprecedented. Rather, they all fall within the long tradition of American debate over the proper powers of the President under the Constitution that began with Alexander Hamilton and James Madison and continues to this day.

In this short comment, I will briefly review the different understandings of the "unitary executive" theory that largely serve as the basis of the panel's criticisms. I will then conclude that while there are pitfalls to a unified presidency directed by a single person, none of the papers convince me that a plausible model of executive administration could exist without the characteristics of secrecy, interpretive independence in constitutional law, and executive control over administration which are the subject of criticism by these papers. I will suggest that the early views of the Obama Administration suggest that the Hamiltonian "unitary" vision is not, as some of the papers suggest, limited to the administration of George W. Bush.

PART I: THE UNITARY EXECUTIVE

Although the idea of a unified executive branch answerable to a single President dates back to, as I have suggested, Alexander Hamilton, the phrase "unitary executive" entered our political and constitutional discourse during the 1980s. The origins of the phrase appear to have been associated with lawyers in the Reagan Administration who used it describe their vision of an active and effective president as chief executive.

The core of unitary executive theory is, as two of its most ardent and influential academic defenders have described it, the President's exclusive constitutional power to appoint and remove officers of the United States government. [2]. The power to appoint and remove officers is crucial to unitary theory since it helps to ensure that the federal government's executive branch, and its increasingly massive bureaucracy, remains answerable to a single executive: the President. Much legal focus has turned to the President's power to remove officers since it is the threat of the removal that ensures his ability to control lower-level officers. Indeed, the U.S. Supreme Court is currently considering an important case challenging the process for appointing and removing officers in a powerful federal agency [3]

Yet unitary theory has also come to be associated with more than just the relatively narrow question of appointments and removal. Especially during the George W. Bush Administration, the phrase "unitary" executive came to stand for an assertive, unilateral executive, especially in the exercise of presidential war powers. Hence, presidents who have sought to limit communications or disclosures about executive decision making to Congress or the public are said to be acting under unitary theory. Presidents who assert the authority to interpret the Constitution against congressional encroachments are also accused of invoking unitary theory. Similarly, unitary theory might also lead to attempts to control the bureaucracy and to limit the ability of Congress or the courts to interfere. Hence, it is this broader version of unitary executive theory that has drawn the most fire from this book's contributions.

PART II: CRITIQUING THE UNITARY EXECUTIVE

In the view of almost all contributors, the modern presidency has aggrandized enormous powers to itself, especially in the control of the U.S. military. These aggrandizements have been exacerbated by a passive Congress and only slightly mitigated by the Supreme Court's cautious decisions limiting presidential power. Combined with efforts by modern presidents to shroud their decision making in secrecy, to unilaterally interpret laws in ways that expand presidential power, and to assert control over the federal bureaucracy, the contributions paint a troubling picture of the modern presidency.

It is not my purpose here to disagree with the contributors' descriptions of how the modern presidency operates. Rather, my disagreement is with the nefarious implications drawn by many of the critics.

For instance, I entirely agree with Fritz Schwarz that the modern executive branch seeks to shield its policy decisions, especially at the presidential level, in secrecy. This includes both the information upon which decisions are made, and the actual decisions themselves, which may remain secret from the public. He goes on to suggest that if presidential decision making was less secretive, and the bureaucracy as a whole, a variety of decisions that were made might have not been made, or at least made better than they were. For instance, he speculates that the 9/11 attacks, the use of the atomic bomb, the war in Vietnam, the Cuban Missile Crisis – all of this might have been avoided had crucial information been made public rather than kept secret.

My disagreement is not that secrecy exists, but simply with the assertion that the executive branch can live without secrecy. This seems especially true when making policy decisions. Although we do in some instances require rulemaking agencies in the executive branch to disclose the basis of their decisions, through the rulemaking process, there are many advantages to privacy and confidentiality in decision making. For instance, when presidents receive advice, it is not hard to understand that they would many times think the advice would be more candid and the discussion more candid if it remains confidential. To take an example from a different branch of government, the Supreme Court does not open up its conferences to reporters because there is a belief that the confidentiality assists in the process of making a decision. The same point applies to lawyers consulting with each other on the strategy for defending their client's interest ("work product") or a doctor giving advice to his patient. In all of these cases, society seems to value the importance of confidentiality as an aid, rather than a problem, for decision making.

If we accept the idea that in some circumstances, secrecy is beneficial to decision making, then the only question is when. In our system, many decisions are public. Congress debates bills in public and votes in public, the Supreme Court publishes their opinions, the executive branch publishes regulations. It seems that we have a balance here and I simply am not convinced that the balance is severely out of whack.

Similarly, Professor Andrew Rudalevidge gently criticizes the efforts by presidents to impose political control on the federal bureaucracy. In other words, he observes that presidents (following unitary theory) have tried to impose policy preferences on the bureaucracy by creating another layer of bureaucracy managed more tightly by the President and his closer advisers. President Reagan made similar, more successful efforts, by focusing more heavily on controlling the personnel process to insert more political appointees in the government. President George W. Bush continued this process through an even more aggressive use of appointees, even recess appointees, and via signing statements and a more flexible employment system. In his administration, the Office of Management and Budget was used aggressively to review agency regulations. Obama has shown some difference on some points, but has also embraced an effort to manage the bureaucracy like his predecessors.

Again, I do not disagree with this narrative. Indeed, I think this paper is very useful for reminding us just how difficult it is for the President to actually direct policy and a reminder of why more presidential control is preferable. It is not shocking that the President, including this one, have sought to control the bureaucracy. After all, Presidents often pay heavy political prices even though they don't actually have control. If President Bush did not control FEMA during Hurricane Katrina, or if President Obama is not actually responsible for the intelligence failures surrounding the Christmas Day bomber in Detroit, then it seems unfair to blame either president for bureaucratic failures. Yet if the presidents can't actually exert control over the bureaucracy, it seems odd to hold them accountable for it. But people do anyway. And would we really want it to be otherwise?

PART III: THE OBAMA ADMINISTRATION AND THE UNITARY EXECUTIVE

As this brief discussion indicates, I differ from many of the contributors to this book on a fundamental level. While I agree with their descriptions of how the modern presidency works, I don't think that the critics of this system have offered a plausible or persuasive account of the feasibility of their alternative model.

In this model, presumably, the President would defer to Congress on all major decisions of military action and policy, disclose all of his deliberations to the public, he would refuse to adopt contrary interpretations of the Constitution from that of Congress, and he would allow the bureaucracy to function independently of political control. This model has attracted little support from presidents throughout history and from presidents of both political parties. As Steven Calabresi and Christopher Yoo have argued recently, almost every single presidential administration from Washington to Bush has asserted the power to remove executive officers at will. [4] Moreover, as John Yoo's recent work suggests, the tradition of aggressive and unilateral presidential actions in military affairs also has a long historical pedigree. [5] This long pattern of presidential practice suggests that the unitary executive is hardly a recent innovation.

Even the broader and more controversial conception of the unitary executive has drawn support throughout history and across partisan divides. In this final section, I will respond to Professor Christopher Kelley's criticism of signing statements to argue that this practice has actually attracted support from presidents throughout history and across partisan divides.

Presidents have at times asserted their independent power to interpret the Constitution in the face of contrary interpretations adopted by the other two branches of the federal government. Aspects of this view manifest themselves today in the increasingly controversial practice of presidential signing statements asserting the authority to refuse to execute laws that, in the President's own judgment, are unconstitutional. The contemporary debate over signing statements of this type, extending through the Bush Administration and into the new Obama Administration, suggests that an executive power to independently interpret constitutional law remains a contested and important question.

As a matter of constitutional text and the original understanding of the U.S.Constitution, this position is perfectly defensible. Nothing in the Constitution's text explicitly grants to any branch of the federal government the power of constitutional interpretation, nor does any provision explicitly make one branch the supreme arbiter of the Constitution's meaning. Members of all three branches, for instance, are required to take the same oath swearing to uphold the Constitution but nothing in these provisions indicates that one branch has a special authority or obligation. The President also is obliged under Article II of the Constitution to "Take Care" that all the laws are faithfully executed, while the Supreme Court and federal courts are granted by Article III the "judicial power" without any explication of the nature of this power.

Lacking both political support and textual authority, Chief Justice Marshall nonetheless laid the foundations for judicial review of constitutional questions in *Marbury v. Madison*, an idea that would in time become an enormously influential and powerful global trend. [6] Although there is historical support for judicial review of constitutional questions, the idea was hardly uncontroversial, and indeed, remains somewhat controversial among modern constitutional scholars.

Yet even after *Marbury*, U.S. presidents continued to assert their independent right to interpret the Constitution. Although they generally agreed to be bound by the Court's interpretation in any case to which it was a party, presidents continued to argue that they had the authority to adopt different interpretations from the Court in other circumstances. As President Andrew Jackson famously asserted in his veto message of the Charter for the Second Bank of the United States,

> The opinion of the judges has no more authority over Congress than the opinion of Congress has over the judges, and on that point the President is independent of both. The authority of the Supreme Court must not, therefore, be permitted to control the Congress or the Executive when acting in their legislative capacities, but to have only such influence as the force of their reasoning may deserve. [7]

The Court has never explicitly rejected this position, although it came closest to doing so in the 1958 decision of *Cooper v. Aaron*, [8] when it asserted the Court's supreme authority over constitutional interpretations vis a vis state governments. Citing Article VI of the U.S. Constitution, which makes the Constitution supreme over state law, and *Marbury*, the Court declared that the principle that "the federal judiciary is supreme in the exposition of the law of the Constitution,[8] has ever since been respected by this Court and the Country as a permanent and indispensable feature of our constitutional system." [9]

Presidential administrations, however, have never fully acquiesced in the idea of judicial supremacy, at least vis-à-vis the executive branch. The most recent manifestation of presidential resistance to judicial supremacy can be found in the presidential assertions of the power to refuse to execute laws that, in the president's own judgment, are unconstitutional.Such assertions have been commonly made in the context of statements attached to presidential signatures of new legislation.

For example, President Obama recently attached the following "signing statement" to legislation objecting to provisions that directed his officers to advocate for certain views when participating in the governance of international financial institutions.

> [Such provisions] would interfere with my constitutional authority to conduct foreign relations by directing the Executive to take certain positions in negotiations or discussions with international organizations and foreign governments, or by requiring consultation with the Congress prior to such negotiations or discussions. I will not treat these provisions as limiting my ability to engage in foreign diplomacy or negotiations. [10]

Like presidents before him, President Obama is asserting a right to simply refuse to follow statutes that he believes are unconstitutional. Although the provisions in the bill in question plainly required the Secretary of the Treasury to adopt certain positions during activities at the International Monetary Fund, President Obama simply declared that he would treat those provisions as nonbinding due to their interference in his inherent constitutional authority. He did so without relying on any Supreme Court precedent for his views.

Such signing statements, especially those attached by President George W. Bush during his presidency, are prototypical examples of the controversial unitary executive theory. Bush's statements drew substantial criticism (including from then-candidate Obama). For instance, the American Bar Association adopted a report in 2006 sharply criticizing the use of such statements, especially by President Bush on questions of constitutional interpretation, [11] The New York Times similarly criticized President Obama's statements, especially those that asserted the independent presidential power to interpret the Constitution. If he wants to assert such a power, the paper editorialized, "then he should be able to point to court decisions or he should find a way to get the issue into court so the judiciary can make a call," [12] Professor Kelley's paper echoes these criticisms. Indeed, House of Representatives has demonstrated its displeasure with President Obama by voting by an overwhelming margin to take away funding for areas over which the President asserted his independent constitutional authority. [13]

To be sure, the dispute over signing statements hardly proves the necessity or correctness of unitary executive theory. But it is still worth noting that a robust assertion of a unitary independent executive lives on today in both Democratic and Republican administrations. At the very least, the bipartisan enthusiasm for unitary executive theory explains the difficulty of finding a replacement or alternative. This is why I believe, with all due respect to my fellow contributors to this book, that the future of presidential powers will strongly resemble the past.

REFERENCES

[1] The Federalist No. 70 (A. Hamilton).
[2] Steven Calabresi and Christopher Yoo, The Unitary Executive: Presidential Power from Washington to Bush (Yale University Press, 2008).
[3] Free Enterprise Fund and Beckstead and Watts LLP v. Public Company Accounting Oversight Board, Docket No. 08-861.
[4] Steven Calabresi and Christopher Yoo, The Unitary Executive: Presidential Power from Washington to Bush (Yale University Press, 2008).
[5] John Yoo, Crisis and Command: A History of Executive Power From George Washington to George W. Bush (Kaplan, 2009).
[6] 5 U.S. (1 Cranch) 137 (1803).
[7] Andrew Jackson, Veto Message Regarding the Second Bank of the United States, 1832.
[8] *Cooper v. Aaron*, 358 U.S. 1, 18 (1958).
[9] *Id.*
[10] Statement on Signing the Supplemental Appropriations Act of 2009, June 24, 2009.

[11] American Bar Association Task Force on Presidential Signing Statements and Separation of Powers, Recommendations, August 2006.
[12] "On Signing Statements," *The New York Times*, March 17, 2009.
[13] Walter Alarkson, "House Overwhelmingly Reject Signing Statements," *The Hill*, July 9, 2009.

ABOUT THE CONTRIBUTORS

DAVID GRAY ADLER is Professor of Political Science at Idaho State University, where he teaches courses on the Constitution and the Presidency. Adler has lectured nationally and internationally on the Constitution and presidential power, and is the author of more than 100 scholarly articles, essays and book chapters. His recent books include *The Presidency and the Law: The Clinton Legacy* (with Michael Genovese, 2002); *American Constitutional Law*, Volume II, 7th ed. (with Louis Fisher, 2007), and the forthcoming books *The Steel Seizure Case*, and *The Constitution and Presidential Power*. He is currently writing a book on *United States v. Curtiss-Wright Export Corp.* and its implications for American constitutional law and presidential power in foreign affairs.

MEENA BOSE is Peter S. Kalikow Chair in Presidential Studies at Hofstra University and Director of Hofstra's Peter S. Kalikow Center for the Study of the American Presidency. She is the author of *Shaping and Signaling Presidential Policy: The National Security Decision Making of Eisenhower and Kennedy* (1998), and editor of the reference volume *The New York Times on the Presidency* (2009), as well as co-editor of several volumes in presidency studies and a reader in American politics. She taught for six years at the United States Military Academy at West Point. Dr. Bose previously taught at Hofstra University from 1996-2000. Long Island Business News selected her as one of the "Top 40 Under 40" leaders on Long Island in 2009.

REBECCA CURRY is Assistant Professor of Public Law at Hofstra University. She received her Ph.D. in Jurisprudence and Social Policy from the University of California at Berkeley (2008), where she also earned her J.D. (2002). Dr. Curry teaches courses on constitutional law, civil liberties, and the judicial process, as well as general courses in American politics. Her scholarly focus is on separation of powers, judicial review, the First Amendment and election law.

LOUIS FISHER is Scholar in Residence at the Constitution Project. Previously he served as Specialist in Constitutional Law at the Law Library, Library of Congress, and before taking that position, he worked for the Congressional Research Service from 1970 to March 2006, specializing in separation of powers. Over his four decades at the Library of Congress he testified more than 50 times on a range of constitutional issues. Publications include twenty books and more than 400 articles in law reviews and political science journals. Recent books include *The Constitution and 9/11: Recurring Threats to America's Freedoms*

(2008) and *On Appreciating Congress: The People's Branch* (2010). He received his Ph.D from the New School for Social Research in 1967 and has taught at a number of universities and law schools.

GENE HEALY is a Vice President at the Cato Institute. His research interests include executive power and the role of the presidency, as well as federalism and overcriminalization. He is the author of *The Cult of the Presidency: America's Dangerous Devotion to Executive Power (2008),* and the editor of *Go Directly to Jail: The Criminalization of Almost Everything*. (2004). Healy is a weekly columnist for the *Washington Examiner, and he also has published in many other publications, including* the *Los Angeles Times,* the *New York Times,* the *Chicago Tribune,* and the *Legal Times*. Healy holds a B.A. from Georgetown University and a J.D. from the University of Chicago Law School.

NANCY KASSOP is Professor in the Department of Political Science and International Relations at the State University of New York at New Paltz. She writes on the presidency and law. Her most recent articles include: "Resolved: Presidents Have Usurped the War Power that Rightfully Belongs to Congress" in *Debating the Presidency*, 2nd ed. (CQ Press, 2010); "The White House Counsel's Office," co-authored with Karen Hult and MaryAnne Borrelli, on http://www.whitehousetransitionproject.org (2009), and "A Political Question By Any Other Name: Government Litigation Strategy in the Enemy Combatant Cases of *Hamdi* and *Padilla*" in Nada Mourtada-Sabbah and Bruce E. Cain, eds., *The Political Question Doctrine and the Supreme Court of the United States* (Lexington Books, 2007).

CHRISTOPHER S. KELLEY is Adjunct Assistant Professor of Political Science at Miami University (OH). His research interests include issues of presidential power, in particular the unitary executive theory of power, as well as the development and use of the presidential signing statement. He has authored and co-authored several papers on presidential power and the signing statement. His next book is a co-edited volume on the theory and practice of the unitary executive.

JULIAN KU is Professor of Law and Associate Dean for Faculty Development at Hofstra Law School. He teaches international, constitutional, and corporate law subjects, and his main research interest is the intersection of international and domestic law. He has recently published articles on the constitutional aspects of foreign relations in the Yale Law Journal, the Supreme Court Review and Constitutional Commentary. He also is a co-founder of the international law weblog Opinio Juris. Professor Ku is a graduate of Yale University and Yale Law School.

ERIC LANE is the Eric J. Schmertz Distinguished Professor of Public Law and Public Service at Hofstra University School of Law, and the Senior Fellow at the Brennan Center for Justice at NYU. He is the author with Michael Oreskes of *The Genius of America: How the Constitution Saved the Country and Why It Can Again* (2007), and with the Honorable Abner J. Mikva of two law school text books, *The Legislative Process*, 3d ed. (2009) and *An Introduction to Statutory Interpretation and the Legislative Process* (1997). Professor Lane is also the author of many articles on government decision making and has served in a number of state and local governmental positions.

ANDREW RUDALEVIGE is the Walter E. Beach '56 Chair of Political Science at Dickinson College. His books include *Managing the President's Program* (2002), which won the national Richard E. Neustadt Award; *The New Imperial Presidency: Renewing Presidential Power after Watergate* (2005); and, most recently, the co-edited volume *The George W. Bush Legacy* (2008). Rudalevige was a fellow at Princeton University's Center for the Study of Democratic Politics in 2004-05, and a visiting professor at the University of East Anglia, England, from 2007-09. In the latter capacity he spoke in a variety of European countries about issues of presidential power and the 2008 elections. He received his B.A. from the University of Chicago and his Ph.D. from Harvard University.

FREDERICK A.O. SCHWARZ, JR., is Chief Counsel of the Brennan Center for Justice at NYU Law School. Along with Elizabeth Goitein, he is working on a book on excessive governmental secrecy to be published by The New Press in 2012. Schwarz was Chief Counsel for the U.S. Senate's "Church" Committee, and author (along with Aziz Z. Huq) of *Unchecked and Unbalanced: Presidential Power in a Time of Terror* (The New Press, 2007; paperback 2008). Other work bearing upon secrecy and secrets in his five decades of public and private work stems from service as Corporation Counsel for the City of New York in Mayor Koch's Administration; as Chair of the City's Charter Revision Commission, which, operating in the open, fundamentally altered the City's constitution or "Charter;" as Chair of New York City's Campaign Finance Board; and from his practice for many years as a litigation partner at the law firm of Cravath, Swaine & Moore.

INDEX

#

20th century, 64
21st century, 99
9/11, viii, ix, x, xiii, 31, 37, 38, 39, 41, 97, 144, 145, 148, 149, 151, 157, 159, 160, 173, 179
9/11 Commission, 145, 148

A

Abraham, vii, x, 3, 18, 27, 28, 44, 45, 46, 63, 147
abstraction, 87
abuse, ix, 19, 20, 28, 30, 34, 39, 88, 92, 100, 110, 112, 116
[illegible], 128
access, 31, 32, 33, 35, 84, 111, 130, 133
accountability, xii, 68, 70, 101, 109, 111, 124
accounting, 114
acts of aggression, 33
Adams, John, 12, 17, 146
Adams, John Quincy, 158, 164
affirming, 12, 54, 112
Afghanistan, 32, 33, 34, 51
age, 7, 20
agencies, viii, xi, 7, 39, 81, 84, 88, 89, 96, 103, 106, 111, 125, 126, 128, 129, 131, 134, 139, 144, 150, 173
aggression, 33
Al Qaeda, 37, 83
ambassadors, 5, 6, 21
ambiguity, 70, 96
American History, 22
American Presidency, xiii, 3, 157, 164, 179
antitrust, 64
anxiety, 64, 157, 161
apex, 14
applications, 53
appointees, 110, 126, 128, 173
appointment process, 128
appointments, xi, 103, 107, 123, 124, 125, 128, 131, 172
Appointments Clause, 72
appropriations, 10, 11, 70, 81, 108, 116
Appropriations Act, 71, 107, 108, 115, 118, 119, 120, 121, 176
architect, 10, 13
Aristotle, 146, 153
armed conflict, 51, 96
armed forces, 6, 67, 75
arrest, 30
Asia, 15
aspiration, 157
[illegible], 100
assertiveness, viii
assessment, viii, xiii, 17, 80, 104
assets, 85, 86, 87
assignment, 7, 9
assumptions, 3, 130
atoms, 149
attachment, 6
attacks, 9, 12, 14, 17, 31, 37, 44, 46, 50, 72, 79, 123, 132, 144, 160, 173
attitudes, 151
Attorney General, 11, 30, 36, 37, 38, 40, 41, 42, 127, 129, 134, 151, 154
authorities, 30, 32, 38, 51, 52, 66, 129
authority, viii, ix, x, xi, xiii, 3, 4, 5, 6, 7, 8, 9, 10, 11, 12, 13, 14, 15, 16, 17, 19, 21, 23, 24, 27, 29, 30, 31, 32, 33, 34, 37, 38, 43, 44, 46, 47, 48, 49, 51, 52, 53, 54, 55, 56, 57, 59, 63, 66, 67, 69, 70, 71, 72, 73, 76, 80, 81, 82, 83, 84, 85, 86, 87, 88, 89, 90, 91, 93, 95, 101, 103, 104, 106, 107, 108, 112, 115, 124, 125, 128, 129, 130, 132, 134, 145, 147, 158, 163, 172, 174, 175, 176
autonomy, 52, 125
availability, 50, 95

aversion, 6, 7, 9
awareness, 116

B

bail, 86
balanced budget, 90
ban, 132
bankruptcy, 86
banks, 86, 87
bargaining, 69
barriers, ix, 81
base, 33
behavior, 64, 83, 84, 99, 100, 109, 133, 135, 157
beliefs, 104, 109
benefits, 57, 88, 131
benign, 27, 129
bias, 95
Bible, 145
Biden, Joseph, 83
binding, 68, 127
birth, 147, 152
blame, 80, 88, 174
blockades, 29
blog, 112, 120
blogger, 112
blogs, 94
blood, 17, 19, 88
blueprint, 4, 6
bone, 47
bones, 124
bounds, 70, 133
brass, 110
breakdown, 158, 163
Britain, 5, 46
bureaucracy, xi, 85, 88, 123, 124, 126, 132, 133, 134, 150, 172, 173, 174
Bush, George W., v, vii, viii, ix, x, xi, xiii, 3, 4, 11, 13, 19, 20, 31, 44, 45, 47, 50, 63, 65, 71, 77, 79, 85, 97, 99, 104, 105, 112, 123, 124, 125, 131, 138, 139, 166, 171, 172, 176, 181
Bush, President, 31, 32, 37, 51, 65, 79, 83, 86, 93, 103, 104, 105, 106, 107, 108, 109, 110, 113, 132, 138, 139, 160, 163, 174, 176

C

cabinet, 125, 131
cabinet members, 126
Cairo, 153
calculus, 111
Cambodia, 15
campaigns, 48, 147
Canada, 35, 41
candidates, 79, 128
Capitol Hill, 82
cargoes, 18
Caribbean, 48
Carter, Jimmy, 4, 13, 15, 159
cast, 150
cell, 34
challenges, xi, 54, 68, 70, 72, 101, 103, 104, 105, 106, 107, 108, 109, 112, 113, 116, 133, 145, 163
channels, 89
chaos, 7
character, 8, 9, 28, 30, 88, 148
charm, 15
checks and balances, viii, xii, 3, 7, 19, 27, 31, 44, 64, 143, 144, 160
Cheney, Dick, 65, 79, 105, 133, 159, 165
Chicago, xiii, 137, 139, 180, 181
Chief Justice, 12, 17, 23, 30, 54, 175
Chief of Staff, 105
children, 35, 47, 164
China, 91
CIA, 34, 38, 41, 143, 144, 147, 148, 150, 151, 154
citizens, 3, 11, 15, 31, 52, 55, 56, 73, 75, 146, 151, 159, 162
citizenship, 162, 164
city, 148, 154, 155, 181
civil law, 131
civil liberties, 46, 47, 48, 49, 50, 55, 56, 58, 91, 163, 179
civil rights, 44, 124
Civil War, vii, x, 18, 27, 29, 30, 44, 45, 46, 49, 52, 56, 64, 147, 152, 154
clarity, 127
classes, 87
classification, 119, 145
Clean Air Act, 85
climate, 85, 131
Clinton Administration, 25
Clinton, Senator Hillary, 83
closure, 133
coercion, 148
Cold War, 144, 149
College Station, 136, 138
commander-in-chief, ix, 10, 13, 14, 15, 44, 45, 48, 56, 157
commerce, 6
common law, 49
communication, 114
communities, 5
community, vii, 91, 153, 161
community support, 91

compensation, 35
competence, 32, 128, 134
competency, 28
competition, xi, 57
compilation, 139
complexity, 161
compliance, 69, 157
complications, 134
concentration, 3, 81, 144
conception, 16, 44, 65, 174
concrete, 47, 161
conference, 3, 37, 67, 75, 120, 164
confessions, 154
confidence, 6, 36, 171
confidentiality, 72, 173
confinement, 32, 60
conflict, viii, 12, 32, 33, 44, 45, 51, 57, 59, 83, 96, 99, 112, 129
confusion, 34
congressional budget, 66
congruence, 99
consciousness, 99
consensus, 44, 55, 82, 159
consent, 26, 53, 124
conservation, 88
Consolidated Appropriations Act, 107, 108, 118, 119
conspiracy, 7, 73
constituents, 88, 90
constitution, v, viii, ix, x, xi, xiii, 3, 4, 5, 6, 7, 8, 10, 11, 12, 13, 14, 15, 16, 18, 19, 20, 21, 22, 23, 24, 25, 26, 27, 28, 29, 30, 32, 33, 37, 38, 41, 43, 46, 47, 48, 49, 53, 54, 56, 58, 64, 65, 67, 74, 75, 80, 81, 82, 84, 85, 90, 93, 95, 101, 102, 103, 104, 107, 109, 111, 112, 116, 117, 123, 124, 129, 130, 132, 144, 146, 147, 151, 152, 153, 155, 159, 160, 162, 164, 165, 166, 171, 172, 174, 175, 176, 179, 180
constitutional amendment, 81, 147
constitutional challenges, 54, 106, 107, 111
constitutional interpretations, 175
constitutional issues, 179
constitutional law, 44, 102, 172, 174, 179
constitutional principles, 4
construction, 4, 18, 101, 112
consulting, 66, 148, 173
continental, 8, 14, 22, 25, 161
continuity, 22
control, 4, 6, 9, 19, 22, 32, 33, 54, 66, 69, 72, 84, 96, 100, 102, 103, 108, 111, 112, 115, 123, 124, 125, 126, 130, 131, 133, 134, 135, 146, 160, 162, 172, 173, 174, 175
controversial, viii, 43, 71, 99, 101, 111, 117, 123, 174, 175, 176
controversies, 49
convention, 13, 18, 124, 158, 161
conviction, 20, 49
coordination, 134, 147
cost, 19, 20, 107, 111, 129, 134
cost-benefit analysis, 134
costs, 88, 125, 129, 131
counsel, 33, 66, 72, 75, 100, 126, 131
country of origin, 46
Court of Appeals, 40, 93, 112
credentials, 126
credibility, 9
credit, 87, 88, 94
crime, 80, 131
criminality, 127
criminals, 148
crises, xii, 45, 79, 85, 144
critical analysis, 16
critical value, 4, 163
criticism, 20, 112, 147, 172, 174, 176
Cuba, 53, 60, 149, 150, 154
Cuban government, 33
cues, 73
cultivation, 164
culture, 90, 92, 150, 151
cycles, 90

D

damages, 35, 36
danger, 53, 81, 96, 130, 144
dating, 4, 104, 116
Dean, John, 20, 126
death, 46
debt, 158
decision making, 3, 6, 19, 153
decision-making process, 150
decisions, 4, 10, 11, 12, 15, 44, 45, 47, 55, 58, 63, 66, 67, 68, 70, 71, 72, 73, 74, 109, 131, 133, 143, 144, 145, 146, 147, 150, 151, 153, 173, 176
defects, 39
defendants, 33, 53
defense, 5, 6, 9, 10, 12, 16, 22, 29, 34, 36, 48, 52, 84, 100, 101, 102, 104, 112, 113, 117, 158
definition, 8, 14, 15, 16, 24, 47, 85, 87, 124, 135
delegates, 6, 9, 10, 22, 70, 101, 146, 161
democracy, xi, xii, 4, 31, 102, 143, 150, 151, 157, 160, 163, 164
denial, ix, 10
Department of Commerce, 136
Department of Defense, 40, 60, 71, 118, 131, 139
Department of Homeland Security, 131

Department of Justice (DOJ), 41, 42, 69, 102, 103, 109, 134, 138, 139
Department of Transportation, 129
deployments, 58
depression, 161
depth, 125
despair, 90
destruction, 155, 160, 161
detachment, 9
detainees, ix, 33, 34, 43, 45, 47, 49, 50, 51, 52, 53, 54, 55, 73, 76, 93, 109, 110, 132
detention, x, 31, 32, 46, 49, 50, 51, 54, 56, 71, 73, 76, 83, 93, 133, 134
dignity, 21, 29, 146
diplomacy, 5, 7, 115, 176
directives, 69, 70, 123, 133
directors, xiii, 128
disappointment, 68
disaster, 7, 64, 83
discipline, 131
disclosure, 34, 130, 154
discourse, 91, 157, 162, 172
disorder, 5, 7
disposition, 80
dissenting opinion, 21, 135
distortions, 160
distress, 10
District of Columbia, 40, 136
divergence, 87
division, 36
DNA, 125
domestic policy, x, 66, 79, 85, 101
dominance, 19, 65, 80, 90
doors, 111, 146
draft, 8, 85, 86, 164
drawing, 81
due process, 50, 56, 73
duration, 59, 80
duties, 4, 11, 19, 44, 48, 49, 52, 55, 56, 65, 81, 108
dynamics, 71, 87

E

earth, 93
echoing, 131
economic crisis, 64, 113
economic downturn, 88
Edgar Allen Poe, 139
education, 108, 119, 153, 163, 164, 166
Eisenhower, Dwight, 149, 163
Eisenhower, Dwight David, 167
El Salvador, 58
election, 19, 83, 103, 109, 179
electronic surveillance, 38
elucidation, 158
emergency, vii, viii, 3, 9, 27, 28, 29, 45, 46, 47, 50, 67, 88, 152
Emergency Economic Stabilization Act, 86, 94
emission, 85
emotional intelligence, 19
employees, 34, 112, 126, 131, 134
employment, 173
endurance, 163
enemies, 32, 52, 126, 148
enemy combatants, ix, 32, 50, 52, 54, 80, 132
energy, vii, viii, xiii, 104, 149, 153, 158, 171
enforcement, 60, 70, 100, 101, 102, 104, 112, 117
engagement, 90
England, 5, 11, 21, 145, 167, 181
enthusiasm, 176
environment, 64, 88, 117
environmental policy, 132
environmental protection, 88
EPA, 85, 93, 139
equality, 46, 81
equating, 109
equilibrium, 57, 64
erosion, 159
espionage, 56
evacuation, 60
evidence, 16, 35, 36, 43, 48, 52, 54, 56, 72, 102, 116, 160
evolution, 100
Ex parte Quirin, 59
execution, 15, 50, 60, 81, 107, 125, 151
executive branch, viii, x, xi, xiii, 19, 34, 36, 39, 45, 46, 50, 52, 54, 55, 56, 63, 66, 68, 69, 70, 72, 73, 83, 84, 85, 86, 87, 88, 89, 91, 95, 100, 102, 103, 104, 106, 107, 108, 110, 111, 112, 114, 115, 116, 117, 123, 126, 127, 131, 132, 133, 134, 139, 143, 150, 151, 171, 172, 173, 175
executive function, 9
Executive Order, 110, 111, 119, 129, 138, 139
executive orders, xi, 69, 70, 89, 102, 103, 104, 119, 125, 131, 133
executive power, ix, x, xi, xii, xiii, 3, 5, 6, 8, 9, 13, 15, 16, 22, 28, 60, 63, 65, 66, 68, 70, 71, 72, 73, 76, 80, 84, 101, 102, 103, 105, 108, 109, 110, 116, 123, 124, 126, 127, 132, 133, 144, 157, 171, 174, 180
exercise, 5, 10, 14, 17, 29, 33, 34, 36, 44, 46, 47, 48, 49, 51, 53, 64, 66, 69, 89, 100, 101, 104, 125, 130, 131, 159, 172
expertise, 19, 26, 32, 150
exposure, 159

F

failure, 80, 86, 87, 89, 110, 116, 159
fairness, 34
faith, 116
families, 7
family, 34, 35, 41
FBI, 35, 109, 143, 144, 147, 151, 154
fear, 6, 16, 81, 151
fears, 15
federal agency, 172
Federal Convention, 21, 165
federal courts, x, 33, 34, 36, 39, 49, 51, 53, 54, 72, 110, 175
Federal Emergency Management Agency (FEMA), 131, 174
federal government, vii, viii, x, 30, 43, 45, 59, 91, 172, 174
Federal Government, 96
federal judiciary, 36, 53, 175
Federal Register, 40, 119, 129
federalism, 96, 180
feelings, 129, 163
Feingold, Senator Russ, 36, 41
Fifth Amendment, 46
fights, 89, 95
financial, 79, 80, 84, 85, 86, 87, 94, 125, 175
financial crisis, 79, 84
financial institutions, 86, 175
First Amendment, 179
FISA, 37, 38, 63, 66, 84, 93, 132
Fish and Wildlife Service, 88
fitness, 12
flank, 51, 114
flaws, 19, 75, 89
flexibility, 108
flight, 4, 35
fluctuations, 65
focusing, 80, 173
food, 148
force, viii, 3, 7, 11, 12, 13, 18, 29, 37, 50, 59, 66, 67, 68, 82, 90, 91, 95, 96, 104, 115, 127, 130, 175
Ford, 4, 13, 15, 57, 58, 100, 102, 105, 129, 135
Ford, Gerald, 4, 13, 15, 135
foreign affairs, ix, xi, 3, 4, 5, 6, 7, 11, 13, 20, 22, 26, 32, 34, 35, 37, 46, 47, 48, 56, 59, 66, 70, 81, 82, 84, 107, 109, 159, 179
foreign policy, ix, 3, 4, 6, 15, 36, 46, 47, 55, 64, 66, 70, 88, 91, 100, 109, 112, 115, 126, 151, 159, 163, 171
foundations, 175
framing, 11
France, 12, 17, 145
Franklin, Benjamin, 22, 158, 163
Fraud Enforcement and Recovery Act, 114, 120
freedom, 31, 91, 147, 153, 163
friction, 134
frustration, 65
functionalism, 44
funding, viii, 66, 88, 90, 116, 164, 176
funds, viii, 28, 31, 116, 127

G

GAO, 140
gene, 116
General Motors, 86
General, Solicitor, 33, 76, 84, 120
generation, 10, 66, 74
Geneva Convention, ix, 32, 53, 73, 93, 154
Georgia, 153
Germany, 33, 34, 149
goals, 84, 87, 103, 128
god, 153
governance, xi, 7, 54, 81, 87, 175
government, 4, 5, 10, 19, 27, 28, 30, 31, 32, 35, 36, 38, 39, 43, 44, 45, 46, 49, 50, 51, 52, 53, 54, 56, 57, 59, 64, 73, 74, 76, 80, 81, 87, 91, 93, 96, 100, 101, 103, 108, 110, 115, 121, 124, 125, 126, 127, 128, 130, 131, 133, 144, 145, 146, 148, 151, 153, 157, 158, 159, 160, 161, 162, 163, 172, 173, 174, 175
government policy, 130, 144
governments, 31, 115, 159, 175
grand jury, 50
grants, ix, 80, 84, 125, 174
greed, 8
greenhouse, 85
Grenada, 24, 130
groups, 110, 111, 150
growth, vii, viii, 4, 79, 80, 90, 125, 143, 144
GSA, 72
Guantanamo, 33, 51, 53, 54, 60, 73, 76, 133
Guantanamo Bay, 51, 53, 54, 60, 133
guardian, 92
guidance, 59, 131, 134
guilt, 49, 50
guilty, 33, 52
Gulf of Mexico, 118

H

habitat, 88
hair, 50
Haiti, 75

Hamilton, Alexander, vii, viii, xiii, 6, 8, 21, 22, 23, 125, 158, 159, 164, 172
Hamiltonian, 172
hands, 4, 5, 9, 14, 23, 65, 66, 80, 116, 127
harm, 27, 36, 79, 89, 143, 144, 148, 150
hazards, 131
health, 91, 159
Health and Human Services (HHS), 108, 119, 137
health care, 91, 159
hegemony, 3, 20
helplessness, 161
history, xii, 6, 14, 16, 34, 46, 48, 50, 53, 57, 64, 67, 71, 73, 74, 79, 105, 124, 143, 144, 145, 148, 150, 159, 161, 162, 164, 174
HIV, 104
hopes, 71, 116, 151
host, 79, 88
hostilities, viii, 6, 7, 10, 11, 12, 13, 17, 67, 96, 130
house, 4, 10, 18, 21, 33, 36, 39, 40, 41, 45, 46, 58, 71, 74, 75, 82, 86, 87, 88, 89, 95, 102, 103, 105, 106, 108, 110, 111, 113, 114, 116, 119, 121, 126, 127, 128, 129, 131, 133, 134, 135, 136, 137, 138, 139, 144, 145, 148, 150, 151, 152, 157, 158, 159, 160, 162, 164, 165, 176, 177
House of Representatives, 10, 74, 89, 105, 162, 176
HUD, 138
human, 6, 7, 20, 145, 146, 153, 157, 158, 159, 162
human nature, 145, 146, 157, 158, 159, 162
human virtue, 6, 159
Hurricane Katrina, 125, 131, 174
Hussein, Saddam, 83, 163
hybrid, 103, 113

I

ideal, 109, 123
ideals, 79, 103, 109
identification, 87, 161
identity, 161
ideology, 6, 43, 161
illegal aliens, 46
illiteracy, 164
illusions, 145
imagination, 35, 157
immigration, 35, 46
Immigration and Nationality Act, 95
immunity, 16, 38
impeachment, 11, 64
implementation, 124, 125, 132, 134, 144
imprisonment, 52
inauguration, 28
inclusion, 67
independence, 35, 36, 46, 70, 130, 145, 158, 172
India, 91
indication, 154
indicators, 44, 111
individual rights, 30, 46, 47, 56, 58
individuals, 30, 31, 33, 34, 110, 114, 126
indoctrination, 128
industrial revolution, 164
information sharing, 154
initiation, 11, 17, 18, 48
injury, 13, 72, 95
innocence, 49, 50, 146
innovation, 4, 174
INS, 75, 89, 95
insecurity, 163
institutions, vii, ix, xi, 53, 56, 64, 65, 86, 101, 105, 107, 109, 116, 117, 157, 163, 164
insurance, 87, 94
intelligence, 19, 34, 35, 37, 66, 69, 70, 83, 91, 127, 130, 144, 147, 151, 154, 174
intentions, 20, 70, 108, 146
intercourse, 6, 30
interest groups, 163
interference, 103, 176
international affairs, 70
international communication, 37
international financial institutions, 175
international law, 11, 12, 17, 24, 109, 180
International Monetary Fund (IMF), 116, 134, 176
international relations, 46, 69, 162
international terrorism, 31, 53
interrogations, 71, 132, 133, 134
intervention, 50, 90
intrusions, 103
Iran, 4, 15, 46, 57, 58, 65, 69, 70, 74, 130, 131, 133, 138, 143, 148, 150, 160, 165
Iraq, xi, 19, 82, 83, 88, 92, 125, 130, 160, 161, 163
Iraq War, 82, 83, 88
issues, x, xiii, 46, 48, 49, 55, 56, 128, 129, 130, 133, 135, 146, 147, 150, 171, 180, 181

J

Jackson Lee, Sheila, 108
Jackson, Andrew, 175, 176
Jay, John, 7, 117, 158, 161, 165, 166
Jefferson, Thomas, 7, 146, 165
jobs, 164
Johnson, Andrew, 74
Johnson, Lyndon, 4, 13, 83, 149, 159
Johnson, President Lyndon B., 15
judges, 19, 27, 30, 31, 32, 34, 35, 36, 80, 82, 84, 89, 108, 112, 123, 153, 175

judgment, 6, 15, 19, 20, 22, 26, 29, 32, 67, 127, 143, 174, 175
judicial branch, 49
judicial interpretation, 47
judicial power, 48, 52, 54, 175
judiciary, x, 17, 30, 32, 33, 35, 36, 49, 50, 51, 52, 53, 55, 56, 57, 59, 89, 101, 175, 176
Judiciary Committee, 36, 71, 119
juries, 153
jurisdiction, 33, 34, 36, 47, 53, 54, 60, 73, 93, 143
justice, 7, 45, 48, 49, 50, 52, 93, 171
justification, 13, 24, 38, 69, 71, 101, 110, 113, 133

K

Kagan, Elena, 84, 93, 101, 110, 120, 124, 134, 135
Kennedy, John F., 149
kill, 134
killing, 12
Korea, 19, 23, 31
Kuwait, 34

L

labor, 80
land, 16, 47, 81, 162
landscape, 3
language, 30, 43, 53, 70, 73, 84, 85, 86, 88, 89, 105, 106, 126, 127, 131, 145
languages, 145
law enforcement, viii, 100
laws, vii, xi, 3, 6, 12, 15, 29, 30, 32, 38, 46, 63, 65, 66, 69, 81, 83, 87, 88, 89, 94, 95, 96, 101, 102, 105, 107, 108, 124, 125, 129, 131, 133, 145, 147, 160, 173, 174, 175
lawyers, 38, 44, 82, 102, 112, 132, 172, 173
lead, 7, 20, 57, 64, 81, 82, 100, 112, 123, 133, 145, 172
leadership, vii, viii, ix, x, xii, 163
leaks, 146
learning, 74, 138
Lebanon, 24, 34, 130, 138
legality, 37, 54
legislation, x, xi, 29, 30, 36, 65, 66, 68, 70, 71, 80, 81, 83, 85, 86, 103, 104, 108, 112, 113, 129, 133, 134, 162, 175
legislative authority, 12, 19, 27, 81, 84
liberty, vii, 30, 54, 73, 80, 81, 144, 158, 164
light, 4, 5, 70, 148, 164
likelihood, 9, 143
Lincoln, Abraham, vii, x, 3, 18, 27, 28, 44, 45, 46, 63, 147
line, 18, 34, 45, 47, 48, 56, 93, 102, 103, 106, 111, 159
linkage, 128
links, 37
listening, 143, 146
literacy, xii, 152, 162, 164
litigation, 31, 32, 34, 55, 89, 181
local government, 180
locus, 17
logging, 88
Lott, Senator Trent, 152
love, 7, 158
loyalty, 87, 125, 126, 131
lying, 160

M

Macedonia, 34
machinery, 64, 71, 126, 134
Madison, James, xiv, 4, 6, 8, 22, 57, 61, 80, 92, 101, 117, 146, 151, 153, 164, 165, 166, 167, 172
magazines, 99
magnitude, 74
maintenance, 4
major decisions, 174
majority, 18, 29, 52, 53, 54, 55, 58, 60, 71, 73, 83, 88, 89, 133, 158, 163
malaise, 79
man, 10, 18, 20, 34, 81, 87, 88, 94, 135, 160, 161, 171
management, 4, 125, 128, 131, 160
mandates, 151
manners, 6, 158
market, 86, 94, 162
market economy, 162
marketing, 160
Marshall, John, 12
Maryland, 60
mass, 109, 119, 125, 160
materials, 28, 131, 153
matter, 18, 21, 29, 50, 51, 64, 65, 80, 99, 109, 153, 174
McCain, Senator John, 79, 105, 120
meanings, 24
measures, 28, 56, 90, 146
meat, 134
media, 41, 88, 95, 100, 157, 163
mediation, 41
Medicare, 96
memory, 19, 120, 149
men, 10, 39, 135, 144, 152, 158, 163
metaphor, 149
Mexico, 17, 18, 48, 118

Miami, 180
militarization, 91
military, viii, x, 3, 4, 5, 6, 7, 11, 12, 13, 14, 15, 17, 19, 28, 31, 32, 33, 34, 37, 43, 45, 47, 48, 49, 50, 51, 52, 53, 54, 55, 57, 59, 60, 67, 68, 71, 72, 73, 74, 83, 90, 91, 93, 104, 105, 110, 125, 130, 131, 132, 148, 150, 160, 172, 174
military aid, 31
Military Order, 92
military spending, 105
military tribunals, x, 3, 31, 43, 45, 52, 83, 110, 132
militia, 10, 81
minority, 65, 160
misconceptions, 146
mission, 130, 157
Missouri, 46, 57
model, 5, 6, 7, 21, 123, 128, 172, 174
modifications, 111
momentum, 150
money, 35, 86, 116
Monroe, James, 102, 153
mood, 28
mortgage-backed securities, 86
Moses, 145
motion, 8, 9
motives, 7, 81
movement, 155, 159
muscles, 64

N

naming, 116
nation, 3, 5, 6, 8, 10, 11, 12, 13, 18, 20, 29, 30, 35, 46, 59, 65, 84, 86, 87, 95, 109, 127, 144, 145, 146, 148, 149, 150, 158, 162, 163
National Defense Authorization Act, 71, 118
national emergency, 47, 50, 67
National Intelligence Estimate, 82
national security, viii, ix, 4, 7, 13, 15, 19, 26, 27, 34, 35, 36, 37, 43, 44, 45, 46, 47, 48, 49, 51, 52, 53, 55, 56, 57, 66, 68, 71, 72, 73, 82, 86, 108, 130, 134, 144, 160
National Security Agency, 31, 42, 132, 139
National Security Council, 34, 126, 130, 147
nationalism, 19
natural disaster, 80
Nazi Germany, 149
negotiating, 157, 158
negotiation, 128
neutral, 11, 35, 50, 51, 53, 128
New Deal, 4, 84, 166
New England, 167
newspapers, 99, 146
Nicaragua, 31, 69, 133
Nixon, Richard, 4, 13, 15, 31, 65, 74, 126, 133, 144, 159
Nixon, Richard Milhous, 144
nominee, 126
noncitizens, 31, 33, 55
NSA, 31, 37, 38, 84, 132
nuclear weapons, 20

O

Obama, xi, 36, 41, 71, 79, 80, 85, 92, 94, 99, 100, 101, 109, 110, 111, 112, 113, 114, 115, 116, 117, 119, 120, 121, 123, 124, 133, 134, 139, 172, 173, 174, 176
Obama Administration, 41, 172, 174
Obama, President, xi, 84, 85, 93, 110, 111, 112, 113, 114, 115, 116, 117, 134, 152, 164, 174, 175, 176
objectives, 116
obligation, 103, 130, 131, 151, 159, 162, 163, 164, 175
observations, 25
obstacles, 90, 159
obstruction, 81
Office of Management and Budget, xi, 102, 126, 173
officials, viii, 27, 31, 34, 35, 39, 44, 46, 59, 69, 72, 87, 115, 143, 144, 147, 148, 150, 154, 160
Omnibus Appropriations Act,, 120
openness, 4, 114, 121, 133, 145, 148, 150, 160
operations, 3, 12, 14, 24, 27, 66, 68, 69, 70, 126
opportunism, 127
opportunities, 73
oppression, 18, 46
order, 3, 11, 13, 21, 28, 30, 31, 32, 38, 44, 46, 49, 54, 67, 71, 73, 79, 80, 82, 83, 84, 86, 88, 89, 92, 93, 102, 104, 110, 111, 115, 116, 117, 130, 131, 132, 133, 134, 152, 154, 161
organ, 13, 32, 37, 45
organize, 127
overlap, 128
oversight, 66, 91, 96, 108
ownership, 134

P

PAA, 84, 93
Pacific, 48, 88
Padilla, Jose, 32
Panama, 23
Pandemic Influenza Act, 118
parallel, 33, 53, 74
parameters, 84

parents, 35
Parliament, 145
participants, xiii, 147
partnership, 6, 86, 159
passive, 53, 88, 173
pathology, 91
Patriot Act, 41
patriotism, 19
peace, x, 5, 6, 7, 8, 9, 11, 12, 13, 14, 15, 18, 19, 24, 81, 84, 88, 130
peacekeeping, 130
pedigree, 174
penalties, 56, 60
Pentagon, 71, 73, 148
performance, 81, 108, 131, 157, 162
permit, 10, 16, 72, 160
Persian Gulf, 58, 130
personality, 21, 133
Philadelphia, 3, 5, 13, 14, 138, 146, 165
photographs, 110
planning, 128
plants, 85
playing, 123
pleasure, 18, 145
polarization, 124
police, 35
policy, viii, ix, xii, 3, 4, 5, 6, 14, 15, 19, 20, 26, 29, 32, 34, 36, 38, 39, 45, 46, 47, 51, 53, 54, 55, 57, 64, 65, 66, 69, 70, 72, 79, 81, 85, 87, 88, 90, 91, 96, 100, 101, 109, 112, 115, 124, 125, 126, 127, 128, 130, 132, 133, 134, 135, 139, 143, 144, 146, 147, 150, 151, 158, 159, 163, 171, 173, 174
policy choice, 144
policy issues, 146, 147
policy making, ix, xii, 159
policy options, 133
political enemies, 126
political participation, 163, 164
political parties, 174
political power, 158
political problems, 112
political system, 105, 123
politics, vii, viii, ix, xii, xiii, 7, 45, 56, 66, 90, 94, 109, 120, 121, 150, 179
Polk, James K., 17
pollution, 127
poor, 26
ports, 29
potential benefits, 129
POWER, v
power plants, 85
power sharing, 159
precedent, 16, 17, 18, 25, 46, 52, 54, 105, 108, 113, 133, 176
precedents, 3, 11, 16, 55, 124
predicate, 23
preference, 6
preparation, 164
pre-planning, 111
presidency, xi, xii, 3, 5, 10, 19, 25, 46, 63, 64, 65, 71, 73, 74, 79, 80, 83, 84, 90, 91, 99, 100, 102, 103, 104, 105, 107, 108, 109, 117, 124, 125, 126, 129, 135, 151, 159, 160, 161, 171, 172, 173, 174, 176, 179, 180
President Clinton, 89, 103, 104, 105, 110, 111, 113, 133, 159
President Obama, xi, 84, 85, 93, 110, 111, 112, 113, 114, 115, 116, 117, 134, 152, 164, 174, 175, 176
Presidential Administration, 93, 110, 117, 135, 139
presidential advisors, 152
presidential authority, 6, 23, 34, 43, 47, 55, 68
presidential campaign, 83, 157, 158
presidential politics, ix, xii
presidential veto, 87
pressure, 105, 109
prestige, 102
prices, 85, 174
primacy, 26, 164
principles, 3, 4, 32, 44, 53, 55, 59, 63, 64, 72, 103, 104, 107, 112, 124, 153, 162, 171
prisoners, 30, 33, 56, 60, 148, 154
prisoners of war, 148
prisons, 33
privacy, 173
privatization, 159
program, 37, 38, 39, 60, 84, 85, 119, 126, 127, 128, 131, 133, 134
progress reports, 136
project, viii, ix, 131
proliferation, 68
property rights, 48
proposition, 12, 84, 96, 162
protection, vii, 5, 19, 21, 34, 46, 53, 88, 112, 113, 115
prototypes, 43, 44
psychologist, 161
public affairs, 145
Public Company Accounting Oversight Board, 176
public education, xii, 153, 164
public interest, xii, 72, 106, 163
public officials, 163
public opinion, 109, 161, 162, 163
public policy, 135, 146, 147
public schools, 164
public sector, 125

public support, xii, 160
purity, 128

Q

qualifications, 47, 58, 101
questioning, 127

R

race, 79
radar, 107
radio, 37
range, 125, 132, 133
ratification, 28, 68, 81, 146, 147, 152
rating agencies, 131
reactions, ix
reading, 6, 48, 83
Reagan, Ronald, 4, 13, 19, 113, 120, 150
reality, 70, 162
reason, 20, 28, 29, 38, 49, 51, 55, 74, 80, 81, 85, 90, 94, 106, 149, 151, 154
reasoning, 10, 37, 39, 44, 51, 52, 55, 60, 175
recall, 20, 87
recalling, 38
reception, 21
recession, 163
recognition, 46, 70, 145
recommendations, 89, 107
reelection, 97
reflection, 4
reform, xi, 63, 64, 65, 68, 88, 96, 119, 128, 152, 164
reforms, 63, 71, 89, 95
refugees, 134
regulation, 10, 85, 111, 125, 129
regulations, 84, 89, 90, 111, 117, 126, 129, 131, 173
regulatory affairs, 134
regulatory agencies, 85, 111
rejection, 5, 63, 79, 160
relationship, 124, 163
relief, 35, 50
religion, 129
rendition, x, 3, 31, 34, 35, 38, 51, 110, 134
reporters, 173
requirements, 66, 67, 68, 69, 73, 95, 130, 131, 132, 133
resentment, 129
resistance, 175
resolution, 8, 9, 11, 32, 66, 67, 82, 83, 89
resources, 126, 135
respect, 9, 18, 24, 28, 33, 46, 47, 51, 55, 56, 74, 82, 96, 132, 145, 176
response, 43, 44, 47, 53, 63, 72, 111, 115, 134, 144, 163
responsiveness, 131, 134
restrictions, x, 3, 29, 66, 67, 69, 85, 136
retaliation, 13
retaliatory action, 74
returns, 29
rewards, 91
rhetoric, 162
rights, 5, 8, 15, 30, 32, 44, 46, 47, 48, 49, 54, 56, 57, 58, 73, 82, 87, 93, 123, 124, 126, 129, 131
risk, viii, 20, 27, 34, 36, 146, 148, 150
Roosevelt, Franklin, 45, 147, 149
Roosevelt, Franklin Delano, 144, 161, 166
Roosevelt, Theodore, 19, 48
root, 128, 143, 151
roots, 80
rowing, 11
rubber, 50
rule of law, viii, 3, 7, 27, 31, 38, 39, 52, 157, 162
rules, 10, 44, 45, 46, 47, 48, 49, 56, 83, 89, 96, 111
Russia, 104

S

sabotage, 56
sanctions, 129
SAP, 114, 115
satisfaction, 24
savings, 87, 94, 128
scandal, 65, 69, 70
school, 11, 47, 48, 65, 157, 164, 180
science, 7, 48, 93, 164, 179
scope, viii, 15, 16, 45, 73, 108, 125, 132, 147, 151
scores, 25
search, 35
Secretary of the Treasury, 176
securities, 86
security, vii, 4, 6, 7, 12, 13, 15, 19, 22, 26, 27, 34, 35, 36, 37, 43, 44, 45, 46, 47, 48, 49, 51, 52, 53, 55, 56, 57, 66, 69, 71, 72, 73, 81, 82, 86, 87, 94, 108, 130, 134, 144, 147, 159, 164
seizure, 13
selectivity, 102
self-interest, 158
senate, 4, 6, 8, 9, 21, 22, 36, 38, 39, 42, 67, 71, 74, 75, 81, 82, 86, 89, 124, 127, 136, 145, 152, 162, 165, 181
Senate Foreign Relations Committee, 75
separation, 3, 5, 7, 10, 19, 23, 32, 43, 44, 48, 51, 53, 72, 81, 88, 126, 145, 158
September 11, 44, 50, 72, 79, 83, 123, 132, 134, 148, 160

shape, 79, 85, 100, 125, 159
shaping, 143, 144, 150
shares, 6, 86
short-term memory, 120
shoulders, 82
showing, 95
signs, 99
skills, 128, 164
skimming, 150
social security, 159
society, 38, 125, 129, 146, 153, 164, 173
soil, 17, 50, 51, 52, 93
Solicitor General, 33, 76, 84, 120
solution, 68, 90, 149, 159
Southeast Asia, 15
sovereignty, 18, 29, 33, 46
Soviet Union, 149
space, 44, 117, 158
specialists, 150
species, 13
specter, 161
spectrum, 13, 44
speech, 14, 39, 112, 154
speed, 131
spending, 88, 105, 112, 127, 128, 134, 149
Spring, 97, 152
stability, 86, 94
staff members, 129
staffing, 126
standards, 50, 52, 59, 72, 128
state, xii, 4, 5, 7, 10, 11, 12, 13, 17, 18, 23, 27, 31, 32, 34, 35, 36, 38, 41, 45, 46, 50, 57, 59, 71, 84, 91, 105, 124, 125, 130, 134, 143, 144, 145, 175, 180
state of emergency, 45
states, xi, 9, 11, 29, 46, 81, 107, 147, 160
statute, 17, 33, 37, 39, 54, 60, 67, 68, 69, 72, 73, 86, 90, 96, 123, 130, 132
statutes, 17, 31, 34, 38, 46, 66, 68, 70, 84, 86, 89, 160, 176
statutory authority, 93
statutory provisions, 72, 89, 112
steel, 13, 31
stock, 71
strategies, 123, 124, 128, 133
strategy, 117, 126, 127, 129, 131, 133, 134, 160, 173
strength, 14, 45, 47, 48, 54, 102
strictures, 66
structure, xii, 6, 14, 57, 64, 65, 74, 81, 87
students, 157, 163
style, 54, 89, 91
substitution, 9
succession, 80, 135
summer, 84, 146
superiority, 26
supernatural, 153
supervision, 85
supervisor, 128
Supreme Court, x, 10, 11, 12, 13, 17, 21, 23, 29, 31, 32, 33, 35, 36, 37, 39, 40, 43, 44, 45, 46, 47, 48, 49, 50, 51, 52, 53, 55, 56, 57, 58, 61, 63, 68, 71, 72, 83, 84, 85, 89, 93, 105, 113, 123, 124, 134, 136, 137, 144, 150, 153, 162, 164, 172, 173, 175, 176, 180
surveillance, ix, x, 31, 37, 38, 66, 79, 83, 84, 126, 132, 133, 151
survival, 157
suspects, 31, 46, 71, 83, 93
Syria, 35, 41

T

tactics, 91, 125, 126, 148, 149, 150, 154
takeover, 89
Taliban, 32
tanks, 128
target, 90
targets, 84
teaching, 157
techniques, 148
technological advances, 91
technology, 149
teens, 162
telecommunications, 35
television, 165
temperament, 19, 159
tenure, 72, 105, 108
territory, 12, 17, 18, 33, 87, 94, 126
terrorism, 31, 34, 38, 53, 59, 157
terrorist organization, 35, 37, 160
terrorists, x, 32, 151, 161
testing, 164
theatre, 14
thinking, 43, 90, 123, 134, 158, 161, 164
Third Reich, 39
threat, 35, 43, 49, 75, 82, 85, 127, 149, 161, 172
threats, ix, x, xii, 44, 46, 53, 80
tides, 5
time frame, 64
tin, 105
torture, xiii, 3, 31, 33, 34, 35, 105, 132, 143, 148, 150, 154, 160
tracking, 91
trade, 85, 116
trade-off, 116
tradition, 5, 15, 16, 171, 174

traditions, 46
training, 126
trajectory, 4
transactions, 5, 146
transition, 128
translation, 145
transparency, xii, 102, 114
treasury, 28, 85, 176
Treasury Secretary, 85
treaties, 3, 4, 5, 7, 21, 34, 38, 46, 68, 108
treatment, ix, 31, 46, 56, 71, 80, 106, 109, 132
trends, 90, 113
Trent Lott, 152
trial, 31, 34, 48, 49, 52, 54, 55, 56, 93, 134
trust, 36, 81, 91
Turkey, 149
twist, 116

U

U.S. history, 34, 79
U.S. immigration law, 46
U.S. policy, 130
uncertainty, 44
unilateralism, 4, 7, 103, 109, 110, 124, 126, 171
united, vii, 6, 7, 8, 11, 12, 13, 14, 15, 17, 18, 19, 20, 21, 22, 25, 27, 29, 31, 32, 33, 34, 35, 37, 38, 39, 40, 41, 50, 51, 58, 67, 69, 75, 79, 81, 82, 83, 84, 86, 87, 90, 91, 92, 93, 94, 95, 107, 109, 110, 127, 129, 130, 134, 146, 147, 148, 149, 151, 152, 154, 159, 164, 165, 166, 172, 175, 176, 179, 180
United Nations (UN), 82, 83
United States, vii, 6, 7, 8, 11, 12, 13, 14, 15, 17, 18, 19, 20, 21, 22, 25, 27, 29, 31, 32, 33, 34, 35, 37, 38, 39, 40, 41, 50, 51, 58, 67, 69, 75, 79, 81, 82, 83, 84, 86, 87, 90, 91, 92, 93, 94, 95, 107, 109, 110, 127, 129, 130, 134, 146, 147, 148, 149, 151, 152, 154, 159, 164, 165, 166, 172, 175, 176, 179, 180
universities, 180
USA, 71
USA PATRIOT Act, 71
USSR, 91

V

vein, 46, 113, 116
venue, 50, 56
vessels, 18, 25, 29
veto, 67, 81, 89, 95, 105, 112, 113, 127, 129, 136, 175
Vice President, 79, 105, 106, 132, 149, 159, 180
Vietnam, 10, 15, 19, 23, 24, 25, 26, 47, 65, 66, 69, 71, 83, 88, 91, 96, 127, 149, 150, 154, 173
Viking, 58
vision, 80, 81, 90, 108, 159, 162, 172
visions, 157, 158
vocabulary, 126
voice, 7, 157
vote, 8, 9, 10, 18, 74, 82, 83, 86, 89, 91, 147
voters, 83, 88, 90
voting, ix, 44, 47, 176

W

war, viii, ix, x, xi, 3, 4, 5, 6, 7, 8, 9, 10, 11, 12, 13, 14, 15, 16, 17, 18, 19, 20, 22, 23, 24, 25, 29, 30, 31, 32, 33, 34, 43, 44, 45, 46, 47, 48, 49, 50, 52, 53, 54, 55, 56, 57, 58, 59, 64, 65, 67, 70, 74, 81, 82, 83, 88, 89, 90, 93, 124, 125, 127, 130, 148, 149, 157, 159, 160, 161, 163, 172, 173
War on Terror, 21, 105, 110, 135, 139
warrants, 84, 132
Warren, Earl, 17
Washington, xiii, 14, 25, 40, 41, 82, 91, 92, 94, 96, 100, 117, 119, 124, 129, 135, 136, 137, 138, 139, 146, 148, 149, 154, 155, 158, 161, 165, 166, 174, 176, 180
Washington, George, xiii, 14, 25, 146, 148, 154, 158, 165, 166, 176
waste, 85, 88, 128
water, 46, 127
weapons, viii, 20, 160
weapons of mass destruction, 160
web, 112, 162
weblog, 180
welfare, 130
welfare state, 130
West Wing, 129
Whigs, 17, 133
White House, viii, x, xi, xii, xiii, 4, 21, 33, 40, 41, 45, 46, 71, 86, 87, 88, 102, 103, 105, 106, 108, 110, 111, 113, 114, 126, 127, 128, 129, 131, 133, 134, 135, 136, 137, 138, 139, 144, 148, 150, 151, 157, 158, 159, 160, 165, 180
WHO, 128
wholesale, 96, 160
Wilson, Woodrow, 19, 158, 164
wind, 88
wiretaps, 71, 93, 132
witnesses, 144
women, 147, 152
workers, 125
World Bank, 116, 134
World Trade Center, 148

World War I, viii, 46, 59, 64, 83, 84, 144, 147, 148, 149, 154, 163
worry, 109
writing, 10, 17, 38, 55, 124, 153
wrongdoing, 70

Y

Yale University, xiii, 40, 61, 74, 94, 95, 117, 135, 154, 166, 167, 176, 180